Professor José Anderson has produced a wonderful biography of Charles Hamilton Houston, the pioneer in the fight for desegregating America and the mentor to Justice Thurgood Marshall. The book is a must-read for anyone interested in the history of the civil rights movement and in the quest for "a more perfect Union."

Richard L. Revesz
AnBryce Professor of Law and Dean Emeritus
New York University School of Law

Brown v. Board of Education is the best-known Supreme Court decision of the 20th century. Thurgood Marshall is the jurist most associated with that decision. What is less well known is the lawyer who devised the long-range, carefully-orchestrated legal strategy. Charles Houston was the visionary who developed and implemented the legal strategy. Professor José Anderson's engaging, carefully researched and thorough examination of Houston's profound contributions finally gives the credit that is due to this "genius for justice."

Leland Ware
Louis L. Redding Chair of Law and Public Policy
University of Delaware

Professor Anderson provides powerful legal insight into the driving force behind Thurgood Marshall and the civil rights court battles he waged by shining remarkable, informative and overdue light on his little-known mentor Charles Houston... A must read!

Chief Judge Wanda Keyes Heard
Circuit Court for Baltimore City (Retired)

Before Black Lives Matter, Martin Luther King, Jr., and Thurgood Marshall, there was Charles Hamilton Houston. With *Genius for Justice,* José Anderson has written a fresh and captivating look at one of the architects of the modern civil rights movement, while providing an essential read for anyone interested in the long crusade for racial justice in America

Mick Caouette
Film Producer
Mr Civil Rights: Thurgood Marshall and the NAACP

Charles H. Houston was the most brilliant and courageous legal freedom fighter in 20th-century America. His peerless intellect and matchless will to fight for justice set a high standard that even his more famous student, the great Thurgood Marshall, aspired to. This magisterial book lays bare the sheer genius and profound love of Black and vulnerable people that sit at the center of Houston's life. His prophetic Christian fire led to his early death, but we should never forget his gifts to Black freedom and American democracy!

Dr. Cornel West
Professor Emeritus
Princeton University

Genius for Justice

Genius for Justice

Charles Hamilton Houston and
the Reform of American Law

JOSÉ FELIPÉ ANDERSON

With a foreword by Charles Hamilton Houston, Jr.

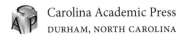 Carolina Academic Press
DURHAM, NORTH CAROLINA

LIBRARY OF CONGRESS CATALOGING-IN-PUBLICATION DATA

Names: Anderson, José Felipé, author.
Title: Genius for justice : Charles Hamilton Houston and the reform of
    American law / by José Felipé Anderson.
Description: Durham, North Carolina : Carolina Academic Press, LLC, [2021]
Identifiers: LCCN 2021021410 (print) | LCCN 2021021411 (ebook) |
    ISBN 9781594609855 (paperback) | ISBN 9781531022730 (ebook)
Subjects: LCSH: Houston, Charles Hamilton, 1895-1950. | African American
    lawyers--Biography. | Civil rights workers--United States--Biography. |
    Law reform--United States. | United States. Supreme Court.
Classification: LCC KF373.H644 A53 2021 (print) | LCC KF373.H644 (ebook) |
    DDC 340.092 [B]--dc23
LC record available at https://lccn.loc.gov/2021021410
LC ebook record available at https://lccn.loc.gov/2021021411

Carolina Academic Press
700 Kent Street
Durham, North Carolina 27701
Telephone (919) 489-7486
www.cap-press.com

Printed in the United States of America

To all the plaintiffs, law students, and lawyers who made themselves available to support the justice vision of the genius Charles Hamilton Houston. I firmly believe this is who he would want me to thank.

Contents

Foreword

Few Americans outside of the legal profession or in rarified academic circles know of my father. Those who have heard of him usually recall his role as the man who mentored Thurgood Marshall. Marshall went on to serve with distinction on the Supreme Court of the United States as its first African American Justice. As the architect of the *Brown v. Board of Education* cases, my father devised the strategy that destroyed legally sanctioned racial segregation in this country.

The *Brown* case is often referred to as the most important legal decision in United States history because it led to the transformation of America and made possible a more inclusive society. Even the election in 2008 of the first African American president, Barack Obama, may not have been possible without the lawyers in *Brown* who blazed the trail toward an egalitarian society.

My father's contributions, however, go far beyond *Brown* and his role in shaping the career of Thurgood Marshall and many other great lawyers and judges. Professor Anderson discusses many interesting things about my father's life and extraordinary legal career in the biography that follows. Those details reveal a brilliant, compassionate man with many interests, a love of America and a passion for the people he served.

My father was born in Washington, D.C., in 1895, when slavery was still a living memory. Both of his paternal grandparents had been born slaves in Missouri and Kentucky, respectively, and had liberated themselves. He attended Washington's famous M Street High School, where he received an excellent education. It was the first academic high school in the country for African American students; its faculty included many Ph.Ds. who were unable to find teaching positions elsewhere because of racial segregation and discrimination.

In 1911 he matriculated at Amherst College, where he was elected to Phi Beta Kappa. Graduating in 1915 at age nineteen, my father was undecided about his career path. He loved playing the piano, however, and, according to my mother, wanted to become a concert pianist, but his father, William L. Houston, a successful and pragmatic practicing attorney, saw no future in it. Therefore, with his Amherst degree in English literature in hand, my father became a lecturer in the Department of English at Howard University, where he also developed a course in African American literature.

Above: Charles H. Houston and family and friends at Highland Beach, Maryland, in the summer of 1947.
Left: Charles H. Houston, Jr. ("Bo"), at Highland Beach, 1947.
COURTESY OF THE CHARLES H. HOUSTON, JR., FAMILY COLLECTION

Teaching at Howard in 1917, when Woodrow Wilson led the United States into World War I to "save the world for Democracy," my father joined with young men at Howard and at other historically black colleges to protest the government's refusal to train black military officers to lead black troops. The protests worked, and consequently my father became one of the first black officers commissioned during the war, with the rank of First Lieutenant in the army infantry. Subsequently, however, my father and several of his fellow black officers objected to the army's policy of excluding black soldiers from artillery training. Military officials considered black people to be too unintelligent to do the mathematical calculations required of artillery officers. My father and several of his fellow protesters resigned their infantry commissions and applied for artillery training. Again, the protest paid off. He was accepted in artillery school, completed the training and was re-commissioned a second lieutenant of artillery.

Before he was shipped to France, my father had a life-altering experience. He was ordered to serve as judge advocate in the prosecution of a black career army sergeant who was charged with a minor infraction of military regulations. Investigating the charges, my father determined that the sergeant had an excellent military records and, moreover, that the charges against him were groundless. Unwilling to spoil the sergeant's outstanding record and ruin his career, my father reported his findings to his white superior officer with the recommendation that the charges be dismissed. For his initiative, my father was severely reprimanded. He was told that his job was not to investigate the facts but to secure a conviction. It was at this moment, my mother later told me, that my father decided to study the law so that he could fight for men who could not strike back for themselves.

In France during the first world war, my father experienced a more dangerous form of American racism. One evening he and a fellow black officer were returning from a concert, through the darkened streets of the seaport town of Vanne, France. They encountered another black officer who was accompanied by two French women. Stopping to chat, my father and his two fellow officers soon found themselves surrounded by a large group of white American enlisted men who were enraged to find black men in the company of white women. The fact that the black men were officers notwithstanding, the mob threatened to lynch them. Violence was averted only by the timely arrival of a captain of the military police, who had been attracted by the commotion. He ordered the mob to disperse and threatened to arrest anyone who did not comply. This experience later led my father to remark bitterly that he was glad that he had not laid down his life for his country.

My father was demobilized during the "Red Summer" of 1919. It was a time marked by widespread racial and labor violence across the country. He made good his commitment to study the law. He enrolled in Harvard Law School, where he became the first black person to serve as an editor of the *Harvard Law Review* and received his law degree in 1922. In 1923 he earned a doctor of juridical science degree and was awarded a Sheldon Fellowship that allowed him to travel to the University of Madrid in Spain to study Spanish civil law. Returning to his hometown of Washington, D.C., in 1924, he began to practice law with his father William L. Houston, who had been a lawyer in Washington since 1892. My father also joined my grandfather as a part-time faculty member in Howard's law school night program.

My father's early years of practice coincided with the rise of a new spirit of militancy and racial pride among black Americans. Shortly after beginning to practice law, he joined the national legal committee of the National Association for the Advancement of Colored People (NAACP). The committee planned legal action to secure civil rights for people of color. This was the age of the "New Negro," when African Americans were migrating out of the South to the North and West, where they became more assertive and showed new racial pride in themselves and their culture. During the 1920s, the NAACP's leadership, for the first time since its founding in 1909, was beginning to shift from white to black. Noted black poet, author, diplomat, playwright and activist James Weldon Johnson was named executive secretary in 1920 and appointed Walter White assistant secretary.

The NAACP was not the only black institution to reflect the racial pride and self-confidence of the New Negro movement. In 1926 Mordecai Johnson became the first black president of Howard University. That same year, Johnson gave a speech at the NAACP annual convention in which he spelled out his agenda for the historically black institution. He said the time had come to demonstrate to the world that the accomplishments of black people were equal to those of any other people. To do this, he explained, he would transform Howard into a first-rate university, second to none. Johnson would appoint as department heads individuals who were leaders in their fields, even if he had to raid other black institutions to find the very best talent. Three years later, he chose my father to lead Howard's law school and charged him with the task of transforming it from an unaccredited night school to a fully accredited day school.

Johnson's plan coincided with my father's conviction that the time had come for black lawyers to lead the fight for civil rights. Under his leadership, the law school became fully accredited and newly dedicated to training young black civil rights lawyers.

The same year that my father was hired to transform Howard University School of Law, the NAACP also underwent a momentous transformation. In 1929, the association received a $100,000 grant from the American Fund for Public Service (AFPS), established by Charles Garland, a young socialist who believed it was immoral to keep money he had not earned. Garland formed the AFPS to give away a $1,000,000 inheritance from his father to organizations promoting radical social change. The grant to the NAACP changed the association's mission. It had been founded in 1909 as a vigilance organization, dedicated to the investigation and reporting of lynching, lobbying for a federal anti-lynching law and to providing pro-bono legal representation by volunteer white attorneys in cases of judicial lynching.

The AFPS grant in 1929 enabled the association for the first time to shift from a reactive to a proactive stance. After much debate, representatives of the fund and the association agreed the money should be spent on a litigation campaign attacking segregation and discrimination across a wide spectrum of issues, including housing, jobs, public accommodation and education.

This ambitious plan, however, was curtailed by the stock market crash of 1929. Because the grant to the association was in stocks, the crash shrank the amount of the grant to $30,000. With reduced resources, the association narrowed the focus of the campaign to end discrimination in education, because equal access to education was considered to be essential in order for black people to compete in a modern industrial society.

My father left Howard's law school in 1935 to become the first black special counsel for the NAACP, having transformed the law school into an institution dedicated to training young black civil rights attorneys. At that time he turned his attention to implementing the NAACP's legal campaign against segregated education. Required by a limited budget to "make bricks without straw," my father started his attack on segregated education where it would meet the least resistance: tax-supported graduate and professional schools. His early strategy was to demand full implementation of the separate-but-equal doctrine, thereby demonstrating that *Plessy v. Ferguson* was, in practice, a fiction and that southern states would not and indeed could not spend the money to equalize graduate and professional school facilities or resources. Southern state officials would always require separate facilities but would never make them equal.

In the early days of the litigation campaign my father rarely attempted to integrate tax-supported elementary schools because he knew southern segregationists would staunchly resist any attempt to integrate children in schools, especially young black boys with little white girls. His ultimate goal, of course, was to achieve recognition that we were all equal members of the human race.

My father's greatest legacy was his commitment to building a civil rights movement that would improve the quality of life not only for his people but for all people. He conceived the plan and began implementing it long before he was named special counsel to the NAACP in 1935. He began by rigorously preparing himself as a legal advocate so that he could fight for the marginalized and powerless. He trained and mentored young black civil rights attorneys at Howard and around the country so that they could join the fight for racial equality and social justice, and by planning and implementing the nation's first sustained and ultimately successful litigation campaign against *de jure* segregation.

The movement my father built was not merely a litigation movement but was more broadly a civil rights movement, with several underlying objectives. First, my father realized that social change cannot simply be legislated or adjudicated. The law reflects social attitudes, not the other way around. He used press coverage of the cases, therefore, to educate a great majority of white people outside the South, who had little knowledge of black people or of racial segregation, with the aim of gradually winning their support. Second, he recognized that a movement required grassroots support in the national black community. My father therefore used black press coverage of the cases to demonstrate how the law could be used to attack Jim Crow segregation. Third, he used the cases to overcome southern black fear and apathy about challenging the racial status quo, by appealing to local black communities through NAACP branch leaders, ministers and lawyers, for members of the community to put themselves forward as prospective plaintiffs. Early courtroom victories encouraged others to step forward and agitate for their rights. Fourth, my father recognized that negative stereotypes of black people were detrimental to black civil rights aspirations.

Consequently, he used the cases to force the white press to provide dignified coverage of black plaintiffs and their attorneys involved in state and federal courtroom proceedings. Through the rigor with which he and his fellow lawyers prepared their cases, my father also used press coverage to overcome negative stereotypes of black lawyers as inept and incompetent. Finally, my father wanted the fight for civil rights to be self-sustaining. He realized that any individual leader might fall before victory was achieved, posing the risk that the campaign might falter and fail. To avoid such a consequence, he mentored outstanding young lawyers like Thurgood Marshall and Oliver Hill who could continue the struggle if he should fall in the fight.

Despite his remarkable accomplishments, his legacy has languished in the shadows of history. My mother told me that my father was not better known because he always considered himself a better "inside" man than an "outside" man, that he was more effective behind the scenes than out in front.

After getting the NAACP's school desegregation campaign up and running, he returned to private practice. Free of the NAACP's budget constraints and political considerations, my father tried a variety of cases over a wide range of issues beyond school desegregation. These issues included labor, restrictive real estate covenants, criminal law, desegregation of the military and First Amendment rights. He decided to leave the NAACP in 1938 because he felt as an independent lawyer he could do more by selecting areas of legal reform without the need for approval of a committee. At the same time, he remained a vigorous and active supporter of the NAACP's legal cases and served on its legal committee until his death in 1950. Over the last twelve years of his life he won some victories and lost others, but in all his legal fights he set a standard of excellence that is still admired in the legal profession and beyond, almost seven decades after his untimely death at the age of 54.

Although I was six years old when my father died, I do have some memories of him. Fragmented and anecdotal, my recollections are a combination of things I remember and things my mother told me when I was a boy. Nevertheless, I like to think they afford me some insight into his character. Though my father traveled frequently, I have fond memories of the time we spent together. On summer evenings, he would take me to the hillside below New York Avenue in Washington, D.C., overlooking the train yard at Union Station, where we would watch trains come and go, making the earth tremble as they rumbled past. My father loved trains, a potent symbol of America's industrial might. We had at home a model train set—an American Flyer freight train with a locomotive that puffed smoke—and he sometimes would let me operate the controls.

He told me once about a railroad case he had handled. Black locomotive firemen in the South were being pulled off trains in remote woods by white mobs that attacked them, because the whites wanted their jobs. My father fought to protect the black railroad firemen.

In fact, my father spoke frequently with my mother in my presence about the cases he had handled. What I gleaned from these conversations was that Negroes were victims and underdogs. One evening, as we were driving home after picking up my father from his office, I asked my parents what we were,

Negro or white. My mother turned her head to look at me in the back seat and said, "What do you think we are?" "White," I replied, reasoning intuitively that Negroes were always in trouble, and we were not. My parents corrected me, and they were more than a little amused by my misapprehension. I was sorely disappointed to find out we were "Negroes," among the underdogs, and did not understand why my parents found this so amusing.

My father also had a strong protective instinct. As we were driving home one evening after visiting my maternal grandmother, we passed the block where my father and I got our hair cut. Several doors away from the barbershop a two-story building seemed to be on fire. A doorway stood ajar and smoke poured out. As my father stopped the car and pulled on the emergency brake, my mother implored him to stay in the car and then, in her most command-ing voice, forbade him to investigate the smoking doorway. Saying something reassuring to my mother, father got out of the car, crossed the street, and dis-appeared through the doorway. He emerged a few moments later, saying the problem was a smoking stove. But the potential fire he now faced was his wife who sat next to him on the front seat of our car, upset he had taken the risk.

My father did his utmost to protect me, and when he could not, he avenged me. One bright day we were in our backyard. My father was tending his rose bushes, which he kept so my mother could have fresh flowers on the dining room table. I was playing with our dog, when a bee stung me on the back of my neck. I must have screamed in pain, because my father swept me up in his arms and carried me into the safety of our basement. He put a wet compress on my neck and tried to calm me, but I was inconsolable. Try as he might, he could not persuade me to return to the yard. Explaining that he had to leave me for a moment but would be right back, he disappeared into the bright light beyond the doorway. A few moments later he returned. With his handkerchief balled up in has fist, he told me that he had killed the bee that stung me and that it was safe to return to the yard.

My father, however, sought to protect me from something more harmful than a bee sting, and when he could not, he was devastated. One day I walked with him the block and a half to our neighborhood Peoples Drug Store. As he was transacting his business with a cashier, I left his side, ran over to the soda-fountain counter and climbed up on one of the barstools. When he real-ized what was happening, my father rushed over but not in time to prevent the "soda jerk" from telling me rudely to get down. My father was upset and said something to the young man about my being just a little boy. As we walked home, my little hand in his big one, he apologized to me.

My mother told me later that when we arrived home, my father was weeping.

My father was a patriot who demonstrated his love of country in countless ways, both large and small. He volunteered to serve his country during World War I and spent the rest of his life fighting to make his country live up to its democratic ideals. He took my mother and me on vacation to destinations that symbolized our nation's greatness: Niagara Falls, Yellowstone National Park, the Grand Canyon, and Yosemite National Park. Whenever we were in the car, no matter how short the trip, we sang songs that reflected the spirit of America like, "Oh! Susannah," On Top of Old Smokey," "She'll be Coming 'Round the Mountain" and "Darling Clementine."

I remember my parents one evening talking with some trepidation about government investigations of individuals and concern that my father would come under scrutiny. Only later did I learn the context for this conversation: my father represented the "Hollywood Ten," screen writers and actors who were being investigated by the House Un-American Activities Committee for suspected Communist affiliations.

In what must have been the last few months of his life, my father took me to the grounds of the National Botanical Gardens, where the government had put on display a Japanese kamikaze airplane. I remember my father's explaining to me what a kamikaze pilot did: how they said goodbye to their family, climbed into the cockpit of a plane whose landing gear would fall away after takeoff, and flew away on a suicide mission for love of their country.

I remember the day my father died, April 22, 1950. My mother and I were in Baton Rouge, Louisiana, staying with my mother's youngest sister, Eva Mae Taylor, and her husband, Tommy, who was commandant of ROTC at Southern University. My father, hospitalized in Washington, D.C., with a heart attack, had sent us away because my mother had suffered a nervous breakdown when he was stricken, and he was concerned about her welfare and mine. The day he died, I was playing with friends in a drainage ditch in front of Uncle Tommy and Aunt Eva's cabin, when my uncle stepped out onto the porch and asked me to come inside.

My mother was sprawled in an armchair, flailing her arms and wailing in grief. My aunt and uncle were bent over my mother, trying in vain to comfort her. One of them turned and told me my father had died and then told me to go back outside. Full of self-importance, I announced to my playmates that my father had died. I sensed that my life had changed, but I had no idea how much.

Charles Houston and Charles Jr. at their final Christmas in 1949.
COURTESY OF THE CHARLES H. HOUSTON, JR., FAMILY COLLECTION

The next day or so my mother left for Washington to attend my father's funeral. She did not take me. The family decided the funeral would be too traumatic for a child. I never got a chance to say goodbye or to grieve properly. So, I grieve still. Nevertheless, I take pride in my father's accomplishments and consolation in the knowledge that his life's work expanded American democracy, created opportunities for me and countless others, and helped make possible the election of Barack Obama as the 44th, and first African American, president of the United States.

Charles Hamilton Houston, Jr.
Baltimore, Maryland
July 2016

Genius for Justice

Lawyer Charlie Houston Is Coming!

We know the only way to ensure freedom for ourselves is to fight for freedom no matter whose freedom is involved.

—Charles Hamilton Houston

In many American cities at the middle of the twentieth century, a bustling downtown shopping district served by department stores sustained the local economy; Baltimore, Maryland, was no exception. Merchants would gladly take money from the community of "Negro"[1] shoppers, but would not allow them to work on the sales floor, try on clothing items in the dressing rooms, or place hats on their heads before they were purchased. Even some in the white community were enraged by such practices. Peggy Ewing Waxter, wife of a prominent Baltimore City judge, "bristled" at store management when her African American shopping companion was told she could not try on clothes or hats. Years later, Thomas Waxter, Jr., her then school-aged son with her during the incident, recalled that his mother was not arrested for advocating for her friend's rights, but they did end up in the department store office after she complained.[2]

Lillie May Carroll Jackson had also grown tired of the disrespect, but she wanted to do more than get angry. She called lawyer Charles Hamilton Houston as she had done on other occasions to help her fix it. As head of the Baltimore branch of the National Association for the Advancement of Colored People, (NAACP), Jackson was growing weary of such racist practices and was not hesitant to act.[3] She was a woman "full of rebellion" who felt racial segregation was an "un-Godly sin."[4] Houston, a native of nearby Washington, D.C., had no problem coming over to lend a hand. Houston hated segregation in all its forms. He once commented that "[w]e are born in segregated hospitals, educated in segregated schools, forced to travel in inferior segregated coaches, take inferior segregated jobs. We have to search for God in segregated churches and wait for judgment day in segregated cemeteries."[5]

At the time of Mrs. Jackson's call for help, no lawyer in the nation, white or black, was more feared or respected for courtroom skill than "Charlie"[6] Houston, as he was affectionately known to his friends. It had been said that Houston's "eyes were almost too pretty for a man's face, but there was nothing unmanly about his bearing...his deep baritone made him more of an arresting presence."[7] He was known to make public officials squirm under the barrage of his questioning. His eloquent arguments could draw "either vociferous applause or laughter from admiring courtroom audiences."[8] He could, "by magic of his personality transform a seething inferno of race hatred into a place of serenity where the same people who came to threaten and to scorn returned to listen and admire."[9] Even a Southern racist onlooker at a case Houston handled would feel compelled to acknowledge his lawyering excellence, commenting, "[y]ou have got to give it to him.... He knows what he's talking about even if he is a nigger."[10]

By the 1930s he had already won several cases in the Supreme Court, testified before Congress on several issues,[11] and challenged General Douglas MacArthur for his discriminatory practices in the military.[12] A national black trade union even called upon President Franklin Delano Roosevelt to name Houston to the Supreme Court of the United States.[13]

The stores that were discriminating against black shoppers acted very differently on the day of Houston's arrival.[14] On that occasion he, Lillie Jackson, daughter Juanita Jackson, and some other NAACP members went to several stores demanding to try on items of clothing. Their plan was to be denied and perhaps arrested so they could file a lawsuit against the stores. Houston decided he would ask to try on some underwear.[15] Dr. J.E.T. Camper, a member of the group of protesters, recalled that the stores did not stop them that day, "[b]ecause they knew...Charlie Houston as a lawyer."[16] Lillie Jackson was aware that Houston wanted to get a "case for us so that we could carry it to the Supreme Court.... But we didn't get any case because all the stores cooperated."[17] The protesting shoppers had intimidated the store owners and made an important point. Unfortunately, the cooperation did not last long. Dr. Camper lamented that after the stores discovered that "Houston was gone; they reverted back to the same procedures."[18]

This episode was just one example of Charlie Houston's ability to shake the foundations of a community by the mere possibility of his advocacy in a courtroom. He was able to get the attention of the "powers that be" and generate fear and respect. Houston sought no special treatment for black people; instead, he thought a person should "be judged on his individual merit and conduct as a human being."[19] It was believed by some NAACP protesters in Baltimore that someone from the black community must have warned the downtown department stores about Houston's planned confrontation designed to create a "test case" for a civil rights lawsuit.[20] Houston would return to Baltimore again and again for many other important legal battles, including one that is consider his first major courtroom victory over "Jim Crow."

In a 1935 case known as *Pearson v. Murray*,[21] Charles Hamilton Houston, Thurgood Marshall, and another Baltimore attorney named William I. Gosnell teamed up to secure a court ruling that ordered the University of Maryland School of Law to admit an African American, Donald Gaines Murray.[22] Again, Lillie Jackson encouraged Houston to sue "Jim Crow out of Maryland."[23] Jackson promised she would be there to back him all the way with the local branch of the NAACP.[24] She would also rally the support of several black preachers and churches of the Interdenominational Ministerial Alliance to support Houston's strategy. Publisher Carl Murphy of the Afro-American Newspapers would aid the Baltimore chapter of the NAACP to become the largest and most influential in the country by the mid-1940s.[25]

In just a few decades after "Charlie Houston" started his important work as one of the greatest courtroom advocates in American history he would be all but forgotten. Not long after his untimely death, people would stand "before audiences and receive recognition for his work, or projects he inspired, without mention of his name."[26] The generations that benefited most from his skill would rarely see him noted in school history books. This exceptional lawyer, in his brief season on earth, helped to make the kind of change that other great men and women attempted but had fallen short of accomplishing. By taking a closer look at Houston's education, nurturing, philosophy and theology, a fascinating picture of the unique person who became one of America's great change agents emerges.

Charles Hamilton Houston was packed up from his home in Washington, D.C., by his loving father and mother in 1911 and sent to Amherst College at sixteen years old.[27] He graduated Amherst as a class valedictorian and was awarded a Phi Beta Kappa key in 1915.[28] He was commissioned an artillery officer in 1917 and served his country honorably during World War I in Europe. After the war, he returned to study law at Harvard, following his father in the profession. Houston would distinguish himself as one of the school's finest students of all time, becoming the first African American elected to the prestigious *Harvard Law Review*.[29] He earned both a law degree and later an advanced doctorate in juridical science, the first time an African American in the United States had achieved that honor.[30]

Amherst College class photo of Houston (circled)
COURTESY OF THE CHARLES H. HOUSTON, JR., FAMILY COLLECTION

In the following year he was awarded a fellowship to pursue yet another doctorate degree in civil law at the University of Madrid in Spain.[31] His Harvard professors and its law dean were in awe of Houston's ability to both excel in the classroom and get along with his peers.[32] After achieving these educational accolades, Houston began the practice of law in 1924 at his father's Washington, D.C., firm. Along his professional journey, Charles Houston built a nationally recognized law school and took on state officials, the military, Congress and United States presidents. He would also fight in the courts at every level, creating more impact than any other lawyer of his time.

In a little over twenty-five years after becoming "lawyer Charlie Houston" he would die, exhausted from achievements that would have taken a dozen other good lawyers at least twice as long to accomplish. What happened in his brief, but extraordinary, quarter-century legal career challenged every part of the world's most powerful democracy. Charles Houston willingly worked himself to death for the causes in which he believed. He not only changed the law but also transformed many of those who worked with and even against him. He was a rarity in the human experience, a true genius with high ethical values, selfless and committed to justice. He was a "sacrificial man" who gave the best of his life for others.

The word "genius" is often overused when describing admirable men and women of accomplishment. It is a difficult word to define. Some have said it is not something one might possess, but a trait that "possesses you."[33] Under almost any definition, however, Charles Houston would be fairly identified as a genius. This "genius for justice" had keen insight into how he could move the legal system to new places.

The law has very few completely original concepts to develop. All societies have adopted rules to carry on basic government operating and decision-making functions. The idea of changing rules through a system of courtroom litigation, which, of course, does not require military coup, change of office-holders by election, or overthrow of a ruling monarch, was Houston's special contribution to the nation.

As noted constitutional scholar Leland Ware put it, "Houston foresaw a means of eliminating formal segregation at a time when most Americans accepted it as a permanent way of life. It was Houston's insight, together with his ability to orchestrate a coordinated campaign over a several-year period that resulted in the elimination of segregation laws."[34] In the same way mathematical genius Sir Isaac Newton acknowledged that if he saw further than others, it was because he "stood on the shoulders of giants,"[35] Charles Houston took the lessons of his teachers and applied them to his own vision. It is in what he added to those lessons that his true gifts were displayed. It has been said that true genius is "to recognize what others have seen but not grasped, have observed but not fully understood, and to then put everything together so that it makes a new kind of sense."[36]

The ability to take what others had "seen but not grasped" and reassemble those things to make legal change is, in my view, what distinguished Houston. He knew where he wanted to take the law and how to persuade others to follow. Whether his audience was an all-white jury, a lawyer on his trial team, opposing counsel, a skeptical politician or a reluctant southern judge, Houston possessed an amazing ability to get people to listen when they were opposed to his views. He was able to take advantage of small openings in the thought process of those he wanted to persuade. He displayed this trait throughout his life on practically every issue he confronted.

Examples of his ability to persuade are numerous. At college he was permitted to give a memorable commencement address about black poet Paul Lawrence Dunbar, to a nearly all-white Amherst, Massachusetts, audience.[37] At Harvard Law School, he persuaded a southern student on scholarship from the United Daughters of the Confederacy to work on a project with him.[38] He convinced opposing counsel in a Virginia death penalty cases to give him greater access to information during a high-profile interracial murder trial.[39]

He conducted secret discussions about federal legislation with former Ku Klux Klan member Hugo Black, when Black was a United States Senator from Alabama in the 1930s. Furthermore, he convinced the senator to support education initiatives for Negroes and the poor.[40] Years later, when Hugo Black was on the Supreme Court, he would serve as an honorary pallbearer at Houston's funeral.[41] Charlie Houston once convinced an entire southern appellate court to set free from death row a Negro convict, swaying the group to unanimously disbelieve the testimony of two white witnesses.[42] He argued successfully to a United States president at the White House to change national government discrimination policies in the military and war industries.[43]

In the pages that follow, these and other examples of Charles Houston's genius will be described in some detail. Of course, he was not perfect. He had some notable failures. However, when measured against the battles he willingly took on, Houston's record of success is extraordinary. Although most often associated with developing the strategy that led to the Supreme Court's historic decision in *Brown v. Board of Education*,[44] and the dismantling of legal "Jim Crow" in America, his career was so much more than that important episode.

Some statistical information helps illustrate his impact. Houston was actually counsel or co-counsel in nine Supreme Court cases, seven of which he won. Indeed, in his career, he established over 70 precedent-setting appellate decisions in state and federal courts. He tried many of those cases himself and developed each step of the legal theories he advanced. He argued cases in every part of the United States, from as far east as Massachusetts, to Alabama in the Deep South, to California on the West Coast and in Midwestern states like Michigan. Houston also waged court battles for civil rights in places like Tennessee and Missouri. He traveled across the nation, logging thousands of miles by train, airplane, and automobile, and made hundreds of personal appearances, particularly at churches and civic organizations. For example, in 1937 Charles Houston travelled 14,589 miles and attended 63 meetings[45] at the same time that he maintained full dockets of court cases.

He also often chronicled his legal experiences in the national press. All of this was done in an era of manual typewriters and "carbon paper" copies. Legal briefs had to be printed in an expensive and time-consuming "typesetting" process like that of the newspapers of his time. Houston also worked with many organizations to achieve change. He was a board member of the legal committees of all three of the country's most influential courtroom advocacy groups. He was chair of the NAACP Legal Committee for most of his career,[46] while also serving on the board of the American Civil Liberties Union.[47] In 1937 Houston as was elected a vice president of the National Lawyers Guild, making him the first African American to serve as an officer of a racially integrated bar association in the nation's history.[48]

While conducting his reform efforts he also practiced law with his father, distinguishing himself in even the most routine client matters on behalf of businesses and labor unions in private civil litigation and criminal law. Although his life was relatively short, his list of political contacts spanned the decades, from the Woodrow Wilson administration in the early twentieth century to a Minnesota senator who would later become a United States vice president during the 1960s, Hubert H. Humphrey.[49] Humphrey, influenced by his contact with Houston, was instrumental in passing major civil rights legislation during the 1960s that still governs America.[50]

Twenty-two years before the famed "Little Rock Nine" integrated Arkansas public schools, Houston filed briefs to aid two Arkansas Negro youths condemned to death on rape charges, unsubstantiated by physical evidence or even the testimony of the victim's companion on the night in question.[51] Long before Dr. Martin Luther King's efforts for civil rights, Houston was organizing church congregations to become engaged in the civil rights struggle, holding "mass meetings" on discrimination as early as the early 1930s.[52] During the "Jim Crow Era" he formed integrated committees that included United States senators, congressmen and even Supreme Court Justice Louis Brandies to advance the goals of job creation for Negroes in public utilities.[53]

Almost 15 years before Rosa Parks refused to give up her seat on a Montgomery, Alabama, city bus, Charles Houston represented a woman named Natalie Marmion, who was arrested for refusing to give up her seat on a Virginia bus.[54] In the 1940s, four decades before famed O.J. Simpson lawyer

Johnny Cochran represented Rodney King in a lawsuit for his beating by Los Angeles police, Houston filed police brutality suits for injuries to young black men shot by police after being taken into custody. In that case he argued that the police have a duty of care to deliver a prisoner safely to jail.[55]

Houston not only mentored Thurgood Marshall, the nation's first black Supreme Court Justice,[56] he also guided the careers of many others, including the first black woman to become a state supreme court justice[57] and the first male[58] and female African Americans to become federal judges.[59] An NAACP colleague and later director counsel, Jack Greenberg, said of Houston's influence on the civil rights work, "his shadow was across everything we did."[60] John Payton, another lawyer who followed Houston as chief of the NAACP's litigation arm described him as the only "indispensable" figure in the courtroom struggle for civil rights.[61] Justice Thurgood Marshall showered praise on Charles Houston until the end of his life, once commenting, "I was never chief counsel in any case that Charlie took part in."[62] Marshall lamented, "[a] lot of people have forgotten Charlie, but I ain't about to forget him."[63]

It should be part of our collective national shame that so few people know of him. In this world of instant news through social media, historical memory has, unfortunately, become a luxury. This biography is my humble effort to tell a part of the story of arguably the most extraordinary lawyer of the twentieth century. By any measure, except perhaps financial success, Charlie Houston was the greatest lawyer of his era. This opinion was almost universally shared by the great legal thinkers of his time of all races who witnessed his work firsthand. Both legal scholars[64] and courtroom lawyers had the highest regard for his ability.[65] Many Supreme Court Justices who heard his advocacy respected and admired him. Justice William O. Douglas, the longest-serving Justice in the history of the United States Supreme Court, was convinced that Charles Houston was one of the finest lawyers to ever appear before the court of any race.[66] The fact that by accident of his birth Houston happened to be African American adds an interesting perspective to the magnitude of his accomplishments.

Houston's race, an important aspect of his identity, helps us understand the times he influenced, the people he affected and the choices he made. The fights he willingly took on were more like the twelve labors of the mythical Hercules.[67] He opposed powerful people and institutions in society for the benefit of the lowly, despised and disenfranchised. He came along at a time of incredible national and international turmoil. By devoting his legal skill to those without power or voice, he forever released the law as tool for the people. He gave the law its place as an enabling force in the lives of ordinary men and women. His lasting contribution was to demonstrate how to use the courts when there seemed no other way for the powerless to obtain justice.

One newspaper writer in the 1930s described Charles Houston as "an unusually well-trained servant of the Negro race in America, whose ... brilliant achievements may well serve as a standard not only for his contemporaries but for those who come after."[68] Houston, however, always believed his work went well beyond the racial issues he confronted. He once said that although "we work directly on questions effecting Negro rights ... we also recognize the essential unity between the problems affecting.... Negro citizens and those affecting ... white citizens. We stand for common solutions to common problems."[69]

In the words of the great American jurist A. Leon Higginbotham, "Charles Houston's life was devoted to the cause of freedom. His accomplishments cannot be viewed as aiding only blacks, instead, he helped save all of America.... His career is an extraordinary counter balance to our forefather's failures in the racial human rights arena."[70] His body of reform litigation also influenced the national development of the law in criminal, labor, business, personal injury, estates and trusts and voting rights. Indeed, even removing from his resume the influential work on race, Houston's accomplishments still would rank him as one of the most important legal figures of the twentieth century.

While bringing Howard University School of Law to national prominence, he re-invented legal education, mentored a generation of the most important legal minds in American history and laid the foundation for generations of lawyers who would use the courts to enforce individual rights of all kinds. Indeed, any lawyer who has asked any court to recognize a constitutional right since 1940 must thank Houston for the road map. He took the design of what became a "living constitution" and breathed life into the non-working parts of its Bill of Rights.

Houston began his reform of the law when the nation was in a crisis for its very political stability and economic survival. His adult life was lived between the arc of two world wars, and the peak of his legal career occurred in the midst of a paralyzing national financial system depression.[71] Even with these obstacles, he used the courts as a tool for social change, skillfully navigating the political, racial and economic tide.

He treated friend and foe with the same blunt candor. For example, he could praise the Catholic Church for a progressive stance it had taken on some racial discrimination issues during the 1940s, while at the same time condemning Catholic University of America for having its black students "bring their lunches in paper bags because they were not admitted to the student cafeteria"[72] Throughout his career, he worked with Catholic priests, Jewish rabbis, Protestant church ministers and other religious leaders to advance his equal justice initiatives.[73]

Although Charles Houston described his belief in Christ as "Savior" during his life, he did not have much use for religious leaders who were "all talk and no action." Instead, he admired what he called "a very simple unadorned...militant Christianity"[74] to support multi-racial direct action against injustice. He once wrote openly of his admiration for white ministers who protested with black people against segregation in public transportation in North Carolina during the 1940s. Foreshadowing the civil rights movement of the 1960s and the freedom rides, he argued that such Christian "brotherhood" could bring change even to racism in the American South.[75] Houston acknowledged that "sometimes we react so violently to prejudice and the discrimination imposed on us by some white people that we forget there are other thousands of white church people...who are ceaselessly fighting every form of discrimination."[76]

Charles Houston also made sharp attacks on black preachers who did not see fit to appropriately address issues of social justice. He complained that only a few were "preaching a practical social gospel...many of them are still wondering the shores of Galilee with little to say about misery, bad housing, job discrimination and segregation in their own communities."[77]

Houston abhorred discrimination, even criticizing his own occasional lack of sensitivity to the plight of at-risk groups. A profound example of his earnest quest for fair treatment of all people resulted from a civil rights speech he gave in Minneapolis, Minnesota, in the 1940s. After the meeting, a man came to greet him who was not looking directly at him when speaking. After a few moments Houston realized that the man was blind. He later expressed embarrassment for not mentioning the plight of the blind during his remarks to the Minneapolis Human Relations Council. The blind man was "a member of the white majority, set apart by the loss of sight...he had a problem different from the rest of the people at the meeting. I thought about how minority problems can multiply themselves.... I apologized and promised to never forget the blind again."[78] This was an active display of the principles held by Charles Houston. He was a man always open to identifying both the best and worst in people, including himself.

Even as a member of the board of directors of the American Civil Liberties Union, Houston would clash with his colleague, attorney and ACLU founder Roger Baldwin, on issues of race when he felt the organization's stance did not line up with the best strategy for obtaining justice.[79] When longtime ally A. Philip Randolph, head of the nation's largest black labor union, suggested that a racial protest march during the 1940s not include white supporters of the cause, Houston vigorously disagreed.[80]

He was not merely a strategist; he was personally ready to take up the struggle by placing himself at risk. In 1933, decades before the era of "passive mass resistance" as a form of civil rights protest in America, Houston remarked that Negro leaders must be willing to get "their heads cracked in order that progress may be made."[81] He participated in symbolic public protests of lynching by wearing a noose around his neck with other marchers during the 1930s.[82] He wrote boldly about his intentions to defeat Jim Crow and other social ills and taught scores of others who studied under him how to do the same.

Houston's influence on other lawyers of his time is unmistakable. By traveling the country encouraging them to get involved in the civil rights struggle, he would develop and expand the impact of his litigation strategy to many communities. In Atlanta, he worked with lawyers like Austin Thomas ("A.T.") Walden fighting segregation and acknowledged those helping him, "at the risk of their personal safety."[83] Walden later became the first black judge in the state of Georgia.[84]

Houston would tell prospective law students "if you are looking for ease, comfort and security the law is not the field for you…but if you like a good fight, if you are able to take it on the chin and come up smiling, if you are looking for an opportunity to serve, then come into the law."[85] Whether driving through the Deep South to record terrible conditions suffered by black students in public schools with a movie camera, or battling in a distant courthouse before an all-white jury, Houston spent time on the front lines of his many transformative legal battles.

Although he was considered to be one of the finest lawyers of his time, he did not escape the personal scars of the humiliation of racial discrimination. Lawyers who worked with him, like the legendary Herbert Wechsler, one of the founders of the prestigious American Law Institute,[86] recalled that when he joined with Houston in argument before the Supreme Court during the 1930s, both would experience great disappointment. Describing Houston as a "charming and delightful man,"[87] they suffered the indignity of knowing that because "Jim Crow" was practiced in the nation's capital, the courtroom advocates had to walk to "Union Station to lunch together during the recess" because it was one of the few places they could eat together near the Supreme Court building.[88]

Other lawyers tell similar stories of Houston, after arguing a case, being unable to have a meal with admiring white colleagues.[89] Perhaps the most heartbreaking public disgrace he suffered was with his child only child, Charles Jr., at a drug store soda fountain counter.[90] A young employee working the counter told the young Houston to get down from the stool, referring to the boy as a "nigger."[91]

Prior to attending law school, while in the army, he would not be offered the respect of white officers of equal rank.[92] Houston's outrage was not limited to personal or family insults but extended to circumstances when other esteemed black professionals were disgraced. For example, he lashed out in his *Baltimore Afro-American* newspaper column when a distinguished member of the Philadelphia Bar, Dr. Sadie T. M. Alexander, was told she would have to take a glass of milk she purchased from Washington National Airport, "and drink it in the lobby, the ladies' room or some other place."[93]

Such events took an emotional toll on him but he would rebound again and again to continue the struggle against injustice. He would, however, express his personal outage from time to time, once criticizing "misguided white people who think they can go on hogging all the best things in the world for themselves."[94] He also complained that "the white man has made no effort to get along with other people. He has sat up in the driver's seat with whip, reins and guns giving orders."[95]

With all his expressions of anger, however, Charles Houston would assure his allies in the struggle that ultimately, they would prevail. "We may not win today," he would say, but the prejudice of many whites would eventually be "swept away, because they have repudiated the brotherhood of man."[96] His occasional bitter outbursts about "white supremacy" were also tempered by his obvious recognition that he had many Caucasian allies. He was aware "a lot of white people who believe in democracy and are willing to fight for it. I am always glad to get their help."[97]

Black America had no president or senators or even a Supreme Court Justice during the first part of the twentieth century, but it had an unofficial leader in the battle for justice in Charles Hamilton Houston. Like other influential world leaders, he worked both publicly and behind the scenes to accomplish his important goals. He was the only black leader of his time to influence all three branches of government. Houston changed both the public and private law of the nation. He served as general and soldier, doing whatever was necessary to carry out his reform of American law. His goal was that all people might receive the full benefit of our flawed, yet remarkable Constitution. Charles Houston's legal career was a peerless example of excellence and purpose on behalf of all mankind.

Endnotes

1. Throughout this book my references to African descendent people will shift in both description and use according to my assessment of the time period and manner that seems appropriate. How people have used the English language to describe themselves is a matter of great complexity and controversy. The terms "Negro," "Colored," "black," "African American" and "Person of Color," among others, have been invoked at different times and for different reasons to identify people who are often the subject of these pages. It is beyond the scope of this work to debate which descriptive terms are most appropriate. I have attempted to be sensitive to those differences and to be as accurate as possible in describing the events that comprise this biography.

My use of a racial description may differ if I am speaking as the author or attempting to describe how a quoted person used the descriptive word or might have described themselves. Ultimately, I am certain that my choices will not be agreeable to all. Some may even vehemently disagree or be offended by my choices. It is not my intention to offend anyone, only to attempt to capture the best way to accurately recount the extraordinary life of the biography subject, Dr. Charles Hamilton Houston.

2. Jacques Kelly, "Champion of Social Causes for Eight Decades," *Baltimore Sun*, September 20, 2007.

3. Elizabeth Fee and Linda Shopes, *Baltimore Book: New Views of Local History* 76 (Philadelphia: Temple University Press 1993).

4. Juanita Jackson Mitchell, University of Virginia Library, William A. Elwood Civil Rights Project, Oral History, video recording September 1, 1988.

5. Charles H. Houston, "Along the Highway," *Baltimore Afro-American*, June 12, 1948, p. 4.

6. J. Clay Smith, *Emancipation: The Making of the Black Lawyer 1844–1944* 3 (Philadelphia: University of Pennsylvania Press 1993).

7. Richard Kluger, *Simple Justice: The History of* Brown v. Board of Education *and Black America's Struggle for Equality* 105 (New York: Alfred A. Knopf 1977).

8. "May Lift Ban on Anderson," *Baltimore Afro-American*, March 4, 1939, p. 1, col. 5.

9. Ralph Matthews, "This Week," *Baltimore Afro-American*, May 5, 1950.

10. Walter White, *A Man Called White* 155 (The Viking Press New York 1948). *See also*, Diana Kienabow and Franklin L. Jonas, *People's Lawyers: Crusaders for Justice in America* 220 (New York: M. E. Sharp 2003). The occasional full reference to the use of the "N" word in this biography is certainly not intended to offend but only to capture the bitterness of racial attitudes held at the time the references were made. *See comment*, note 1, *supra*.

11. Statement of Charles Hamilton Houston, representing the NAACP, to the House Ways and Means Committee on the Economic Security Act (commonly known as the "Social Security Act.").

12. "Dean Houston Flays Gen. MacArthur for Upholding Jim Crow Army," *Chicago Defender* Sept. 8, 1934, p. 1. (In a news article Houston declared that "the records of the War department…reflect simply a policy of discrimination and nothing more.")

13. "Urge Negro for Supreme Court," *New York Times*, November 20, 1939, p. 11.

14. Fee and Shopes, *The Baltimore Book*, p. 74.

15. Ibid.

16. Ibid.

17. Ibid.

18. Ibid.

19. Charles H. Houston, "Along the Highway," *Baltimore Afro-American*, December 18, 1948.

20. Dr. J. E. T. Camper, oral history interview OH 8134, McKeldin-Jackson Oral History Collection, Maryland Historical Society, July 2, 1976.

21. *Murray v. Pearson*, 169 Md. 478, 182 A. 590 (1936).

22. Ibid.

23. C. Fraser Smith, *Here Lies Jim Crow: Civil Rights in Maryland* 99 (Baltimore: Johns Hopkins University Press 2008).

24. Smith, *Here Lies Jim Crow*, p. 88.

25. Edward Orser, *Blockbusting in Baltimore: The Edmondson Village Story* 70 (University of Kentucky Press 1994).

26. Marjorie McKenzie, "Pursuit of Democracy," *Pittsburgh Courier*, June 23, 1951, p. 22.

27. Genna Rae McNeil, *Groundwork: Charles Hamilton Houston and the Struggle for Civil Rights* 31 (Philadelphia: University of Pennsylvania Press 1983).

28. Ibid., p. 33.

29. Ibid., p. 51.

30. Ibid., p. 53.

31. Ibid., pp. 53–54.

32. Roscoe Pound to Fenton Booth, December 31, 1923, William LePre Houston Family Papers, Manuscripts Division, Library of Congress.

33. Attributed to Malcolm Cowley, assistant editor of the New Republic, public-quotes.com, visited September 17, 2019.

34. Leland B. Ware, "Setting the Stage for *Brown*: The Development and Implementation of the NAACP School Desegregation Campaign, 1930–1950," 52 *Mercer L. Rev.* 631, 632 (2001).

35. Isaac Newton, "Letter from Sir Isaac Newton to Robert Hooke (1675)." Historical Society of Pennsylvania.

36. Tom Burman, *The Dictionary of Misinformation* 69–70 (New York: Ballantine Books 1975).

37. McNeil, *Groundwork*, p. 33.

38. Roscoe Pound to Fenton Booth, December 31, 1923, William LePre Houston Family Papers, Manuscripts Division, Library of Congress .

39. "Defense Delayed," *Washington Post*, November 1, 1933, p. 11.

40. Roger K. Newman, *Hugo Black, A Biography* 225 (New York: Pantheon Books 1994).

41. http://blackhistorynow.com/charles-hamilton-houston/ visited May 14, 2018.

42. *Legions v. Commonwealth*, 181 Va. 89, S.E. 764 (1943).

43. Rawn James, Jr., *Root and Branch: Charles Hamilton Houston, Thurgood Marshall and the Struggle to End Segregation* 179 (New York: Bloomsbury Press 2010).

44. 347 U.S. 483 (1954).

45. NAACP 1937 Annual Report at page 23.

46. Jack Greenberg, *Crusaders in the Courts: How a Band of Dedicated Lawyers Fought for the Civil Rights Revolution* 4 (New York: Harper Collins 1994).

47. Charles Lam Minkmann, *The Noblest Cry* 260 (New York: St. Martins Press 1965).

48. "Lawyers Guild Asks for End to House Probes," *Washington Post*, February 23, 1949.

49. "D.C. Businesses Accused of Maintaining Negro Ghetto," *Washington Post*, December 11, 1948, p. 1.

50. *See generally*, F. Michael Higginbotham, *Ghosts of Jim Crow: Ending Racism in Post Racial America* (New York: New York University Press 2013) (Describing the importance of the civil rights legislation championed by Hubert Humphrey and signed by President Lyndon Baines Johnson under the "Great Society" programs).

51. "NAACP, ILD Unite to Aid Ark. Youths," *The Chicago Defender*, September 21, 1935, p. 1.

52. "Crawford Case Aid Address Mass Meeting," *Washington Post*, November 20, 1933, p. 13.

53. Carolyn Dixon, "Ban to Drive Jim Crow on Washington Buses," *New York Amsterdam News*, November 7, 1942, p. 2.

54. "Tests Bus Jim Crow," *Baltimore Afro-American*, May 17, 1941, p. 8.

55. "Father Sues Cop Who Shot Boy for $25,000," *Baltimore Afro-American*, September 10, 1940, p. 10.

56. Juan Williams, *Thurgood Marshall: American Revolutionary* 338 (Random House, 1998).

57. Jessie Carney Smith, *Black Firsts* 115 (Pennsylvania Supreme Court Judge Juanita Kidd Stout) (Canton, Michigan: Visible Ink Press 1994).

58. Jay P. Pederson, *The African American Almanac* 113 (Federal Judge William H. Hastie) (Farmington: Hills: Gale Research, Sixth ed. 1994).

59. Jay P. Pederson, *The African American Almanac* 115 (Federal Judge Constance Baker Motley) (Farmington: Hills: Gale Research Sixth ed. 1994).

60. Greenberg, *Crusaders*, p. 3.

61. John Payton, "Charles Hamilton Houston: Way Outside the Box," remarks at the grand opening celebration of the Charles Hamilton Houston Institute for Race and Justice, Harvard University, September 15, 2005.

62. Kluger, *Simple Justice*, p. 189.

63. Carl T. Rowen, *Dream Makers, Dream Breakers: The World of Justice Thurgood Marshall* 52 (Boston: Little, Brown 1993).

64. Roscoe Pound to Fenton Booth, December 31, 1923, William LePre Houston Papers, Manuscript Division, Library of Congress.

65. McNeil, *Groundwork*, p. 77.

66. William O. Douglas, *The Court Years 1939–1975* 185 (Random House: New York 1980).

67. *See generally*, Alister Banshard, *Hercules: A Heroic Life* (London: Granta Press 2005).

68. A. M. Wendall Malliet, "Story Behind Retirement of Houston Told," *The New York Amsterdam News*, July 30, 1938, p. A3.

69. Ibid.

70. McNeil, *Groundwork*, p. xviii.

71. For a detailed and textured examination of the Great Depression in America consider Studs Terkel, *Hard Times: An Oral History of the Great Depression* (New York: The New Press 1986).

72. J. Robert Smith, "Sen. Wagner Appeals to Kudsen to Check Jim Crowism in Defense Program," *New York Amsterdam News*, January 25, 1941, p. 6.

73. "Confab Meets This Weekend," *New York Amsterdam News*, March 29, 1941, p. 3.

74. Charles H. Houston, "The Highway," *Baltimore Afro-American*, June 14, 1947, p. 4.

75. Charles H. Houston, "The Highway," *Baltimore Afro-American*, June 4, 1947, p. 4.

76. Charles H. Houston, "Along the Highway," *Baltimore Afro-American*, December 25, 1948, p. 4.

77. Charles H. Houston, "Our Civil Rights," *Baltimore Afro-American*, January 22, 1949, p. 4.

78. Charles H. Houston, "Our Civil Rights," *Baltimore Afro-American*, January 15, 1949, p. 4.

79. Letter Charles H. Houston to Roger Baldwin March 21, 1940, Moorland-Spingarn Research Center, Houston Family Papers, Howard University.

80. Letter Charles H. Houston to A. Philip Randolph May 20, 1940, Moorland-Spingarn Research Center, Houston Family Papers, Howard University.

81. "Crawford Case Aids Address Mass Meeting," *Washington Post*, November 20, 1933, p. 13.

82. "Mob Violence Hit in Crime Program," *Chicago Defender*, December 29, 1934, p. 5.

83. Tomiko Brown-Nagin, *Courage to Dissent: Atlanta and the Long History of the Civil Rights Movement* 20 (Oxford University Press 2011).

84. Ibid., at p. 17.

85. "Alabama Has 4 Lawyers, Va. 57: Law for Those Who Like to Fight," *Baltimore Afro-American*, April 21, 1934, p. 23.

86. The American Law Institute (ALI), a prestigious body of lawyers, professors and judges, is well known for its legal work on various Restatements of Law, the Model Penal Code and the Uniform Commercial Code. It has been a place where Supreme Court Chief Justices often make public pronouncements about the Court at the ALI annual meeting. *See*, Jeff Shesol, *Supreme Power: Franklin Roosevelt v. The Supreme Court* 212 (New York: Norton Press 2010).

87. Kluger, *Simple Justice*, p. 129.

88. Herbert Wechsler, "Beyond Neutral Principles of Constitutional Law," 73 *Harv. L. Rev.* 1, 34 (1959).

89. Barbara Mills, "*...And Justice for All: The Double Life of Fred Weisgal, Attorney and Musician* 75 (Baltimore: American Literary Press 2000).

90. Kluger, *Simple Justice*, p. 278.

91. Ibid.

92. https://biography.com /people/charles-h-houston-9344795, visited May 9, 2018.

93. Charles H. Houston, "Along the Highway," *Baltimore Afro-American*, October 30, 1948, p. 4.

94. Charles H. Houston, "The Highway," *Richmond Afro-American*, May 3, 1947, p. 4.

95. Charles H. Houston, "The Highway," *Baltimore Afro-American*, August 23, 1947, p. 4.

96. Charles H. Houston, "The Highway," *Baltimore Afro-American*, June 21, 1947, p. 4.

97. Charles H. Houston, "The Highway," *Baltimore Afro-American*, October 18, 1947, p. 4.

II

Making of a Mentor

The Early Years

I made up my mind that I would never get caught again without knowing something about my rights; that if... I got through this war, I would study law and use my time fighting for those who could not strike back.

—Lieutenant Charles Hamilton Houston, United States Army,
Camp Meade, Maryland, 1918

Charles Hamilton Houston was born on September 3, 1895, in post-Civil War America. When he entered the world, "Negroes," as they were referred to at that time, had little representation in any legislature, state or federal, and few were actually able to vote. They had no extensive influence over American commerce or industry. In his hometown, the segregated nation's capital, there was little political incentive for white America to change any of those facts. It could be said, without fear of contradiction, that Charles Houston was literally born into a world of abject racial inequality. That year, one of the great progressive voices against race prejudice, Frederick Douglass, died.[1] Other voices would emerge.

Shortly after, the controversial black educator Booker T. Washington presented his famous speech at the Atlanta Cotton Exposition where he would encourage black people to remain as "separate as the fingers" in all things social from whites.[2] Washington's comments drew praise from segregation proponents everywhere. That speech was accurately characterized by Pulitzer Prize-winning biographer David Levering Lewis as "one of the most consequential pronouncements"[3] in American history. After his highly publicized comments, American race relations in the country would never be "quite the same again."[4] Booker Washington's proposal was seen by some black observers as surrendering even the possibility of equal treatment under law. Into these dire circumstances, Charles was born to William LePré and Mary Ethel Houston as their only child. His birth record merely identified him as No. 91,593 at the Health Department of the District of Columbia.[5]

Before Charles Houston's first birthday, the Supreme Court of the United States announced its infamous *Plessy v. Ferguson* decision,[6] which allowed states to maintain racially separate public accommodations of all kinds and doomed African Americans and other non-Caucasians to second-class citizenship because "separate" was rarely equal.

As a child, Charles would also be cared for by his paternal grandfather Thomas Jefferson Houston, who had stolen himself out of slavery. Thomas Houston would have a "religious encounter" as a young man and answered his call to the ministry of the gospel in 1849.[7] He married and eventually settled in Washington, D.C., where he pastored the First Baptist Church of Bladensburg, Maryland, nearby.[8]

During the years after his religious conversion, "T.J." Houston became an active member of the so-called "Underground Railroad" aiding runaway slaves coming north.[9] He freed members of his own family, then returned to free others.[10] During the first few years of young Charlie's life his former slave grandfather was a consistent "care provider and playmate."[11] Reverend T.J. Houston's death on February 19, 1899, was not only a tragedy for his family and young Charles, but the entire community. Over a thousand people attended his funeral.[12] T.J.'s love and care for his grandson in the early years provided Charles a sense of destiny and a preacher's faith for the battles he would face.

Often described as a "private" and "serious" child, Charles was considered a "bookworm."[13] He loved the zoo but could still hold his own in outdoor sports with his cousins and playmates.[14] He would develop a love for theatre and music early in life, a love instilled by his mother. He desired one day to have a career as a concert pianist or symphony director.[15] One childhood observer recalled that as a youngster Charles was "attractive, alert and intelligent."[16] He spent "more time at the piano than in the rough-and-tumble of outside sports."[17] Charles Houston became a prolific reader, often preferring a book to playing with other children.[18] The Houston household's financial situation permitted him to attend private nursery school.[19] Thereafter, he went to Garrison Elementary School in the District of Columbia, where he could learn at his own pace. He was bright enough to complete eight primary grades by age 12.[20]

Well prepared in grade school, he was ready for the prestigious M Street School in Washington, D.C., the first college preparatory high school for black students in the nation. Although Charles did well in many subjects, he was not a perfect student. He sometimes played pranks in algebra and study hall that prompted a teacher to write his mother about Charles being "trifling"[21] and her need to deal with some of his "nonsense."[22] Ironically, the future Supreme Court advocate would only get a grade of "C" in public speaking class.[23] Still, he did well enough to have prospects for a good college and enjoyed extra-curricular activities like the military cadet organization at the school where he would become a first lieutenant.[24]

Charles H. Houston's Military Cadet Photo, from the famous M Street High School in Washington, D.C. It was the first college preparatory high school for "colored" students in the nation.
COURTESY OF THE CHARLES H. HOUSTON, JR., FAMILY COLLECTION

His cousin William Hastie, who would later become the nation's first African American federal circuit court judge, described Charles as a "spoiled and self-centered only child, living a rather comfortable and somewhat secluded life and not very acutely or painfully disturbed by American racism."[25] No one could have predicted that one day he would shake the very foundations of his birthplace. The legally imposed inferiority of non-Caucasian people was not merely a way of life in the era of Charles Houston's childhood, it was knitted into the very fabric of the federal Constitution which imposed slavery at the founding of the nation.[26] He graduated from M Street High School at 15 years old. With the encouragement of his father, Charles turned down a scholarship to the University of Pittsburgh and instead decided to attended the prestigious Amherst College in Massachusetts, where he began his studies in September of 1911.[27]

The Influence of Loving Parents

By the end of his life Charles Houston would be remembered as one of the greatest legal mentors in American history. He guided the careers of many great lawyers and judges. How did Charles Houston become so effective at advising other influential people? The answer to this question lies in the rearing he received from his parents. Charles would ultimately use those skills to develop an army of lawyers to transform the nation. His protégés would have many "historical firsts" and would often credit him for their success.

It would have been an amazing accomplishment for any two black men in the same family to become lawyers under any circumstances in the early 1900s. To explain the genius of Charles Houston's mentoring skill, a detailed look at the life of his father, William LePré Houston, is necessary. Referred to by his co-workers and others close to him as "W.L.,"[28] The elder Houston was a multi-dimensional man. He could be described as part lawyer, part politician, doting father, community activist and teacher. He was a man capable of extremes. He could argue important civil rights cases asserting equal protection of the law,[29] while on another occasion vote as a member of the D.C. School Board, against married women working as teachers, believing they should be in the home performing domestic duties.[30] Ironically, William was only able to build his early law practice because of his wife's successful hair stylist business. Among her clients were the wives of U.S. senators and diplomats.[31] "W. L." ultimately built a thriving business with many labor, business and commercial clients. He represented several railroad unions and even established a branch law office in Chicago, Illinois.[32]

He was actively involved in the national leadership of the Odd Fellows fraternity, rising to the level of national Grand Master, the organization's highest position. William presided over the fraternity at a time when its branches had grown by 1,220 chapters and 40,000 members.[33] As the organization's leader, he commanded much respect. One lodge member, upon missing a scheduled meeting, wrote "My Dear Grand Master, I beg to ask your pardon on bended knees for my failure to respond more promptly to your very kind letter of July 4; moreover I beg pardon still more profoundly for my failure to be present Monday night, July 6, at the meeting of Corinthian Lodge, No. 38575,... of which I have the honor to be [a] humble but earnest member."[34] William's longstanding leadership role with the Odd Fellows organization ended when he was removed in 1922 after being accused of stirring up "dissent among the membership."[35]

William LePré Houston
COURTESY OF THE CHARLES H. HOUSTON, JR., FAMILY COLLECTION

A stern and disciplined man, he had been a former high school principal in Indiana before coming to Washington.[36] He first worked in a federal civil service job. He then earned a law degree attending Howard University School of Law at night.[37] He later sent for his wife to join him in Washington after deciding that there was enough opportunity for the both of them to make it their permanent home.[38] Although William Houston was an extremely confident man, he was generally modest.

He handled many types of cases involving business, domestic relations, property and estates. The firm's financial records indicated that only about 10% of its work was for criminal matters.[39] The few criminal cases William Houston handled usually involved important civil rights issues like the failure of police to protect black citizens.[40] Active in both local and national politics, William was at times a Republican, and on other occasions worked for Democrats, depending on the amount of influence he could wield by supporting specific candidates. He sometimes travelled across the country as a surrogate to speak on politics for one candidate or another.[41]

On November 12, 1912, for example, William spoke in Schenectady, New York, at the invitation of one of its local Republican clubs. An advertisement of that event described him as "The brilliant colored orator...Counselor at Law, of Washington, D.C., especially engaged for this meeting." His topic for that event involved, "The Issues as They Affect us as a Race in This Campaign."[42] It is interesting to note that, considering full rights for women to vote had not yet been established in those years, "ladies were especially invited to attend" the political event.[43]

William Houston would often find himself at the intersection of important times in American history. His reputation as a person of respect and influence caught the attention of famed Harvard-trained sociologist Dr. W.E.B. Dubois, who wrote to the elder Houston in 1905 and again on March 27, 1906, urging him to become part of the discussions that formed the "Niagara Movement."[44] The Dubois meetings would lay the foundation for the NAACP, which was founded a few years later in 1909.[45]

"W.L." Houston would also have contact with another influential Negro of the early century, Booker T. Washington. William Houston represented a cousin, Daniel Houston, in a contract dispute against Booker Washington and the Tuskegee Institute, where Daniel was on the faculty.[46] Daniel wished to terminate his teaching contract with the school, but Washington would not allow it. Concerned about Booker T. Washington's reputation for retaliation, Daniel Houston told William that he "feared Washington's influence...for he could ruin me by discharging me."[47] Ultimately, William secured Daniel Houston's release from Tuskegee without penalty.

By the early 1920s, William Houston had become so well known in Washington and Chicago that the *Chicago Defender* newspaper reported the headline "Atty. Houston on Crutches" from an injured foot caused by stepping on a nail.[48] He served from 1937 to 1942 as a special assistant United States attorney general in the Antitrust Division of the Department of Justice.[49] William also served for decades on the part-time law faculty at Howard University, teaching many courses including Insurance Law.[50]

William Houston wielded considerable political influence well into the end of his six-decade legal career. At one point he was one of a handful of influential African Americans considered to be advisors to President Franklin Delano

Roosevelt as part of his so-called "Black Cabinet."[51] William also was present at the first integrated inaugural presidential dinner, held for Harry S. Truman in the late 1940s at Washington, D.C.'s famous Mayflower Hotel.[52]

Even with all the activity connected with his busy law practice, there was little doubt that he was still very devoted to his wife and son Charles.[53] From a young age, it was clear that William intended to have Charles exposed to a wide range of social, cultural and educational opportunities, like speeches and musical concerts.[54] When William Houston was away on business he frequently corresponded with his wife and son, often questioning why letters were not answered within a day or two.[55] These letters provide insight into how Charles Houston would acquire his remarkable mentoring ability that influenced some of the greatest legal minds of his time.

William's correspondences to Charles covered a wide range of topics from encouragement on schoolwork[56] to advice on what should be done if Charles were to contract a sexually transmitted disease.[57] The letters demonstrate a relationship of great trust between father and son. Their relationship was open enough to be useful, firm enough to provide guidance and detailed enough to give clear structure. The letters started very early in Charles' life and often opened with the greeting, "My Dear Son ..."[58]

In November of 1909 William wrote Charles from his Chicago law office during the Thanksgiving season when he could not be home. The elder Houston gently scolded his son for failing to send him a Thanksgiving card.[59] In the same letter, however, William also demonstrated understanding, "I know you are busy with your studies endeavoring to make a good record.... Mother informs me you look very well indeed in your cadet suit and overcoat."[60] The letters sometimes directed young Charles to perform tasks for his father that supported his Odd Fellows fraternity work.

Always a careful planner, William rarely left any detail to chance. In a letter dated January 10, 1910, William requested some reports regarding the fraternal organization's business that he had left at his District of Columbia home. William instructed Charles in very specific detail: "Dear Charles.... On the floor underneath the bottom drawer of the closet in the hall on the third floor, are tied together in two or three different packages [are] some Odd Fellow books I desire.... wrap them up in good, stout paper and send them to me at once by express."[61] He cautioned, "take all the papers...out" from between the pages. William would further advise his son to "get mama to assist you in order that no mistakes or omissions will be made."[62] He would direct Charles to "[s]end the books to my residence, #2710 Dearborn Street, I want to use them at the house, so don't send them to the office as I would have to carry them home.... Show this [letter] to mama."[63]

The detail of the instructions given by William to Charles reflected a life lesson that even small jobs matter, and all tasks should be performed with great care. Although rigid and methodical as a practicing lawyer, William enjoyed occasional cultural activities. He was often a guest at noted social parties of his day. William once served as master of ceremonies at a "Patriotic Musical program" for a United States congressman.[64]

Although not as dedicated to civil rights as his son Charles would become, some social activism was a vital part of the elder Houston's legal career. By virtue of his status as a lawyer in a time when there were so few black lawyers, William was often called upon to draw clear lines against racial segregation and other injustices. If he had not been mindful of these issues he never could have been elected president of the National Bar Association, the group of African American lawyers who championed opportunity for themselves.[65] One example of William Houston's efforts to advance civil rights was when he joined forces with the leadership of the National Lawyers Guild to denounce the policy of racial discrimination in the American Bar Association. When William was a luncheon speaker at New York City's Rosoff Hotel in August of 1939, civil rights took center stage.[66] During his remarks, William joined Stanley M. Isaacs, the president of the Guild, charging that the ABA had "heaped 'lasting disgrace' upon itself for 'setting up a color barrier' against Negro applicants."[67]

William took great pride in the quality of his legal work, particularly the fact that he represented both Negro and white clients. In a letter to his wife, while she was attending a family reunion in Ohio, William wrote, "I think you would have felt some real satisfaction if you could have been present when I argued the case last week before the Interstate Commerce Commission; when I stood there before the highest Railroad Court in the United States and argued a case on behalf of thousands of railroad men and every man for whom I spoke was a white man."[68] William related the satisfaction of the union leaders in the quality of the representation he provided. "The officers of the Order of Railroad Station Agents...are very generous in their expressions of praise for my efforts. They say their cases in the future shall be given to me."[69] Always with the eye on the bottom line of his business, William made clear, "I charged them a nice fee, which they cheerfully paid."[70]

"W.L." was clearly at the helm of all Houston family activities, but because of his vigorous court and travel schedule, Mary Houston provided much of the moral support and guidance that young Charles needed. She developed his taste for art and culture. They traveled, often by ferry, along the Potomac River and Chesapeake Bay to historic sites like Harper's Ferry, Virginia.[71] It is clear from many of Charles Houston's letters that he cherished his mother, as she often smoothed the sharp edges of W.L.'s strict style. She provided him encouragement and taught him sensitivity for others.

His parents were a complimentary team raising their son. Each added support for his educational efforts. Both offered advice that fit into the tapestry of wisdom that aided Charles' own ability to persuade and inform. The combination of parenting styles resulted in a dignified and respectful young man who was continuously encouraged. This rearing made him capable of concentrating on his studies and developed his ability to get along with a wide range of people. The letters from his parents were particularly important during his college years at Amherst, when the pressures were great on a fifteen-year-old having his first experience away from home alone.

At college, Charles Houston, though reserved and somewhat withdrawn, was well-liked by his classmates.[72] Amherst was quite an adjustment for him. His first semester report card yielded some victories and some disappointments. Grades of "A" in both Latin and Greek showed his considerable promise for academic success. However, the "C" in English resulted in a letter from his father to the college dean.[73] On February 12, 1913, William wrote his son to offer encouragement. "I believe you can do better; I hope you will.... Your promise to buckle down and improve your record is pleasing news to your mother and me."[74]

William maintained much of the practical communication with Charles, like cautioning about his spending. "Now we come to our usual trouble, your expense account. Amherst is making a pauper out of me.... You better readjust your expenses so that you will be able to come within the amount designated."[75] His father also provided him pragmatic advice about cultivating relationships at the nearly "all white" school. William cautioned Charles, "you will become lonesome at Amherst but I am inclined to believe that you are far better off being there alone. It will lead to the formation of friendships among the whites that will stand you in good stead in years after."[76] William was careful to explain to his son how to develop those relationships. He advised, "while I do not wish you to cringe, fawn or thrust yourself upon the students, still you must place yourself in a receptive attitude for their proffered friendship and association."[77]

During his years at Amherst, Charles received many compliments for his thesis on African American poet Paul Lawrence Dunbar. Somehow, his father had occasion to mention his presentation to the late poet's widow, Alice N. Dunbar, who was living in Wilmington, Delaware, at the time. On June 24, 1915, Charles received an inspiring letter "congratulating him on his work and…choice of subject." Ms. Dunbar wrote, "[i]t takes courage for a man to honor his race in a college of men of the other race, and I feel like commending you for such courage."[78] She continued, "[w]hen we honor our own men, commend our own deeds and show the members of other races who we associate with that we are not afraid or ashamed of our own, we are doing much to give our race its proper place in the sun."[79]

In a letter to his mother, Charles would tell her about being asked to serve on the finance committee for a student group, "it means only that I am some sort of collector…. The thing I like most about it is that it came unexpected; Dick Pratt came up to me in chapel one morning and asked me to take it."[80] Charles would describe in letters to his mother details of his active campus life. "Every morning I am up in the shower by 6:30 except when I play tennis; there I get up at 5:30 and bathe at 7. I can mess up a mean tank too (swim); can't go so fast but I can keep going."[81] In the 1915 Amherst year book it was written that "Charlie was known as a hard worker who led a very quiet life during his stay."[82] He would keep updates on his mother's spiritual development and let her know about his own, once commenting in response to a letter "you are becoming a regular church goer."[83] He once excitedly reported, "I wish you could hear some of these sermons, then your appreciation for the church would increase twofold."[84]

The constant encouragement paid off. Charles Houston would participate in the Hardy Prize Debates in 1915, discussing a question of whether the United States should enter into the first World War.[85] Charles Houston would be one of the few students awarded the prestigious Phi Beta Kappa key at graduation.[86] By the time Charles Houston returned to D.C. from college, William and Mary Houston had already built into their son a full set of advice-giving skills.

Return to Washington

When Charles returned from Amherst, life slowed down for him. He no longer had the bustle of college activity. Like all Houston men before him, he needed a job. His father helped him secure a teaching position at Howard University. He began teaching English and various remedial courses at the liberal arts college.[87] Charles loved teaching, and his students loved him. He had a gift for communicating that they willingly received. "His tenure as an instructor of English at Howard lasted two years from 1915–1917."[88] Charles Houston also developed "the first course in black literature at Howard."[89] Among the stated goals of the course from the university's catalog was "to teach the students to give adequate written and oral expression to his thoughts; second, to develop the student's culture and broaden his outlook; third, to train the student to stand before an audience and give utterance to his thoughts."[90]

Like all young people, Charles pondered his future, however all plans would have to wait because of World War I. Charles became restless, and talk of the European conflict was growing more intense. He sought to serve his country. His pursuit of military service would be one of the great turning points in his life. Because he was a college graduate, he would seek to be commissioned as an officer. He had no intention of entering the army to merely lead a manual labor detail; he wanted to fight. He sought to be trained in the science of artillery. Because of the discrimination practiced by the army, Charles was told that artillery was not available, but he eventually secured those skills.[91]

He was first sent off to Camp Des Moines, Iowa.[92] After artillery training, Charles was stationed at Camp Meade, Maryland. It would be there that he would learn a profound lesson about the unequal administration of justice. He would encounter a military officer who resented Charles's advocacy on behalf of Colored troops. That officer's solution to Houston's caring approach was to appoint him judge advocate general, where he would be responsible for prosecuting Negro soldiers for rules violations.[93] In a particularly painful case, his assignment required him to charge a soldier for minor infractions.[94] That career soldier, a family man, lost rank and was severely punished under the Code of Military Justice.[95] The event broke Charles Houston's spirit so much that he went to see the punished soldier in the military "lock up" to apologize for the outcome of the case.[96] Charles Houston vowed that if he were fortunate enough to get out of the war alive he would study law and "strike back" for those who could not fight for themselves.[97]

Soon after that traumatic experience, Charles learned he would be deployed overseas. In Europe he would both broaden his global perspective and also see racism that he would battle for the rest of his life. He did have some enriching personal experiences while abroad, like performing with a military choral group.[98] In this endeavor he also showed a modest, somewhat insecure side when he passed on an opportunity to perform a piano solo for one of the concerts.[99] While serving in Brest, France, Houston would experience humiliation not from his enemies but from white superior officers.[100] Blacks were removed from the battleship *Virginia* after being assigned there and placed on a tug boat "with the explanation that no colored troops had ever traveled on board a United States battleship."[101] The black troops were served their meals at a different "mess hour" than their white comrades.[102]

French officers, allies of the United States, were not permitted to eat with or shake hands with Negro officers. French officers were puzzled by these directives from the United States command staff and often ignored them.[103] The French respected the Colored officers because many spoke to them in their native tongue, with proficiency that was often superior to that of the white army officers.[104] Furthermore, Negroes were absolutely forbidden, under threat of arrest, from speaking with French women. This rule led to a confrontation between black and white military officers.[105]

Decades after the war Charles Houston's cousin William Hastie commented that Charles' negative experiences in the military give him a "new sense of kinship with his black brothers."[106] Hastie explained that Charles "came out [of the army] a much wiser and tougher man with a hatred for American racism that he never wore on his sleeve but would retain as a motivational force."[107]

Charles informed his mother that his experience in the military had made him resilient, "[t]his Army has taught me that the man with only one trick or trade has a hard time. I have tried everything from splitting a target to making French dressing."[108]

The war not only left Charles with emotional scars, but physical ones as well. He contracted a respiratory illness in the army. His weakened breathing would later prove to be major factor in declining health during his later years.[109] At the end of his tour of duty, he became anxious to return home. His letters reflected guarded optimism that he would soon resume his role as a private citizen. Again, writing his mother from France he told her that he found souvenirs for she and his father. Charles purchased what he humorously described as "a French preparation for dad's hair guaranteed to kill or cure."[110] Anxious to get home he lamented, "my heart has descended from my mouth to the depths of my stomach; my will has buckled . . . when we will move, where we will move . . . I am leaving to the higher command; and it doesn't seem in a hurry to let us know."[111]

In Christmas of 1918, Charles took respite from the toils of war and tensions of racial discrimination. In a cold barrack with little extra food he felt grateful that the war appeared to be coming to an end. The American engineers had erected a huge cross on the highest hill near camp and wired it with high powered lights so bright they lit the entire countryside. Grateful his life had been spared, he viewed the Christmas Eve lights with special meaning.[112] Years later he recalled "that night standing in the mud, conscious that peace was spread over the land like the benediction from the cross; I got my first realization of what Christmas should mean."[113] In a letter to his mother at Christmas of 1918 Charles wrote "[t]he cross added an air of solemnity up there on the skyline shining in the midst of the night…to me this Christmas seemed a Christmas of peace and rest and all my burdens were at the foot of the cross."[114]

Before leaving France, Charles had a brief time to take in the culture and have some escape from discrimination in public accommodations. He would be able to ride in taxis, eat breakfast at Parisian cafés and take in a burlesque show without the segregation practiced in the United States.[115] Charles commented, "[f]or the early evening we sat on the sidewalk outside the cafés on the Boulevards. We saw every nationality: soldiers of every Allied country."[116] Soon he returned home and reunited with his family.

On to Harvard

After his discharge from the army, Charles pursued the law as he had planned. He attended Harvard University, considered by many the nation's finest law school. His father would spare no expense in an effort to make sure his son would succeed. William arranged for him to live in an apartment close to campus in Cambridge, Massachusetts. It had sleeping quarters and an additional room to serve as a study.[117] Charles embraced the study of law. He pondered broader social ideas in Roscoe Pound's Jurisprudence class. His class notes reflect a keen interest in the "moral" principles of law and justice.[118]

He also absorbed the detailed precision in Commercial Law by the legendary Felix Frankfurter.[119] Frankfurter would later become an important Justice of the Supreme Court of the United States.[120] He was also an indispensable figure in Houston's professional development. The Eastern European Jewish scholar would notice Houston's sharp mind and treated him as a favored student. Frankfurter spent additional time with Charles, socializing outside of class in less formal settings. Frankfurter would recall that Houston "was one of my students who I saw intimately."[121] He would enjoy dinners at the Frankfurter home prepared by the professor's wife.[122] Attorney William T. Coleman, who worked for Justice Frankfurter as the first African American judicial law clerk at the United States Supreme Court, explained Frankfurter's influence on Houston. At Harvard the professor "provided Charles the intellectual confidence to excel against any lawyer in any case."[123] Coleman would recall that Frankfurter had a particularly profound effect on the few African American students he mentored. Students exposed to Frankfurter's "training in analysis...could examine and explain any legal problem."[124] William Coleman would also share that when he was personally confronting an important career decision, Charlie Houston had given him some of the "soundest advice he had ever received."[125]

Charles' intellectual vigor was astonishing. A review of his law school notebooks reflects a capacity not only to comprehend the law, but to absorb it and recount it in extraordinary quantity. He would keep his notes in large cloth-bound, "accountant style" ledgers neatly written in fountain pen. Each page contains portions of the legal rules in the margins and reveal dozens of written questions he placed beside the legal definitions and other comments on the assigned cases. These questions reflected the thoughts of either the professor, classmates or his own analysis. It is sometimes difficult to tell whose ideas Houston was analyzing in his notes. What is clear, however, is that he was recording a high quality, high-speed, multi-level legal dialogue in his head as he sorted through what was discussed in his classes.

One of the most stunning examples of this intellectual prowess is demonstrated in the magnitude of his constitutional law notebook. The several hundred page behemoth was neatly arranged with fold-out charts glued to the ledger written in multi-colored fountain pen. The notes were so detailed and comprehensive, they read more like a professor's scholarly critique than a student's renderings. No matter which subject Charles was recording in his notes, they retained the characteristics of clarity, precision and order. These traits would soon become the hallmarks of his professional career.

His father William took a great interest in Charles' law school progress, sometimes talking directly to his professors. In a 1920 letter his father wrote "I hope you made even a better mark than you now have reason to believe in your examination in Contracts. I am very anxious that you distinguish yourself in your examinations. I came away from Harvard much elated over the report that Messrs. Williston and Warren made to me of you."[126] William would even check on the academic progress of his ward and Charles's future wife Gladys Moran while she was in college. Upon her receiving a poor but passing mark in a class at Howard University, William wrote her instructor who responded that "he was not impressed that she was a strong student" in his particular class.[127] The professor, making no apologies for his "high standards,"[128] added that he thought Gladys was "in every respect a fine young women"[129] and that her grade was "no disparagement of her general ability."[130]

Charles' life as a Harvard law student was not perfect. He wrote his parents to tell them of his first unsuccessful academic effort, "The Editors on the Review didn't want me on this fall. . . .But I still go on my way alone."[131] He was ultimately selected to join; his superior academic performance would lead to an invitation to become a member of the prestigious editorial board of the *Harvard Law Review*.[132] This honor, only offered to Harvard law's finest students, would be among the several "firsts" for Charles for as an African American.[133] While he was at Harvard he also helped sponsor an event where the controversial black nationalist leader Marcus Garvey was invited to the campus as a guest speaker.[134] He loved interaction with the few other African American students at Harvard both from the law school and other parts of the university.

Charles would try to help other black students who were struggling with their academic work. One student, Earl Brown, recalls that Charles made him come to study sessions in his apartment to keep him from being academically dismissed.[135] Brown described himself as a distracted freshman. The dean of Harvard College summoned Brown to his office to warn him that he was in serious academic trouble. "Charlie took direct and extreme action when he learned of my academic crisis."[136] Fearing that Brown did not know how to study, Houston pressed him to improve, "[m]aybe I can't make you study but I'm going to try."[137] In the weeks that followed Brown came to Charlie's apartment every night to study for three or four hours. Their contact continued even after Brown finished Harvard. "He was always ready and willing to go out of his way to advise, help and lead me in any undertaking in which I was engaged."[138]

After graduating with honors from the law school, Charles was encouraged to complete a graduate degree in law. The Doctor of Juridical Science (J.S.D.) was offered at Harvard for advanced study for those who might contemplate a career as a law professor. In his application to the doctorate program, he expressed his goal that "his desire for further study" might lead to "a Negro Lawyer in every community . . . the great majority [of whom] must come from Negro schools . . . [and] Negro Teachers."[139] Charles was encouraged by members of the Harvard faculty to pursue the prestigious academic credential. His doctoral thesis was entitled, "Functional Study of the Requirements of Notice and Hearing in Governmental Action in the United States."[140]

During his graduate work, other influential people in the academic community took notice of him, and he was encouraged to apply for a Sheldon Fellowship, which supported expenses and tuition to study law in Europe. After receiving letters of recommendation from Professor Frankfurter and Dean Pound, Charles learned he would receive the fellowship to study in Madrid,

Spain.[141] The trip was transformational for Charles. He was able to immerse himself in a totally new culture and dissect a foreign legal system. Not only would he receive another doctorate degree in civil law from the University of Madrid, but he was also able to use his cultivated language skills in Spanish, German, and French. This experience would provide valuable perspective on the United States legal system that he would be destined to reform through legal attacks in the future.

Houston's travels also enriched his views on international affairs, which would become an important part of his advocacy in the later years of his life. Charles' journey through Europe and North Africa would again (like he experienced in France during WWI) expose him to social integration in a way he had not experienced in America. He could eat in restaurants, use public transportation freely and enjoy operas from the orchestra section rather than the balcony.[142]

These rich academic, cultural and travel experiences helped him become a "well-rounded" sage for advice giving. His global perspective helped him see the full potential of a constitutional government that, if operated properly, could give equal protection of the law. After the intellectual stimulation of higher learning and world travel, Charles would prepare to return to the United States to join his father in the practice of law.

Endnotes

1. William S. McFeely, *Frederick Douglass* 381 (New York: W.W. Norton & Company 1995).

2. David Levering Lewis, *W. E. B. Du Bois: A Biography of a Race 1868–1919* 174 (New York: Henry Holt & Company 1993).

3. Ibid.

4. Ibid.

5. Health Department of the District of Columbia, Birth Certificate No. 91,539, William LePre Houston Family Papers, Manuscript Division, Library of Congress, Box 4.

6. 163 U.S. 537 (1896).

7. Genna Rae McNeil, *Groundwork: Charles Hamilton Houston and the Struggle for Civil Rights* 19 (Philadelphia: University of Pennsylvania Press 1983).

8. Ibid.

9. Ibid.

10. Geraldine R. Segal, *In Any Fight Some Fall* 15–16 (Rockville: Mercury Press 1975).

11. McNeil, *Groundwork*, p. 25.

12. Ibid.

13. Ibid.

14. Ibid., p. 25–26.

15. Ibid.

16. Ibid.

17. Ibid., p. 25.

18. Segal, *In Any Fight*, p. 22.

19. McNeil, *Groundwork*, p. 25.

20. Ibid.

21. Ibid.

22. Ibid., p. 30.

23. Ibid.

24. Ibid.

25. Segal, *In Any Fight*, p. 6.

26. As one insightful observer explained, "the ability of the white majority to impose the institution of slavery was a prime example of the destructive power of factions." *See* Michael M. Meyerson, *Liberty's Blueprint: How Madison and Hamilton Wrote the Federalist Papers, Defined the Constitution, and Made Democracy Safe for the World* 169 (New York: Basic Books 2008).

27. McNeil, *Groundwork*, p. 30.

28. "A Symposium on Charles Hamilton Houston: Oral History Hon. Margaret A. Haywood," 27 *New Eng. L. Rev.* 616 (1993).

29. *Dent v. Swilley* No. 46 United States Supreme Court, October Term 1927.

30. "Would Bar Married Women as Teachers in School," *Washington Post*, October 18, 1923, p. 2.

31. McNeil, *Groundwork*, p. 27.

32. Letter William L. Houston to Charles H. Houston, January 29, 1910, from 185 Dearborn Street offices of Edward H. Morris & William L. Houston, Chicago, William LePre Family Houston Papers, Manuscript Division, Library of Congress, Box 19.

33. "Odd Fellows Are Thriving," *Baltimore Afro-American*, June 13, 1908, p. 1.

34. Letter to W. L. Houston, Grandmaster July 14, 1908, William LePre Houston Family Papers, Manuscript Division, Library of Congress, Box 21.

35. "Houston Is Expelled by Odd Fellows," *Chicago Defender*, Feb. 22, 1922, p. 3.

36. McNeil, *Groundwork*, p. 21.

37. Ibid., p. 22.

38. Ibid., p. 22.

39. Ibid., p. 23.

40. *Laney v. United States*, 294 F. 412 (D.C. Cir. 1923) (William defended a criminal case regarding a shooting during a race riot).

41. William L. Houston to Mary Ethel Houston, October 20, 1920, William LePre Houston Family Papers, Manuscript Division, Library of Congress, Box 5.

42. Broadside, (N. Haskins President), William LePre Houston Family Papers, Manuscript Division, Library of Congress, Box 10.

43. Ibid.

44.   Letter DuBois to William L. Houston, March 27, 1906, William LePre Houston Family Papers, Manuscript Division, Library of Congress, Box 4.

45.   *See generally*, Gibbs Smith, *NAACP: Celebrating a Century, 100 Years in Pictures* 12–13 (Layton, Utah: Gibbs Smith Publisher 2009).

46.   Letter, Daniel Houston to William L. Houston, September 9, 1906, William LePre Houston Family Papers, Manuscript Division, Library of Congress, Box 4.

47.   Ibid.

48.   "Atty. Houston on Crutches," *Chicago Defender*, July 27, 1923.

49.   "Houston Will Retire from Atty. General Office," *Chicago Defender*, August 29, 1942, p. 3.

50.   Insurance Law Examination, Howard University Law Department, May 28, 1921, William LePre Houston Family Papers, Manuscript Division, Library of Congress, Box 26.

51.   Charles M. Christian, *Black Saga: The African American Experience* 355 (Boston: Houghton-Mifflin 1995).

52.   Edward T. Folliard, "2500 Hail President at $15 Banquet: Truman Asks Aid of All Americans to Achieve Peace," *Washington Post*, January 19, 1949, p. 1.

53.   William L. Houston to Charles H. Houston, April 15, 1914, William LePre Houston Family Papers, Manuscript Division, Library of Congress, Box 21.

54.   Ibid.

55.   William L. Houston to Charles H. Houston, November 9, 1910, William LePre Houston Family Papers, Manuscript Division, Library of Congress, Box 4.

56.   Ibid.

57.   William L. Houston to Charles H. Houston, April 19, 1910, William LePre Houston Family Papers, Manuscript Division, Library of Congress, Box 4.

58.   Ibid.

59.   William L. Houston to Charles H. Houston, November 9, 1910, William LePre Houston Family Papers, Manuscript Division, Library of Congress, Box 4.

60.   Ibid.

61.   William L. Houston to Charles H. Houston, January 29, 1910, William LePre Houston Papers, Manuscript Division, Library of Congress, Box 19.

62.   Ibid.

63.   Ibid.

64.   "DePriest Backs Concert in D.C.," *Atlanta Daily World*, February 25, 1934, p. 1.

65.   Larry Gibson, *Young Thurgood: The Making of a Supreme Court Justice* 269 (New York: Prometheus Book 2012).

66.   "Bar Group Scored for Color Barrier," *New York Times*, August 19, 1939, p. 15.

67.   Ibid.

68.   William Houston to Mary Ethel Houston, Letter of October 6, 1920, William LePre Houston Family Papers, Manuscript Division. Library of Congress, Box 21.

69.   Ibid.

70.   Ibid.

71.   William L. Houston to Charles H. Houston, August 10, 1910, William LePre Houston Family Papers, Manuscript Division, Library of Congress, Box 19.

72.   Segal, *In Any Fight*, p. 23.

73. Amherst College report of standings, Charles Hamilton Houston first semester 1911–1912.

74. William L. Houston to Charles H. Houston, February 12, 1913, William LePre Houston Family Papers, Manuscript Division, Library of Congress, Box 19.

75. Ibid.

76. Ibid.

77. Ibid.

78. Alice N. Dunbar to Charles H. Houston, April 19, 1910, William LePre Houston Family Papers, Manuscript Division, Library of Congress, Box 19.

79. Ibid.

80. Charles H. Houston to Mary Ethel Houston, May 3, 1914, William LePre Houston Family Papers, Manuscript Division, Library of Congress, Box 5.

81. Ibid.

82. Segal, *In Any Fight*, p. 24.

83. Charles H. Houston to Mary Ethel Houston, February 12, 1914, William LePre Houston Family Papers, Manuscript Division, Library of Congress, Box 5.

84. Ibid.

85. Hardy Prize Debate Program, June 11, 1915, College Hall, William LePre Houston Family Papers, Manuscript Division, Library of Congress, Box 26.

86. *Amherst Student Monday*, March 15, 1915, p. 1.

87. William L. Houston to Charles H. Houston, June 20, 1917, William LePre Houston Family Papers, Manuscript Division, Library of Congress.

88. Christel N. Temple, "Charles Hamilton Houston and Post-New Negro Movement Authority: The Socio-Literary History of a Legal Warrior," Collected in Ed. James H. Conyers, Jr., *Charles H. Houston: An Interdisciplinary Study of Civil Rights History* 175 (New York: Lexington Books 2012).

89. Ibid.

90. *Howard University Catalog*, 1914–1915, p. 55.

91. Charles H. Houston, "Saving World for Democracy," *Pittsburgh Courier*, July 27, 1940, p. 13.

92. Bernard F. Harris, "Chipping Away at the Bedrock of Racial Intolerance: Fort Des Moines and Black Officer Training, 1917–1918." *The Annals of Iowa* 77 (2018), p. 231–262.

93. Charles H. Houston, "Saving World for Democracy," *Pittsburgh Courier*, August 24, 1940, p. 13.

94. Ibid.

95. Ibid.

96. Ibid.

97. Ibid.

98. Music Program, "The Burleigh Glee Club, Camp Meucon, France," January 3, 1919, William LePre Houston Family Papers, Manuscript Division, Library of Congress.

99. Ibid. (Charles wrote his mother that he passed on playing the "Raging Scales" piano solo listed in the program).

100. Charles H. Houston, "Saving World for Democracy," *Pittsburgh Courier*, September 14, 1940, p. 13.

101.   Segal, *In Any Fight*, p. 26.

102.   Ibid.

103.   Ibid., p. 27.

104.   Charles H. Houston, "Saving World for Democracy," *Pittsburgh Courier*, September 14, 1940, p. 13.

105.   Ibid.

106.   Segal, *In Any Fight*, p. 26.

107.   Ibid.

108.   Charles H. Houston letter to Mary Ethel Houston, December 27, 1918, America Expeditionary Forces, Meucon, France, William LePre Houston Family Papers, Manuscript Division, Library of Congress.

109.   Treasury Department, Bureau of War Risk Insurance Award of Compensation to Charles H. Houston, C-430826, August 10, 1920. William LePre Houston Family Papers, Manuscript Division, Library of Congress.

110.   Charles H. Houston to Mary Ethel Houston December 12, 1918. William LePre Houston Family Papers, Manuscript Division, Library of Congress.

111.   Ibid.

112.   Charles H. Houston, "The Highway," *Baltimore Afro-American*, December 20, 1947, p. 4.

113.   Ibid.

114.   Letter of Charles H. Houston to Mary Ethel Houston, December 27, 1918, from Camp Meucon, France, William LePre Houston Family Papers, Manuscript Division, Library of Congress.

115.   Ibid.

116.   Charles H. Houston to Mary Ethel Houston, December 12, 1918, William LePre Houston Family Papers, Manuscript Division, Library of Congress.

117.   McNeil, *Groundwork*, p. 52.

118.   Charles H. Houston, Roscoe Pound Jurisprudence, hand written class notes, William LePre Houston Family Papers, Manuscript Division, Library of Congress.

119.   Felix Frankfurter to Charles H. Houston, January 3, 1924, William LePre Houston Family Papers, Manuscript Division, Library of Congress.

120.   Paul F. Murphy, "Felix Frankfurter" in, *The Oxford Companion to the Supreme Court of the United States* 364 (Kermit L. Hall 2nd ed. 2005).

121.   Richard Kluger, *Simple Justice: The History of* Brown v. Board of Education *and Black America's Struggle for Equality* 115 (New York: Alfred A. Knopf 1977).

122.   Ibid.

123.   Author's Interview with William T. Coleman, May 17, 2004, Mayflower Hotel, Washington, D.C.

124.   Ibid.

125.   Ibid.

126.   William Houston to Charles Houston, Letter of June 5, 1920, William LePre Houston Family Papers, Manuscript Division, Library of Congress, Box 21.

127.   Letter of Dean Dwight O. W. Holmes to William Houston, February 16, 1921, William LePre Houston Family Papers, Manuscript Division, Library of Congress, Box 21.

128. Ibid.

129. Ibid.

130. Ibid.

131. Genna Rae McNeil, "In Tribute: Charles Hamilton Houston," 111 *Harv. L. Rev.* 2167, 2168 (1998).

132. 34 *Harvard L. Rev.* 450 (1922).

133. Howard Ball, *A Defiant Life: Thurgood Marshall and the Persistence of Racism in America* 29 (New York: Random House 2011).

134. John M. Fitzgerald and Otey M. Scruggs, "A Note on Marcus Garvey at Harvard, 1922: A Recollection of John M. Fitzgerald," 63 *Journal of Negro History* 157 (April 1978).

135. Earl Brown, "Tribute to Charles H. Houston," *New York Amsterdam News*, May 6, 1950, p. 8.

136. Ibid.

137. Ibid.

138. Ibid.

139. McNeil, *Groundwork*, p. 52.

140. Ibid.

141. Ibid.

142. Michael D. Davis and Hunter R. Clark, *Thurgood Marshall: Warrior at the Bar, Rebel on the Bench* 52 (New York: Birch Lane Press 1992).

III

The Calling

Building Lawyers for Battle

A lawyer is either a social engineer or a parasite on society.

—Charles H. Houston

harles Houston returned from Europe for a second time during his 20s, not as a soldier but a scholar. He completed studies in Madrid, Spain, earning a doctorate degree in civil law. Now he prepared himself for a more routine life as a practicing attorney in the nation's capital. His father was proud to have his son home and in practice with him. The start of "Houston and Houston" was the culmination of a long-held dream for William. He made no secret of his desire that they work together. After Charles was admitted to law school in April of 1920, William Houston "felt mighty proud" to see his son's name enrolled among the Harvard students "and best of all when I see it on our door and stationary."[1] In the spring of 1924, Charles took the District of Columbia bar examination and was sworn in as an attorney on June 9th of that year.[2] Soon after, he married Gladys Moran of Baltimore, who his parents had helped raise. Charles had taken a romantic interest in her before he left for war.[3]

He returned to his alma mater, Dunbar High School, to address junior and senior college-bound students about his travels and their future. The *Washington Post* summarized his remarks as a discussion of "practical and spiritual values of higher education and their importance in the development and progress of the American Negro."[4] Even before returning to Washington after his international studies, Charles was not completely settled on a career practicing law in his hometown. He contemplated the possibility of either entering foreign service or practicing law abroad. In July 1922, he wrote to the Brazilian Embassy in Washington, D.C., to inquire about opportunities in Brazil for a lawyer. He was informed "he must pass an examination before the Brazilian bar."[5]

He worked with his father on a host of routine legal matters that were part of the daily law practice William Houston had engaged in for over two decades. The cases he handled represented the needs of the black middle class, who could afford to pay for legal services.[6] For example, there were cases involving financial institutions. In the fall of 1925, Charles Houston was counsel in a court battle regarding assets of a defunct bank. Charles filed a lawsuit against the general partner of the bank and his wife, alleging that they failed to properly account for bank assets.[7] He desired to have the widow of the general partner file a financial bond to protect what remained.[8]

Always impatient for a challenge, Charles began to seek to practice law at the highest level. He worked on a case with a prominent black lawyer from New England. That attorney, William Henry Lewis, became the first African American nominated by President William Howard Taft as a federal assistant attorney general in 1911.[9] Lewis was among the first African Americans to be admitted to the American Bar Association.[10] Lewis mentored Houston early in his career, including allowing him to participate in a Supreme Court case in the 1920s.[11] In *New York Central v. Chisholm*, Lewis and Houston sought damages for the estate of a man named McTier, for fatal injuries he sustained while working as a railroad employee on a train line between Malone, New York, and Montreal, Canada.[12] The estate sued under an employer workers' compensation provision authorized under the federal law of the United States. The Supreme Court rejected the claim on the procedural ground that the law "contains no words which definitely disclose an intention to give it extraterritorial effect."[13] Accordingly, a lawsuit across international lines was not authorized.

Charles also worked on a wrongful death case in the Supreme Court with Harvard classmate Samuel Horowitz, involving a work-related injury under a Utah workmen's compensation law.[14] The case sought payment to a widow for her husband's death, despite the Bountiful Brick Company's contention that the worker was negligent in crossing the railroad tracks near work. Giles, the employee, was killed by an approaching train. Since all employees had to cross the tracks, the company could not avoid legal responsibility. In its opinion, the court wrote, "the only way of access to its brickyard...was across the railroad tracks, the company necessarily contemplated the crossing of them by its employees."[15] The court reasoned that part of the workplace is the "ingress and egress" by which the employee reaches work.[16] With this decision, Charles Houston shared a first Supreme Court victory.

Between these occasional opportunities to participate in the Supreme Court "lime-light," there were plenty of ordinary law firm cases to complete. Charles collected money for construction projects[17] and represented employment agencies in negligence cases,[18] the kind of steady legal work designed to pay the bills and sustain the day-to-day operation of a vibrant law office. Many of the correspondences between father and son discussed the details of cases while catching up on various personal matters.[19] In one correspondence, Charles suggested to his father "[i]f you have spare time on Saturday and want an outing…I would suggest you motor over to Newark, and locate Mrs. Teemer and get the necessary information from her; also drive up in Harlem [New York] and see Mrs. Johnson, so that you can put your hands on them to sign the deed if necessary."[20] The work was often tedious and time consuming because the Houston firm had such a reputation for quality. W.L. would require documents with one error to be completely retyped rather than correcting an error on the incorrect page.[21] Part of this desire for precision was due to the professional elitism Charles and his father shared.

Indeed, Charles could be particularly blunt when it came to the poor quality work of Washington, D.C.'s "night school trained" black lawyers. He once said, "[t]hey do not know how to study and are too shiftless to learn."[22] It was at this point in his career that Charles Houston started to truly understand that "[c]ourtrooms were public market places where black lawyers bought and sold prestige as well as money and legal services."[23] On the one hand, being the best among black lawyers meant a future of personal security for family and future. On the other hand, the progress of the race was also linked to advancing social justice issues to provide a chance for racial uplift for all black people. For the present, however, the work of "Houston and Houston" had to take priority.

The firm also ran a tight financial ship, as William Houston accounted for every penny, according to former employees of his office.[24] He once called a staff member's home at 11p.m. to assure that a $15 client deposit was received.[25] Of course, Charles sometimes accepted civil rights work for little or no payment, notwithstanding his father's frugal habits. Juanita Kidd Stout, a former legal secretary for the Houston firm who became a Pennsylvania Supreme Court Justice, observed if someone came in "with a worthy case and did not have the filing fee,…he [Charles] would pay the fee."[26]

Charles treated cases large and small with equal care. "He emphasized you must drive for perfection…. You should prepare even the smallest case with the same zeal you would prepare a case going to the Supreme Court of the United States."[27] He also had a magnetic personality. "He was the type of person who 'lit up' a room merely by walking in."[28] Charles was also exceedingly ethical, once lecturing a legal secretary on her first day during a walk to the bank about the evil of comingling client funds. "'Never, never, never mix mine and thine'! He explained that keeping clients' funds separate from your own was not only the right thing to do, but that the failure to do so was the major cause of disbarment of lawyers."[29]

As would become Charles Houston's habit, he would work long hours underneath one of his favorite possessions, "an ink and pen rendering" of the Supreme Court Justice Oliver Wendell Holmes. Inscribed on the pictures were the words "for Charles H. Houston" by Justice Holmes.[30] Charles would have occasion to appear before Justice Holmes in the Supreme Court. William Houston would see his son often sat in a chair right across from Holmes's portrait in their law office library. "I used to leave Charlie when I closed my office for the day…it would often be two in the morning before he turned out the lights and started home."[31] So precious was the signed portrait to Charles, that he would take care to have it removed to a safe location when winter heating conditions might damage it. He once wrote to his father from New York, "If you have not done so, please take my picture of Justice Holmes down from the wall over the radiator, so it will not dry out. If necessary please put it back in the storeroom with the files."[32]

For a time early in his legal career, Charles Houston served as president of the Washington Bar Association, a group of black lawyers in the district. In that role, he attended the 42nd anniversary of the admission of Everett J. Waring, the first black attorney admitted to the Baltimore Bar. At that event, on December 9, 1927, at the Bethel African Methodist Episcopal Zion Church in Baltimore, he offered remarks among the practicing lawyers during the celebration.[33] Charles Houston showed an inclination early in his legal career to speak out conspicuously on political issues. In a 1925 "letter to the editor" in the *Washington Post*, Charles Houston criticized the French Air raids on North Africa, writing that those raids were as "deadly to women and children as bombs dropped over London."[34] Noting the undercurrent of potential vengeance brewing among the natives of Tunis, Algeria and Morocco, he suggested the "French may yet feel the boomerang effect of these raids by loss of sympathy and understanding among tribes now friendly to them."[35] Such comments on international political affairs would become more frequent toward the end of his life as he began to share his international vision of human rights. However, during most of the early 1920s, he remained focused on the work of the firm as an energetic young lawyer climbing the ladder of success in the nation's capital.

Charles and his wife occasionally entertained during the early part of their marriage. He had some remnant of a social life, including hosting a medical student from China.[36] The Houstons served supper at their home in Washington, D.C., for Hubert T. Delany, an assistant United States attorney for the Southern District of New York.[37] He also gave a talk to the National Medical Association annual convention in 1932.[38] The excitement of his professional life was, however, occasionally dimmed by the challenges of his personal life. Charles's marriage to Gladys was beginning to deteriorate, even from its early days. He responded to his wife in a letter in August of 1926, addressing whether to accompany her on a trip to New York, where he described the "persistent coldness" of her last two letters written to him.[39] "In view of your attitude toward me I really do not know what to say to you. Most of the day I have been debating whether to come to New York at all, but I had promised Judge Mack...and I wanted to see Professor Frankfurter, so I will be in town Friday."[40]

Although the law practice was thriving, Charles still had a yearning to teach. He wrote to his former professor and mentor Felix Frankfurter about his studies in Madrid. Professor Frankfurter answered his letter on January 3, 1924, excitedly replying, "I am delighted to have your letter, to learn of your well-being and to read your vivid account of Spanish legal education."[41] His letter to his former teacher was not simply to tell stories about Madrid; it was also a request for a recommendation so that Charles could teach at Howard University School of Law. Frankfurter replied, "[o]f course it will be a pleasure for me to write to Dean Fenton Booth of Howard Law School to tell him how admirably equipped you are to give a course on the Interstate Commerce Act."[42]

Roscoe Pound, the dean of the Harvard Law School, also wrote Howard Law Dean Booth on Charles Houston's behalf. Pound described him as a "remarkable man,"[43] noting that the "Faculty of the Harvard Law School have shown their appreciation for his work as a student and their confidence in him by giving him about every honor that it is possible for a law student to take while in the institution."[44] He further explained, "I have rarely met a man who combined a high order of scholarship with solid good sense and a capacity for seeing things are they are as does Dr. Houston."[45] Interestingly, Dean Pound felt compelled to add additional information about Charles Houston's ability to get along with others. "When I tell you he was able to work alongside of and in harmony with a student from North Carolina who held a scholarship granted by the Daughters of the Confederacy, you will understand what I mean."[46]

Another man who would later become a dean of Harvard Law School observed, with admiration, Charles argue a Supreme Court case during the 1930s. Erwin Griswold would later identify Houston in his own memoir as "surely entitled to be included in any list of truly great American lawyers."[47]

In the midst of the work of the firm and the turmoil of his family life, Charles finally received some welcome news: Howard's law school made him an offer to teach. He was excited about the opportunity. From the start of his tenure at the school, he was involved in every stage of its transformation. He understood the reality that the school needed financial recourses to carry out its mission to train competent "Negro men and women lawyers adequately prepared and properly inspired to enter the profession of the law."[48]

He was appointed chairman of the capital campaign committee at the school. In that role, he sent out a personal message to "friends of Howard University Law School to acquaint them with its condition."[49] He explained that "[T]he Law School has before it a great future and unlimited possibilities of service; but with it into this future must go the sympathy and support of its friends."[50] He noted that the school's faculty was made up of "both colored and white instructors" and that in the current year, there were "ninety students, representing twenty states and three foreign countries."[51]

Houston pointed out several problems that the school was experiencing related to funding. He explained to potential donors that the school "had no endowment. It has no student loan fund or scholarships. Most of the professors are only employed part-time; and even the full-time professors'... salaries fall below" salaries of professors at other schools.[52] The major focus of his plea related to the library. He complained that the "law library was not up-to-date, and is perhaps the chief obstacle in the way of recognition of the Howard Law School by the Association of American Law Schools...," an important national accrediting organization.[53]

Charles Houston noted that through the help of his mentor Professor Felix Frankfurter of Harvard the needs of Howard's Law Library were made known to philanthropist Julius Rosenwald, who was a great benefactors of Negro education during the early twentieth century and the driving force behind the Sears and Roebuck retail stores and catalogue.[54] Houston informed potential donors that on January 26, 1926, Mr. Rosenwald pledged a generous gift of $2,500 to support the library as soon as the law school raised $500.00.

Houston urged the friends of the law school to accept the Rosenwald challenge as a point of personal pride. "Mr. Rosenwald does not ask us to match his gift dollar for dollar. He offers to give five dollars to our one. It is up to us to prove…that we sponsor high grade legal education for Negroes and that within the limit of our means we are ready and willing to accept the responsibility for it and contribute to its cost."[55] Later in his life Houston would become a member of the board of directors for the Rosenwald Foundation, which elevated the quality and condition of Negro schools during the Jim Crow years.[56]

Howard University was always a hub of African American intellectual life. The university had its share of the world's greatest thinkers among its ranks. Because of the discrimination that was rampant in the United States in the early 1900s, Howard became the only place that many African Americans could pursue academic creativity and rigor. Its proximity to the national government also enhanced its influence. Howard did, however, have some severe shortcomings.

Supreme Court Justice Louis Brandeis, a vigorous supporter of racial equality, expressed concerns that black lawyers who practiced before his court often submitted legal briefs of inferior quality.[57] He believed that this problem could best be addressed by providing proper training in law school. It was known that the Justice "in his personal relations…treated African-Americans with respect."[58] He told his friend Mordecai Wyatt Johnson, the young president of Howard University, of his concerns. He encouraged him to seek full accreditation for Howard's law school.[59]

Johnson, a native of Tennessee and a Baptist minister, became Howard University's first African American president.[60] Along with his seminary training, Johnson was educated at some of the nation's finest schools, including the University of Chicago and Harvard.[61] Persuaded by Justice Brandies' plea for improvement, President Johnson took swift action and sought a dean who could do the tough job of reforming the law school and gaining full national accreditation. Charles Houston's Harvard training made him an obvious choice.

On June 4, 1929, Charles Houston was hired as the law school's vice dean and promoted from instructor to associate professor.[62] He immediately began his controversial mission to achieve President Johnson's objectives. The first step was to move the school from a part-time night school to a full-time day school.[63] This change would take Howard from its historical roots, as a school that allowes prospective lawyers to study while keeping full-time jobs. This change angered many alumni.[64] One student was even threatened with the possibility of a disciplinary hearing because of his complaints against Houston's plans.[65] Many of its graduates, like Charles' own father William, had come to Washington first to secure government employment so they could earn their law degree at night. One critic expressed "[m]any of the country's best lawyers among our people secured their training by being able to work in the day and attend evening classes. Our economic condition is such that few of our young men have the means to attend college in the daytime."[66] This change would cut off the very opportunity that built the small number of black practicing attorneys. Despite the complaints, Houston pressed forward. There were also several shake ups on the law faculty, where established professors were removed.[67] His actions caused critics to say he was attempting to "Harvardize" Howard's law school.[68]

After making many of the changes required to impress the accreditation committees, the law school's Ivy League-educated dean prepared the school for the final stages of the inspection process.[69] His efforts were overwhelmingly successful. By 1931, Howard received certification from the American Bar Association[70] and was approved for accreditation by the Association of American Law Schools at their annual meeting.[71]

Clearly, eliminating the night school at Howard Law was no small matter. Whittling classes down from in the 30s to six students graduating per year also meant many fewer black lawyers. Creating more part-time lawyers by night while working for the government by day was not Charles Houston's vision for Howard's law school student body. What kind of lawyer did Charles Houston want? The answer was "younger" and "fearless." He wanted lawyers ready to do battle in hostile Southern courtrooms. Experienced black lawyers, with few exceptions, were not waging that type of war. "The older Negro lawyers in the South," Houston said, "have tended to avoid highly inflammable issues.... But the younger lawyers are embracing the opportunity for service and accepting the risks which are bound to accompany any lawyer working on a social frontier."[72] Indeed, he believed those more senior lawyers, working with "white authorities have attempted to cripple the courageous efforts of the younger lawyers by working through influential Negro citizens" who would stifle assertion of full constitutional rights.[73]

Houston's educational innovations, however, did not seek to merely adopt the traditional standard of a first-rate law school, but he made sure law teaching would be "experiential,"[74] including practical training which has become a permanent part of law school training today.[75] Houston experimented with clinical and internship-type experiences like a Criminal Law Laboratory course which included components like psychiatry.[76] Houston "was among the first legal educators to appreciate the importance of practical, real life experience."[77] He brought in guest speakers like the legendary lawyer Clarence Darrow to discuss trial strategy.[78] He took a "hands on" practical approach, like tours to

a federal prison in Lorton, Virginia, inspecting the building and prison conditions.[79] Students visited coroner's offices and police stations in order to gain
important perspective.[80] The lawyers in training would go on field trips to St.
Elizabeth's mental hospital, the United States Attorney's Office, and the Federal
Bureau of Investigation "and learned how they did things."[81]

During a visit to the coroner's office for an autopsy demonstration, star
pupil Thurgood Marshall fainted and fell in the floor.[82] Marshall also described
the sobering experience of the Howard law students visiting a penitentiary
electric chair, taking turns sitting in it, "there's no electricity in there—you
know that.... You can't sit there more than a minute... it's the fear."[83] Howard
students also practiced with the lawyers preparing Supreme Court arguments
on pending civil rights cases as well as serving as research assistants for cases
coming up for trial.[84]

Another key lesson often repeated by Charlie Houston was, "lose your
temper, lose your case,"[85] training students in composure while in the heat
of courtroom battle. During a speech in the 1970s, Justice Marshall recalled
other lessons he learned from his mentor. "Get your law and get it straight. Get
your research and dig deeper. When you plan, plan twice. When you map out
your case, take not [just] the two possibilities but assume two others," Houston
would say.[86] He also reminded his students that "[t]he difference between law
and other professions like medicine, is the doctor's bury their mistakes, but the
lawyers' mistakes are made public."[87]

Houston's goal was to instill the gravity of the lawyer's task. Marshall
remembered, "Charlie Houston was training lawyers to go out in the courts
and fight and die for their people."[88] Yet with all of his stern lessons, Thurgood
fondly recalled Charlie's sensitive and thoughtful side. "He loved people, if he
came to visit you, when you got back... you got a letter thanking you... [he
remembered] your wife—calling her by name; and your children calling them
by name; and your dog, calling him by name."[89]

In this setting Houston began the process of turning lawyers into social
engineers, ready to fight all vestiges of racial discrimination. It was the kind
of training required to identify the legal talent necessary to take on a multi-
year, multi-state legal battle that would transform a nation. What he did
was to use the law school as a "breeding ground" for testing issues on the
faculty with the students' help. For Houston, the United States became his
classroom.[90] The goal was what Justice Brandeis had urged President Mordecai Johnson to pursue and what the Justice William O. Douglas further

urged Charles Houston to implement. "Houston would put the students in his course on constitutional law to work on specific problems, presenting the question as to how to raise, in a trial court, the precise federal constitutional question that would challenge a housing code, or other racist measures, and how to preserve it on appeal."[91]

It was while serving as the leader of the law school that Charles Houston would cultivate his special relationship with his best pupil, Thurgood Marshall. Brilliant and comedic, Thurgood was a unique combination of intellect and wit. Boisterous and likeable, his playful nature had caused him trouble in college at Pennsylvania's Lincoln University for fraternity hazing.[92] He recovered from that setback and decided that he wanted to attend law school. At Frederick Douglass High School in Baltimore City, Marshall learned he had the skill for courtroom work. He was a champion debater.[93] He continued developing those skills at Lincoln University.[94]

What was seen as great potential by Marshall's prior teachers became realized when he encountered Charles H. Houston at Howard. Whatever childishness Marshall displayed in college was evaporated by the rigors of Houston's strict law school regime. The students gave Houston names like "Iron Shoes"[95] and "Cement Pants"[96] but as much as Marshall was known for wanting to "cut up," party, and have a good time, he thrived under Houston's invitation to achieve excellence. Thurgood Marshall admitted "I never worked hard until I got to law school and met Charlie Houston.... I saw this man's dedication, his vision and his willingness to sacrifice, and I told myself you either shape up or ship out."[97]

The two men had great chemistry with each other. Marshall did well in his classroom performance; Charles Houston rewarded him with more opportunities to grow. Houston arranged a part-time job for Thurgood in the law school library, which allowed him more study time,[98] while earning money for he and his wife, affectionately known as "Buster," who was largely financially supporting the couple at the time.[99] Houston took Marshall to bar association meetings with him and introduced him to established black lawyers as his student protégé.[100] Marshall loved the attention and worked hard to impress Houston.

In turn, Houston developed an almost "father-son" relationship with Marshall, although they were not that far apart in age, only about thirteen years. Charles Houston also learned from Thurgood Marshall's father, William Marshall, who was the first black man to serve on a grand jury in Baltimore. He said that during the first two days he served, many of the grand jurors wanted to know if the person under investigation was white or black.[101] If they were informed that the defendant was black they almost always indicted without further inquiry. On the third day William Marshall complained that the question of the race of the defendant should be removed from consideration.[102] The grand jury foreman agreed with him that day and no race inquiry was made during the remainder of that grand jury session.[103]

It was clear that although many Houston-trained lawyers received care and respect, Thurgood was and remained his favorite working partner until Charlie's death. Marshall continued to give Charles Houston due credit for transforming the Constitution, and Marshall's own life, until the end of his days.[104] Although both men were hard working, Houston's sober, direct manner served him well in written correspondences, court documents, and meeting rooms. Thurgood's more affable personal approach was better suited to the kind of coalition building that Houston believed would be needed to support the future legal campaign of the NAACP.[105] With the need to win cases, raise money from donors, and persuade board members of the association that all was well on the front lines, Thurgood appeared to Houston to be a perfect fit one day to be lead "engineer" of the civil rights litigation campaign. Clearly, the two men trusted each other, in much the same way that Charles trusted his own father.

Over seventeen years of letters between the men and many reports of conversations they had with each other support that their bond was unshakable. As former Howard law dean J. Clay Smith noted, "Marshall's devotion to and respect for his mentor lasted a lifetime. Marshall had been baptized into the emancipation movement by Charles Hamilton Houston, the architect of modern civil rights to litigation."[106]

Marshall's law school class would produce another famous protégé, Richmond, Virginia's Oliver Hill. Hill recalled that "Charlie Houston impressed upon us from the first day that a lawyer who is not a social engineer is a parasite upon society. We worked extremely hard, attending law school six days a week. We were told that we would have to appear in the courts not just before some hostile white judges, but that we would also have to litigate cases against some very good white lawyers. Charlie and the faculty required that we give nothing less than our best."[107]

In an interview several decades after Houston's death, Oliver Hill would comment that Houston was given the title "'vice dean,' and he used to say 'they don't pay me enough to take the title of dean.' Of course that wasn't true," Hill recalled. "The fact was they had an old retired white judge that had [the title] dean as a cover."[108] "They thought that somebody white had to be head of every damn thing."[109]

As a law professor, Houston was a man that did not take kindly to student excuses. His former student and later federal circuit judge Spottswood Robinson commented, "[a]s a teacher Houston was an unremitting taskmaster; he rejected out of hand all complaints that the work was too difficult with assignments too long.... His students learned that he was interested only in first rate achievements, not excuses or shortcomings."[110] Houston's use of challenging curriculum and practical application "combined...to provide...students with the necessary tools to fight racism in the courts."[111]

His exceedingly rigorous teaching regimen also extended to exams. Oliver Hill recounted one of Houston's eight-hour finals. "Charlie Houston taught evidence.... When the final exam was given, Charlie told us that if we thought it would help, we could use any books, notes, or even the kitchen stove. However, Charlie gave so many essay questions that your initial reaction was that you would be lucky to read all the questions much less answer them. Other than your brains, extensively using reference materials was not a viable option."[112]

Houston's work at Howard was not merely a teaching enterprise, but a scholarly one as well. While at Howard University, Houston began developing a community of thinkers among other college professors on racial issues. The program was located at Swarthmore College in Pennsylvania in 1933 and included the participation of future Nobel Peace Prize winner Dr. Ralph J. Bunche. It included discussions seeking solutions by bringing "the discipline of scientific methods to the study of race relations."[113] His interest in bringing together people to tackle race discrimination in an interdisciplinary approach was part of a lifelong strategy to transform the law. His hunger to read literature, keep up with the emerging social sciences, and examine new ideas further sparked his interest in how the law could be used to construct better societal outcomes. He yearned to do more, and he would soon get his chance.

With full accreditation satisfied at Howard and an extraordinary faculty assembled, Houston was looking forward to new challenges. He wanted to start moving the nation toward integration but knew it would be a long process that would require patience. He began to consider Walter White's offer to battle Jim Crow full-time with the NAACP.

Endnotes

1. William L. Houston to Charles H. Houston, April 20, 1920, William LePre Houston Family Papers, Manuscript Division, Library of Congress.

2. Genna Rae McNeil, *Groundwork: Charles Hamilton Houston and the Struggle for Civil Rights* 56 (Philadelphia: University of Pennsylvania Press 1983).

3. Ibid., pp. 40, 56.

4. "Higher Studies Urged by Dunbar Speaker," *Washington Post*, January 17, 1926, R12.

5. Letter 1st Secretary of the Brazilian Embassy to Charles H. Houston, July 22, 1922, William LePre Houston Family Papers, Manuscript Division, Library of Congress.

6. "Heirs to Hurst Estate Victors in Suit," *Baltimore Afro-American*, February 6, 1932, p. 23.

7. "Bank Case Take Fight Property into Court," *Chicago Defender*, October 3, 1925, p. 4.

8. Ibid.

9. J. Clay Smith, Jr. *Emancipation: The Making of the Black Lawyer 1844–1944* 106–107 (Philadelphia: University of Pennsylvania Press 1993).

10. Ibid.

11. *New York Central v. Chisholm*, 268 U.S. 29 (1925).

12. Ibid.

13. Ibid., p. 31.

14. *Bountiful Brick Co. v. Giles*, 276 U.S. 154 (1928).

15. Ibid.

16. Ibid.

17. *Weller v. Wolf et al.*, 50 F.2d 1014 (D.C. 1931).

18. *Janoff v. Newsom*, 53 F.2d 149 (D.C. 1931).

19. Charles H. Houston to William L. Houston, August 8, 1929, William LePre Houston Family Papers, Manuscript Division, Library of Congress.

20. Ibid.

21. Hon. Margaret A. Haywood, "A Symposium, Charles Hamilton Houston: Oral History" 27 *New Eng. L. Rev.* 613, 616 (1993).

22. Kenneth W. Mack, *Representing the Race: The Creation of the Civil Rights Lawyer* 60 (Boston: Harvard University Press 2012).

23. Ibid.

24. Haywood, *A Symposium*, p. 616.

25. Ibid.

26. Hon. Juanita Kidd Stout, "A Symposium, Charles Hamilton Houston: Oral History" 27 *New Eng. L. Rev.* 649, 652 (1993).

27. Ibid.

28. Ibid.

29. Ibid.

30. Bill Gibson, "They Tell Me, Baltimore," *Baltimore Afro-American*, March 17, 1951, p. 6.

31. Ibid.

32. Letter Charles H. Houston to William L. Houston, January 4, 1936, William LePre Houston Family Papers, Manuscript Division, Library of Congress.

33. "Under the Capitol Dome," *Chicago Defender*, May 19, 1928, p. A8.

34. Charles H. Houston, "Protests Against Air Raids," *Washington Post*, August 6, 1925, p. 6.

35. Ibid.

36. "Washington Society," *Chicago Defender*, August 3, 1929, p. A3.

37. "Washington Society," *Chicago Defender*, May 31, 1930, p. 20.

38. "Washington Society," *Chicago Defender*, August 27, 1932, p. 4.

39. Charles H. Houston to Gladys Houston, August 2, 1926, Houston Family Papers, Moorland-Spingarn Research Center, Howard University.

40. Ibid.

41. Felix Frankfurter to Charles H. Houston, January 3, 1924, Houston Family Papers, Moorland-Spingarn Research Center, Howard University.

42. Ibid.

43. Roscoe Pound to Judge Fenton W. Booth, December 31, 1923, Houston Family Papers, Moorland-Spingarn Research Center, Howard University.

44. Ibid.

45. Ibid.

46. Ibid.

47. Erwin N. Griswold, *Ould Fields, New Corne* 183 (Eagan, Minnesota: West Publishing Co. 1992).

48. Charles H. Houston, Howard Law School fundraising campaign letter entitled: "A Personal Message to Friends," April 12, 1926, p. 2, William LePre Houston Family Papers, Manuscript Division, Library of Congress, Box 11, School Papers.

49. Ibid., p. 1.

50. Ibid., pp. 2–3.

51. Ibid.

52. Ibid.

53. Ibid.

54. Clarence Page, "Remembering Black America's 'silent partner' at Sears, Julius Rosenwald," *Chicago Tribune*, November 2, 2018.

55. "A Personal Message to Friends," pp. 3–4.

56. "Houston Accepts Fund Drive Post," *Washington Post*, May 11, 1946, p. 6.

57. Richard Kluger, *Simple Justice: The History of* Brown v. Board of Education *and Black America's Struggle for Equality* 123 (New York: Alfred A. Knopf 1977).

58. Jeffery Rosen, *Louis D. Brandeis: American Profit* 19 (New Haven: Yale University Press 2016) (Citing Christopher A. Bracey, "Louis Brandeis and the Race Question," 52 *Ala. L. Rev.* 859, 880, 884 (2001)).

59. Hunter and Clark, *Thurgood Marshall: Warrior at the Bar, Rebel on the Bench* 52 (New York: Birch Lane Press 1992).

60. Ibid., p. 50.

61. Ibid.

62. Appointment Letter as Vice-Dean and Associate Professor, Howard University Secretary Emmitt Scott to Charles H. Houston, August 10, 1929, William LePre Houston Family Papers, Manuscript Division, Library of Congress.

63. McNeil, *Groundwork*, p. 71.

64. "Alumni Protest Abolition of the Night Classes," *Washington Tribune*, June 6, 1930.

65. "H.U. 'Heckler' Case Uncertain," *Philadelphia Tribune*, December 12, 1935, p. 1.

66. Editorial, *Washington Tribune*, June 6, 1930; McNeil, *Groundwork*, p. 72.

67. McNeil, *Groundwork*, p. 73.

68. McNeil, *Groundwork*, p. 74.

69. "Bar Association Adviser Inspects Howard Law School," *Chicago Defender*, October 25, 1930, p. 3.

70. McNeil, *Groundwork*, p. 75.

71. Handbook of the American Association of Law Schools, and Proceedings of the 29th Annual Meeting (December 1931), pp. 197–204.

72. Charles H. Houston, "The Need for Negro Lawyers," *Journal of Negro Education*, 4 No. 1 (January 1935) p. 49, 52.

73. Ibid.

74. Clinical Legal Educ. Ass'n, Comment of Clinical Legal Education on Proposed Standard 303, A.B.A 2 (Jan. 30, 2014). *See also,* José Felipé Anderson, "Simulating the Litigation Experience: How Mentoring Law Students in Local Cases Can Enrich Training for the Twenty-First Century Lawyer," 33 *Review of Litigation* 799 (University of Texas Law School, Austin 2014).

75. Ibid.

76. Mack, *Representing the Race*, p. 45.

77. Note, "A Symposium on Charles Hamilton Houston," 27 *New Eng. L. Rev.*, 595, 600 (1993).

78. "Darrow Is Lecturing at Howard Law School," *Pittsburg Courier*, January 10, 1931, p. A3.

79. "H.U. Law Students See Va. Reformatory," *Baltimore Afro-American*, May 14, 1931, p. 17.

80. Ibid.

81. Oliver W. Hill, Sr., Oral History Interview Transcript, Voices of Freedom, Special Collections and Archives, James Branch Cabell Library, Virginia Commonwealth University, November 13, 2002, p. 2.

82. Thurgood Marshall, "A Symposium on Charles Hamilton Houston, Oral History," 27 *New Eng. L. Rev.* 625, 628 (1993).

83. Ibid.

84. Ibid.

85. Rawn James, Jr., *Root and Branch: Charles Hamilton Houston, Thurgood Marshall and the Struggle to End Segregation* 113 (New York: Bloomsbury Press 2010).

86. Thurgood Marshall, "College Honors Charles Houston," *Amherst Magazine*, Spring 1978, p. 13.

87. Ibid.

88. Ibid.

89. Ibid., p. 12.

90. William A. Elwood, Road to *Brown* Film Transcript, *California Newsreel*. A Presentation of the University of Virginia, p. 2 (1990).

91. William O. Douglas, *Go East Young Man: The Early Years* 443 (Random House 1974).

92. Juan Williams, "The Thurgood Marshall Nobody Knows," *Ebony*, May 1990.

93. Larry S. Gibson, *Young Thurgood: The Making of a Supreme Court Justice* 72 (New York: Prometheus Book 2012).

94. Ibid., p. 94.

95. Richard Kluger, *Simple Justice: The History of* Brown v. Board of Education *and Black America's Struggle for Equality* 128 (New York: Alfred A. Knopf 1977).

96. Ibid.

97. Carl T. Rowen, *Dream Makers, Dream Breakers: The World of Justice Thurgood Marshall* 68 (Boston: Little, Brown 1993).

98. Kluger, *Simple Justice*, p. 179–180.

99. Ibid.

100. Juan Williams, *Thurgood Marshall: American Revolutionary* 58 (New York: Random House, 1998).

101. Charles H. Houston, "The Highway," *Baltimore Afro-American*, December 27, 1947, p. 4.

102. Ibid.

103. Ibid.

104. Carl T. Rowen, *Dream Makers*, p. 52.

105. Hunter and Clark, *Thurgood Marshall: Warrior at the Bar*, p. 103.

106. J. Clay Smith, "Thurgood Marshall an Heir to Charles Hamilton Houston," 20 *Hastings Cost. L. Q.* 503, 511 (1993).

107. Oliver W. Hill, Sr., "Reflections on *Brown* and the Future," 39 *U. Rich. L. Rev.* 1, 2–3 (2004).

108. Oliver W. Hill, Oral History Interview, National Visionary Leadership Project. Transforming Howard Law into a First-Class Law School with Dr. Mordeci Johnson, http://www.visionaryproject.org/hilloliver, visited May 22, 2010.

109. Ibid.

110. Spottswood W. Robinson III, "No Tea for the Feeble: Two Perspectives on Charles Hamilton Houston," 20 *Howard L. J.* 1 (1977).

111. Note, "A Symposium on Charles Hamilton Houston," 27 *New Eng. L. Rev.* 595–600 (1993).

112. Oliver W. Hill, Sr. (Jonathan Kay Stubs, Editor), *The Big Bang:* Brown v. Board of Education *and Beyond* 82 (New York: Grant House Publishers 2007).

113. "Professor Study Relations of Race," *Washington Post*, July 22, 1933, p. R11.

IV

NAACP Years

The Legal Campaign for Education

Finally, we beg you to save young America from the blight of race prejudice. Do not bind the children within the narrow circles of your own lives. Teach them to hear the song without hating the singer. Make them understand that it is just a question of reconciling the want and desires of different human beings, each equally entitled to life, liberty and the pursuit of happiness.

—Charles Hamilton Houston, "An Approach to Better Race Relations," a speech to the National YMCA Convention, May 5, 1934

Walter White eventually convinced Charles Houston to become the first full-time legal counsel for the NAACP. In one of his final speeches as dean of Howard Law, given at the National Young Men's Christian Association (YMCA) convention in Philadelphia, he reminded the audience of its Christian responsibility to treat people fairly, without the evil of race prejudice. A newspaper reporter overheard a female listener in the crowd comment "[t]hat is the danger of educating niggers."[1]

In July 1935, he joined the staff at the New York national headquarters as full-time special counsel.[2] This change in Houston's career and in the fortunes of the NAACP was a critical event in American history. He would soon go on the road to grow the reputation of the organization. In another YMCA event in Berkley, California, Houston would receive a more favorable reception than he had at the annual meeting months before. Speaking not only to the YMCA but the University Club of the University of California, the Alameda Branch of the NAACP, and the First AME Church, "throngs who heard him deemed it a privilege."[3] He made such a great impression that a faculty member from the University of California, "Prof. Perstein of the public speaking department, invited him to take charge of his class for the afternoon."[4] On that same trip, Charles Houston visited San Francisco, Oakland, Monterey, and Los Angeles.[5]

As he swept across the nation, he would be received in places like Chicago, Illinois, where large numbers of admirers would come to the Lincoln Memorial Congregational Church and brave "sub-zero weather"[6] to hear him discuss "the fight for economic, educational, political and social equality."[7] That same month, Houston told a Toledo, Ohio, audience, "Some of you want separate schools so that you can have colored teachers. Schools are for children, not teachers."[8] He explained that if children are educated together during "impressionable" school years it will be hard to consider them "mental inferiors."[9] He gathered with a multitude of black fraternity and sorority members of the Panhellenic Council, at the Metropolitan Baptist Church in Memphis, Tennessee, to urge them to join the NAACP.[10] At the Memphis event, a newspaper described him as "one of the greatest influences for progress the race has ever had."[11]

Charles Houston assisted his youth director, Juanita Jackson, with a problem at the University of Pennsylvania, her alma mater, when they attempted to have segregated women's dormitories. At a forum held at the Friends Meeting House near 15th Street in Philadelphia, he asserted, "our struggle for full civil rights is motivated by the desire for physical advantage for ourselves and to free our white friends from fear of not living up to the teachings of Christianity."[12]

For the first time an African American lawyer would be both the face and brain of the legal assault on racial discrimination. The fledgling civil rights organization was finally mobilizing to strike at the heart of the flawed "Jim Crow" system. He also believed part of his objective was to create more soldiers for the discrimination fight. At Howard's law school, by "making it the West Point of the Civil Rights movement...he was training the foot soldiers."[13] He believed the NAACP "should be the great laboratory for developing Negro leadership wherever possible."[14]

It had become increasingly clear that all facilities in America, when separated, were rarely equal. Houston now had a total commitment to work on the task without the distraction of classes and educational administration. The full force of his remarkable intellect would be unleashed on the nation's most daunting social, legal and political challenge. For several decades prior to Houston taking over the legal campaign, the nightmare of inequality in a "separate but equal" world became all too apparent.[15] African Americans had neither the political ability nor the financial resources to change these living conditions. In large part, this circumstance was caused by the *Plessy v. Ferguson* ruling.[16] In *Plessy*, the Supreme Court considered an 1890 Louisiana law that required rail passengers of different races to ride in separate rail cars.[17] Plessy sat in a rail car reserved for whites. He was asked to leave and was arrested after he refused.[18] Plessy argued that he "was seven-eighths Caucasian, one-eighth African blood...and that he was entitled to every right [of] the white race."[19] In essence, Plessy argued that he was white enough to ride in the first-class car because he could afford the ticket.

The decision rejecting his claim would become a nightmare for Negroes: "Congress and the states could not prohibit racial segregation, [and] the states could compel it."[20] Thus, *Plessy* and the statutes and precedents it spawned "most certainly dammed up and discouraged the democratic values of American life, stunted the political and moral capacity of people, and released and energized the most unworthy, even bigoted forces."[21]

The case encouraged all manner of inferior treatment of black citizens through state law and local custom. There was certainly Jim Crow in the North, but in the South "because few statutes exist[ed] that [were] favorable to the Negro, the white man's mood and spoken word become law. Whatever the Southern white man decided for the Negro ha[d] the sanction of tradition, and against tradition there has been little legal recourse."[22] Although social separation by race was certainly embarrassing, there was a larger problem within the architecture of unequal treatment; it hampered advancement by denying most "Colored" people access to even the most basic educational opportunity. In the United States the denial of learning had a long and painful history.

After the Civil War the South's effort to rebuild was hampered by Northern politicians who were angry about the attempt to leave the Union.[23] Congress offered little financial help to the South for its school systems, with the exception of Reconstruction era policies providing some education for the newly freed slaves.[24] As soon as Reconstruction ended, Southern states provided little or no educational help for African Americans who worked largely supporting the agricultural economy. In no place was the inequality more profoundly demonstrated than in South Carolina. In that state, Charles Houston would begin to lay the foundation for his national attack on educational inequality. He knew that the statistical evidence was fertile soil for a test case. He would take trips to investigate and record movies of the disparities between the white and Colored schools.

For example, "[i]n 1915, South Carolina spent $23.76 on the average white child in public school, [but only] $2.91 on the average Negro child. As late as 1931, six southeastern states (Alabama, Arkansas, Florida, Georgia, [and] North and South Carolina) spent less than a third as much per Negro public school pupil as per white child."[25] While planning his litigation strategy, other private organizations attempted to help. Between 1914 and 1932, almost 5,000 black schools were provided by funds from the Julius Rosenwald Foundation, for which Charles Houston spent time as a board member.[26] Such efforts were welcome but were hardly enough.

During the early 1900s, black citizens were taxed heavily and actually subsidized white schools at a higher rate than they financed their own schools. Black taxpayers literally owned 43.9 percent of the black schools in the South because, "[m]any schools identified as being in the public domain were paid for through the voluntary contributions of black citizens."[27] In Atlanta, Georgia, in 1903 there were four times as many white schools and teachers to accommodate the student population that was only about twice the black population.[28]

The question for Charles Houston was, how should a legal attack on these practices begin? He found his starting point in the 1925 Margold Report. That study, commissioned by the NAACP, described the possibility of filing lawsuits to challenge the validity of "separate but equal."[29] As he would make clear in a *Washington Post* editorial, the blatant constitutional violations under the separate but equal system could not be easily hidden, The "fatal fallacy" he argued, was "that there can be no real effective enforcement of...civil rights here guaranteed as long as flagrant violations of other amendments, just as fundamental, are openly condoned."[30] He would further explain that by "taking in the Constitution and all its amendments, that you are really advancing the cause of civil liberty and true democracy."[31]

Houston knew he would need help for such a big fight. He assembled a band of lawyers, intent on using the courts to help his people out of the quandary of "separate but equal." One legal scholar has noted that not only was Houston a great mentor to the civil rights bar of his day, but he was "keenly attentive to the ramifications of the tactical choices he made as a litigator."[32] Houston was aware that he would need to build strong cases that would give little room for state officials to avoid the consequence of their choices. Some of his help would come from a familiar source, his former star student, Thurgood Marshall. Marshall, who had only recently graduated from Howard's law school, would be the most important building block in the foundation of his litigation army.

After law school, Marshall returned to Baltimore to open a law practice. He was invited to apply for an advanced degree in law at Harvard University, but passed on that opportunity.[33] Being a black attorney during the Depression in Baltimore was tough on Thurgood and his family. He would reach out to Houston for help. Houston would send him clients, referring to him as his "Baltimore associate."[34] Houston occasionally would send a fee or expense money to Marshall which, in the words of Marshall, would help "keep the wolf away from my door."[35]

In June 1936, Charles Houston wrote: "Dear Thurgood: I agree with your letter of June 22 about the suits for tuition and transportation. The only thing I suggest is that you do not solicit the suits yourself to the point where they can charge you with barratry. If you submit a requisition for twenty-five dollars, covering your work this week, I will be glad to approve it."[36] Thurgood felt comfortable enough to say jokingly in correspondence: "Dear Charlie: At last you have been found. Your father and I were offering a reward for your capture dead or alive."[37]

Considering the closeness of their relationship, Houston realized that it made sense to persuade Walter White to hire Marshall as his full-time assistant in the national legal office. In October 1936, Marshall was excited about the opportunity because he "idolized"[38] Houston and Charlie "treated him with respect."[39] Furthermore, Houston felt Marshall was a perfect complement to his own advocacy style. "Marshall's joviality made him extremely adept at the kind of negotiating and conciliating that NAACP office politics required."[40]

As it turned out, it was not that difficult for Houston to get his wish. Thurgood had already caught the attention of Walter White. White commented that the "lanky" and "brash" young Marshall would stay close to Houston. White noted, "I was amazed at [Thurgood's] assertiveness in challenging positions [taken] by Charlie and the other lawyers. But soon I learned of his great value…doing everything he was asked, from research on obscure legal opinions to foraging for coffee and sandwiches."[41] Marshall and Houston had undertaken a huge task, to strike out effectively against a deeply entrenched "Jim Crow" legal system. Marshall would say of his mentor Houston, "[h]e was a perfectionist of the first order. I have seen him writing a brief and spending the whole day looking for one word—just the right word."[42]

The legal strategy was to attack the system at its most obvious weakness; the absence of any graduate education at all for qualified black students in any Southern state. Houston embraced the challenge to find suitable cases. In a survey conducted in 1928 for the 1926–1927 school year, it was reported that there were 13,860 black college students in America and about 75 percent of them were enrolled in private colleges.[43] In a few early cases, the NAACP was unsuccessful because of procedural flaws.[44] Judges would often look for any excuse to avoid reaching the merits of a state's blatantly discriminatory practices. What the association needed was a case to provide a dose of good fortune. That opportunity would come more quickly than either Houston or Marshall would anticipate.

In *Pearson v. Murray*, the new NAACP team gained much needed national attention for the legal campaign.[45] In that 1935 case, the NAACP attempted to desegregate the University of Maryland's law school in Baltimore, Marshall's hometown. Donald Gaines Murray was the grandson of a Baltimore bishop of the African Methodist Episcopal Church.[46] For a brief time, Murray would attend Marshall's alma mater, Lincoln University in Oxford, Pennsylvania.[47] He ultimately transferred and graduated from Charlie Houston's alma mater, Amherst College. Murray wanted to attend the University of Maryland, and many of the local civil rights lawyers and activists in Baltimore were anxious for him to try.[48] One of those local lawyers, William I. Gosnell, first identified Murray as an ideal plaintiff for a test case. Gosnell encouraged Murray to seek admission to the law school, even before Charles Houston and Thurgood Marshall began work on the case.[49]

Gosnell was a 1932 African American graduate of the University of Chicago Law School and prior to that, Lincoln University.[50] Gosnell had Murray begin the application process and made presentations at local meetings to make interested members of the community aware of Murray's plans.[51] Houston was somewhat reluctant when first made aware of Murray's application. He felt that the NAACP might need a case of somewhat lower visibility. Local attorney Bedford Lawson, working with his college fraternity Alpha Phi Alpha, attended meetings to pursue a case against the University of Maryland.[52] Thurgood Marshall learned of these local efforts and stayed in constant contact with Houston about Murray's intention to take the case to court.

Marshall informed Houston about the rapidly unfolding local activity to advance Murray's case while Houston was travelling the country. Houston advised Marshall to tell Gosnell to go to the next community meeting about the case and "take good notes" but make no commitments to file the suit.[53] Gosnell, who did not feel compelled to agree with Houston's suggestion to wait, advised the community group that he would go forward with a lawsuit.[54] After the meeting, Gosnell informed Marshall about what he said at the meeting. A panicked Marshall advised Houston that they needed to move if they were going to take the case as part of the NAACP national legal campaign.[55] Although Bedford Lawson was nudged out of participation in the *Murray* case, he continued to work on projects with Charles Houston later in his career.[56]

Marshall had a deep personal interest in taking on the University of Maryland and its law school. Although no researcher has found evidence that Marshall ever actually made an application to attend Maryland law,[57] it was well known that its admissions policy would have excluded him. In order to become a lawyer, he had to attend Howard University and make the long train commutes each day for three years.[58] Ironically, the downtown Baltimore campus of the law school at Maryland was located just blocks away from Marshall's home and the train station he used to travel to Howard. This circumstance was a lasting reminder that Marshall's own choices were limited by racial discrimination. Marshall also had another reminder of the serious effect discrimination had on his family. To cover his law school expenses, his mother pawned her engagement rings and never got them back.[59]

Taking on school discrimination in Baltimore was no easy matter. During the time of the *Murray* case in the mid-1930s, although the black schools were not equal to the white schools, they were providing a better education to black students than most places in the nation. Indeed, Maryland had one of the best educated black populations of any state in the union.[60] For example, in Baltimore, there were about 10 teachers for every 367 colored students.[61] Those numbers compared favorably to the teacher resources provided to the white population, which was about ten teachers for every 324 white pupils.[62]

"Between 1890 and 1930, Northwest Baltimore had coalesced and matured into a stable, self-contained community. Other than work, most blacks had everything they needed in Northwest Baltimore. Moreover, it was a decent place to live. Children growing up in this community were generally safeguarded from 'day to day' discrimination, and most blacks could live their lives with little outside interference even though the state was largely segregated."[63] The Negro community was "virtually a separate city in which blacks lived and died together ironically... it would be a source of strength in the battle against Jim Crow."[64] Still there were many challenges that flowed from racist thinking.

Some Negroes in rural counties in Maryland had to survive humiliations regarding beliefs white school officials embraced in the 1930s. In one instance, a one-room schoolhouse in Anne Arundel County, with a wood stove for heat and an outdoor toilet, desired some janitorial help and requested funds for that purpose. The official response from the local board of education denied the funds for a part-time janitor because, "the colored children needed the training which they would receive by sweeping the school floors."[65]

The effort to integrate the University of Maryland started in the early 1930s, years before Murray pursued admission. It was known by a few people that in the late 1890s, two Negroes actually attended the University of Maryland Law School before it adopted a formal segregation policy and became a state university. In 1933, African American Harold Arthur Seaborne applied to the law school. On July 13th of that year, Seaborne's effort generated a shocking reaction from W.M. Hillegeist, the university's registrar. He wrote Maryland's law school dean Roger Howell informing him, on university stationary, that "the nigger has applied for admission."[66] The registrar queried whether he should "talk to the President (of the University) before I send the official reply."[67] Seaborne was denied admission, as were several other Negroes over the next few months.[68] By the time of Donald Murray's 1934 application, Charles Houston fully understood that the way to attack "Jim Crow" in the professional schools was to challenge the "equal" portion of the *Plessy* requirement. As Dean Roger A. Fairfax, Jr. suggests, Houston would attack the "soft underbelly" of Jim Crow, which was the lack of any graduate education for black students in the South.[69]

Once Houston was in the case, he directed every phase of it, from the national publicity to the witness strategy. He advised the local community and local church members to dress in their finest attire and attend the trial to help the press take interest.[70] For that task he called upon the local NAACP branch president Lillie Jackson and her daughter Juanita Jackson.[71]

Charles Houston worked closely with the energetic and courageous Juanita Jackson as they were in side-by-side offices at the NAACP in New York. In a postcard from Columbia, South Carolina, after he had filmed the conditions in Southern schoolhouses he wrote, "I want to arrange to show you the films from last summer, as well as those taken on this trip…lots to tell you about things seen and heard."[72] Her job at the national office would be to organize talks for Houston to youth and church groups across the nation to show how they could directly support the NAACP's efforts in court.[73] These multi-day programs would sometimes include classical music, dance recitals and oratorical contests, all presented by Negro college and high school students.[74] Among these activities Charles Houston would speak to the young audiences about the progress of the legal campaign.[75]

Houston would later encourage Juanita Jackson to go the law school where she became the first African American woman to attend the University of Maryland and the first female editor of its law review.[76] She would also be the first African American woman admitted to the Maryland Bar.[77] Mitchell would later recall, "We crowded that courtroom on that day in June, I'll never forget it."[78] She would become one of Maryland's greatest lawyers, working on many precedent-setting civil rights cases of her own.[79]

Once the *Murray* trial began, Houston and Marshall examined the witnesses in court with William Gosnell assisting in the preparation of exhibits and preparing legal memorandum. The case was assigned for trial to the Honorable Eugene O'Dunne of the Supreme Bench of Baltimore. Just a few months before the case, when the National Bar Association (a professional group of black lawyers) held its convention in Baltimore, O'Dunne hosted several of the organization's lawyers in his court chambers. The judge complimented Charles Houston before the group saying; "I see Brother Houston here among us.... He has tried several cases before me, and I had great pleasure in seeing the suave, adroit, courteous, and efficient manner he handled the litigation."[80]

The case presented by the NAACP team on behalf of Murray went forward flawlessly.[81] University officials were quickly pinned down by Houston regarding the absurdity that Murray could not receive a law school education in Maryland at a tax-payer supported institution. Houston's case included a blistering attack on the university's attempt to establish a valid "separate but equal" claim. Under questioning by Houston, after being designated a hostile witness, University President Raymond Pearson admitted that Murray was not accepted "because he was a Negro."[82] Pearson wrote Murray asking him to apply to the Princess Anne Academy, which did not have a law school.[83] Indeed, that school, on Maryland's Eastern Shore, had no law courses at all. It only had one lab table, a few test tubes and a case of butterflies to service its agricultural science curriculum as compared to the well-equipped laboratory building at the University of Maryland's College Park campus.[84] The Eastern Shore branch was considered, at best, a junior college.

President Pearson further admitted that if Murray had been Chinese, Filipino, Indian, Mexican or Japanese he would have been admitted to the law school.[85] In a particularly revealing moment during the testimony, Houston was able to get the university president to make, arguably, his most racist statement. Noting the increase in African American college enrollment during the 1930s, Pearson said there was "a mistaken notion very largely among the leaders, in the Negro race, that they should get an education in the liberal arts and white-collar work, instead of one of the vocations like agriculture, and I am contending against it constantly."[86] Pearson did more than simply assert his own authority as president to deny Murray's application, he urged the University of Maryland Board of Trustees to do the same. Houston had President Pearson read into the trial record the minutes from the April 22, 1935, university trustees meeting announcing, after considering Murray's request, a unanimous decision to deny him admission.[87]

The case was covered widely in the press.[88] Even the famous American literary pundit H. L. Menken wrote an editorial condemning the university's position.[89] After the evidence and arguments were concluded Judge Eugene O'Dunne ruled without leaving the bench that Donald Murray should be admitted to the university's law school.[90] The local black community was ecstatic, and the NAACP national office was excited.

The University of Maryland would appeal the decision to the state's Supreme Court. The red-robed judges upheld O'Dunne's order to admit Murray to the law school. It rejected all the university's arguments, including one suggesting that young white women would be afraid to attend the university in College Park because a black man would be present at the law school in downtown Baltimore over 40 miles away. This argument was advanced by new university president Harry Clifton "Curley" Byrd, who had replaced Raymond Pearson shortly after his trial testimony in the *Murray* case.[91] Agreeing with Judge O'Dunne, Maryland's highest court noted:

> Howard University, in Washington, District of Columbia, provides the law school for Negroes nearest to Baltimore. The yearly tuition fee there is $135, as compared with a fee of $203 in the day school of the University of Maryland, and $153 in its night school.... "[t]o attend Howard University the petitioner, living in Baltimore, would be under the necessity of paying the expenses of daily travel to and fro, with some expenses while in Washington, or of removing to Washington to live during his law school education, and to pay the incidental expenses of thus living away from home; whereas in Baltimore, living at home, he would have no traveling expenses, and comparatively small living expenses.[92]

Going to any law school in the nearest jurisdiction would, then, "involve him in considerable expense even with the aid of one of the scholarships should he chance to receive one."[93] The court further wrote, Murray "could not there have the advantages of study of the law of this state primarily, and of attendance on state courts, where he intends to practice."[94] The court made clear, "this rather slender chance for any one applicant at an opportunity to attend an outside law school, at increased expense, falls short of providing for students of the colored race facilities substantially equal to those furnished to the whites in the law school maintained in Baltimore."[95]

Judge Eugene O'Dunne retired from the bench in 1945 after a long and successful judicial career.[96] At a retirement event held in his honor, Henry L. Mencken, as guest speaker, commented that Judge O'Dunne was "a profoundly serious and earnest man … a judge with a … tremendous respect for common sense and equal justice."[97] O'Dunne would remain a legendary figure with Baltimore's black community.[98]

This victory would be the first of many encounters with the University of Maryland for Charles Houston. The *Murray* case was an important step challenging educational discrimination. The successful litigation gave the NAACP legal campaign national credibility. It demonstrated that the legal system could be used to advance racial progress even in a time of economic hardship during the Great Depression era.

Murray enrolled in the University of Maryland during its very next term and completed his studies largely without incident. He was helped by Carl Murphy of the *Afro-American* newspapers and the Alpha Phi Alpha Fraternity, who made sure that his tuition was paid so he could enter law school without delay.[99] Quiet and "bespectacled," Murray occasionally reported his progress at community meetings around the country. At one NAACP meeting held at New York City's Salem Methodist Episcopal Church, Murray conveyed that the students and faculty seemed friendly.[100] Although he recognized that he was under "close scrutiny" and once received a written threat from the Ku Klux Klan,[101] Murray said that "there was no evidence of discrimination against me in the classroom…. I really keep so busy, I rarely give much thought to it. I do my work that keeps me busy."[102] This was the first NAACP case "to force open, tax supported higher education institutions to colored students through legal action."[103]

Unfortunately, since Houston won *Murray* in Maryland's Supreme Court, and the state did not appeal the decision to the United States Supreme Court, it would not apply in any other state. Houston was soon contacted by other qualified African Americans who wanted to apply to graduate school in other programs of the university. Among those several applicants was a Williams's College and Brown University graduate named Clinton E. Knox. Obliviously a qualified applicant, his inquiry was simply ignored.[104] Upon the third unanswered letter to President Byrd on behalf of the six students seeking graduate or professional education, Charles Houston wrote:

It had been my idea in writing you...to see whether we could handle the matter amicably. I had assumed the decision of the Court of Appeals in *Pearson vs. Murray* would be precedent for all departments of the University of Maryland.... In case you had any doubt, I had thought we might confer about the matter rather than the loss of both time and money in court. As this my third letter, I shall not write again but very reluctantly will have to proceed to take whatever steps may be necessary to preserve these students' rights.[105]

President Byrd maintained, with great passion, his segregationist views by pursuing laws to prevent the admission of "Colored" students to the university. As Byrd wrote:

We contemplate trying to pass such a [segregation] law before the close of the present Legislature in order to protect ourselves for the next two years, because we feel that unless we do we shall have some liberal minded judge granting a Mandamus forcing us to accept some negro student, upon receipt of which I feel that some of us will go to jail.[106]

Byrd continued to law dean Howell:

Don't give up the ship so easily! We are going to battle the *Murray* case right down to the last ditch. Of course, your respect for the decision of the Court and all that it implies is fine, but the fact nevertheless remains that we cannot afford to have Negroes enter the University of Maryland. Perhaps I shall have to go to jail, but I think we have got to keep the Negroes out. [Governor] Nice tells me he does not mind going to jail provided I go with him, so there is some moral support anyway.[107]

President Clifton Byrd's views would dominate Maryland higher education for decades. His later efforts would include summoning William H. Murphy, a well-qualified Oberlin College graduate and potential law school student, to his office. The purpose of the request was to tell him personally that it would "be better for the Negro group as a whole for [him] not to insist upon [his] legal rights."[108] Byrd even offered Murphy a tuition and travel scholarship if he would go to Harvard rather than the University of Maryland Law School.[109] Murphy flatly refused, telling President Byrd, "You've just made up my mind, I'll be coming to your school in the fall."[110] William Murphy entered the University of Maryland Law School, graduated and joined Charles Houston as co-counsel in a criminal case in later years.[111]

The Zimmerman Case

After winning *Murray*, the NAACP moved on to a new, more risky case, that would break from the strategy of seeking access to higher education for adults and focus on high school children. In the 1930s, Baltimore County, Maryland, had no Negro high school. Margaret Williams and her father, a resident and taxpayer of Baltimore County, sought to compel school officials to admit her to the Catonsville High School, a public school maintained in the county for white children only.[112] The county made some provision for high school education of colored children by paying their tuition to high schools in Baltimore City. Houston and Marshall argued that Williams had a constitutional right to the educational facilities within their own county.

The number of white children in Baltimore county were about ten times that of the Negro children.[113] Margaret Williams lived in the county close to the southwest boundary of the city, and about equally distant from Catonsville, and the nearest colored high school in the city.[114] Margaret finished the seventh grade in the county elementary school near her home in June 1934, when she was thirteen years old, and, upon passing an examination given at her school, received from the principal a card certifying that she was "promoted to the eighth grade,"[115] and was recommended as a "very good student."[116] She was officially listed as a graduate of the primary school. She took another examination given by county officials at Catonsville to test her qualifications for sending her to the county high school, but her marks were below the requirements. She nevertheless went to the city high school and was admitted on presentation of the card from her principal, without examination by the city officials, the city schools requiring none. But her tuition not being paid either by her parents or by the county, she returned a month later to repeat the seventh grade. At the end of another year, given a card marked, "promoted to the eighth grade,"[117] and included in the list of graduates, she again took the examination at Catonsville preliminary to being sent to the city high school, and her scores totaled 244 out of a required minimum of 250 and a possible 390.[118] It was in this situation that application for admission to the Catonsville school was made and refused. The trial and appellate court both rejected Williams' claims.[119]

Losing the Baltimore County high school lawsuit was devastating to the availability of educational opportunity in central Maryland. Even with scholarships to the Baltimore City black high schools, only a few hundred students were able to attend.[120] About three years after losing the case, only 104 of the county's nearly 6,000 high school students were black.[121] By 1945, with the construction of three black high schools in the county, "African-American high school enrollment had grown somewhat, to 305, but it was still far outdistanced by white enrollment numbers of 6,436."[122]

Houston had a long-standing interest in the effect of discrimination on children of lower age groups. While dean at Howard, Charlie and Thurgood did extensive research and made films in the South of school conditions between white and black schools. "They toured Virginia, Kentucky, Missouri, Tennessee, the Carolinas, and Mississippi to investigate segregation in schools. The schools were wooden structures, no more than shacks."[123] As Thurgood Marshall described it, "Charlie Houston and I used to type sitting in the car with a typewriter in our laps. . . . The sight of two men investigating segregated schools led to threats from local whites."[124]

"In Mississippi, these concerns were so great that the state NAACP president assigned a funeral hearse, with two riflemen inside, to ride behind Houston and Marshall for protection."[125] After producing the movies about the shocking conditions in the Southern colored schools, he held mass meetings and showed them to integrated audiences, arguing that the Negro "must base his case for complete justice on what is best for the entire country."[126] The message was political as well as legal. "Either relieve the pressure on us in the South, or we will vote against you up here and put you out of power."[127]

Houston had begun to lay the intellectual and evidentiary foundation for the *Brown* case during the early 1930s. Long before the famous "Doll Tests" were used in *Brown v. Board* in the 1950s, a young graduate student in psychology working on a master's degree came to work at the Houston law firm.

Mamie Phipps, a native of Arkansas, had come to Howard University in 1934, where she pursued a degree in psychology and graduated magna cum laude in 1938. During her senior year she married another graduate psychology student, Kenneth Clark, who later was credited with the psychological testing that played such a prominent role in ending discrimination in American schools.[128] According to Mamie, her earlier affiliation with Charles Houston laid the foundation for his ultimate courtroom strategy to prove the harm done to black children by Jim Crow schools.[129]

Although Charles Houston would not live to see his strategy carried out to completion, he certainly played a role in developing the very social science literature that would support the later court cases. Mamie Clark's master's thesis, developed while she worked with Charles Houston, was entitled "The Development of Self-Esteem in Negro Pre-School Children."[130]

Decades later, Mamie Phipps-Clark would comment, "it just happened by sheer accident that I got a job in the office of Charles Houston, and at the time the whole business of segregation cases was just beginning, and in this office came many lawyers, including Thurgood Marshall.... I can't remember all of them, but they converged in his office to prepare these cases, and that was the most marvelous learning experience I ever had."[131] She explained, "the whole sense of urgency...of breaking down the segregation, and the whole sense of really, blasphemy, to blacks, was brought very clearly to me in that office."[132] It was in Houston's office that Phipps-Clark thought about how she might study racial inferiority in order to attack it. She recalled "here was an actual tangible approach to the whole thing."[133]

She and her husband Kenneth Clark would continue their graduate studies together, and she became the first African American woman to earn a Ph.D. in psychology at Columbia University.[134] They would both testify as expert witnesses at later desegregation trials, explaining their research findings that children form a racial identity and internalize society's negative view of blackness at about three years old. The early influence of Charles Houston shaped her entire career.

The *Gaines* Case

After the defeat in the Catonsville High School case, Houston finally had the opportunity to expand on the success of the *Murray* case on a national stage. He testified in Congress in 1937 about the glaring inequities between Negro and white schools. He told a United States Senate subcommittee that in the Southern states the average "outlay for a white child is $44.31 while that for a Colored child was $12.57...more than $300,000 transporting white children to elementary school and only $628 transporting Colored children."[135] He further informed the Senate that not only do most school districts in the South refuse to provide transportation, "many will not let the colored people provide transportation for their children out of their own pockets."[136]

As an example, he cited a Southampton, Virginia, case where a principal lost his job because he directed agitated parents "to get together and provide a bus for the children."[137] On another occasion, Houston reminded Congress that states provided money to ship graduate students off to other states for an education had provided woefully inadequate resources. "Not a single Southern State provides graduate or professional education for colored students." States that did provide scholarship money provided an arbitrary limit, like $150 in Virginia.[138]

The State of Missouri refused admission of a black student to its state law school.[139] Lloyd Gaines was a citizen of Missouri. In August 1935, he graduated with the degree of bachelor of arts at Lincoln University, a Missouri college for the higher education of Negroes. The state had no law school that black students could attend. Upon the filing of his application for admission to the law school of the University of Missouri, the registrar advised him to communicate with the president of Lincoln University, who directed Gaines to a 1929 Missouri law that allowed the state to arrange for attendance of a Negro student at a university of any adjacent state and pay its state tuition and fees.[140]

The Missouri law further provided:

> Pending the full development of the Lincoln university, the board of curators shall have the authority to arrange for the attendance of negro residents of the state of Missouri at the university of any adjacent state to take any course or to study any subjects provided for at the state university of Missouri, and which are not taught at the Lincoln university and to pay the reasonable tuition fees for such attendance; provided that whenever the board of curators deem it advisable they shall have the power to open any necessary school or department.[141]

Gaines sued and the case went to the Supreme Court. The late federal Judge Robert Carter recalled that in *Gaines v. Missouri* "when Houston rose to begin his argument, Justice James McReynolds turned in his chair and kept his back to Houston throughout his presentation."[142] Judge Carter explained, "[i]n retrospect, it seems remarkable that no one witnessing this…discourtesy from an official supposedly representing all Americans, whatever their race, color or ethnicity, reacted with disapproval. Nor do I myself recall feeling any outrage at the time. In 1938 the second-class status of blacks was accepted by both blacks and whites as a fact of life."[143] At another Supreme Court argument, Justice McReynolds had a sharp exchange where Houston was compelled to point out to him an admitted "lack of understanding" of an issue by telling the Justice, "You've never been a Negro."[144]

McReynolds, a known racist and anti-Semite, once referred to D.C.'s Howard as a "nigger university."[145] He also "repeatedly snubbed Justices Brandeis and Cardozo because of their Jewish faith."[146] Despite these blatant racist attitudes, Charles Houston secured the admission of the first African American to the University of Missouri in the *Gaines* case.[147] The Supreme Court reasoned, "[b]y the operation of the laws of Missouri a privilege has been created for white law students which are denied to Negroes by reason of their race.[148] The white resident is afforded legal education within the State; the Negro resident having the same qualifications is refused it there and must go outside the State to obtain it. That is a denial of the equality of legal right to the enjoyment of the privilege which the State has set up, and the provision for the payment of tuition fees in another State does not remove the discrimination."[149] In dissent, Justice McReynolds wrote:

> For a long time Missouri has acted upon the view that the best interest of her people demands separation of whites and Negroes in schools. Under the opinion just announced, I presume she may abandon her law school and thereby disadvantage her white citizens without improving petitioner's opportunities for legal instruction; or she may break down the settled practice concerning separate schools and thereby, as indicated by experience, damnify both races.[150]

Houston was exceedingly optimistic about the potential impact of *Gaines* after the victory. In a newspaper interview he noted that the "decision effects the entire scope of graduate and professional training in 16 Southern States which do not now provide such training within their borders."[151] Some Justices of the Supreme Court began to show impatience with the Jim Crow practices and stalling of the Southern states. One news account reported that during the case of Ada Lois Sipuel, who was seeking admission to University of Oklahoma law school,[152] Justice William O. Douglass "snapped" at the attorney general of Oklahoma when he could not say how long it would take to provide a law school for Ms. Sipuel to attend, stating "she might be an old lady by that time."[153]

The stunning victory had become something of a disappointment, since Lloyd Gaines never attended the University of Missouri law school. Shortly after the Supreme Court victory he was reported missing.[154] To this day it is still a mystery what happened to him. Some have speculated he was killed by some hate group, others have thought that he left the country.[155]

Teacher Pay Cases

An ugly reminder of government-sanctioned racial inferiority was teacher pay inequity during the Jim Crow era. Unashamed of the hypocrisy of the system, about 18 states engaged in the practice of paying black teachers about half what white teachers made.[156] The NAACP decided to challenge the practice. Charles Houston first examined the teacher pay situation in Roanoke, Virginia, in November 1935.[157] Along with his former student Oliver Hill, he planned a

Thanksgiving weekend trip to meet with local teachers of the Black Virginia Teachers Association.[158] The remarks Houston made in his keynote address were described as "brilliant" and "succeeded for the moment in carrying the 500 teachers present up to the verge of the promised land."[159] Recognizing the possibility that taking legal action might lead to a teacher being fired, Charles Houston announced a $1,000 scholarship fund "to support any plaintiff willing to challenge unequal teacher salaries."[160]

Charles Houston and Thurgood Marshall, however, selected a few Maryland counties to make the first court challenge. Similar challenges in other states like North Carolina had failed for lack of an unafraid plaintiff to file the suit.[161] After the Negro teachers had several failed attempts to correct the inequity with the local school board and in the Maryland legislature, they were ready to resort to the courts.[162]

The first plaintiff who stepped forward in Maryland was "a colored teacher employed and paid by the County School Board of Anne Arundel County, Maryland," named Walter Mills.[163] Mills' "complaint alleges that for many years past in this State only white teachers are employed to teach in schools for white children and only colored teachers in the schools for colored children; and that in most of the Counties of the State, including Anne Arundel County, the salaries paid colored teachers in colored schools are materially less [about half] than the amounts paid white teachers in white schools although having equal professional qualifications."[164] Houston called "attention to the Maryland statute which provides a minimum scale of salaries for white teachers, graduated to professional qualifications and years of experience, and a separate statute providing a lower minimum for teachers in colored schools," solely on account of their race.

William Marbury, a partner in one of Maryland's most influential law firms, would encounter Charles Houston while representing the Calvert County school board in a similar teacher pay lawsuit as Mills'. After litigation was filed, the Calvert County, Maryland case was ultimately settled before trial. Although Thurgood Marshall played a key role in many of the teacher pay suits across the state, William Marbury recalls that it was Houston who guided the ultimate outcome. In his memoir Marbury would write that he was "deeply impressed by Dr. Houston's handling of this very delicate situation."[165]

After Houston laid the road map for success in the teacher pay cases, Marshall was able to follow that blueprint for success in both state and federal courts. After winning equal pay in a federal court, Marshall filed contempt proceedings against another local school board official who said to the trial court, "I will not be a party to paying a nigger the same money I pay a white person. And I refuse to do it."[166] Marshall was successful in getting that official to change his mind after the higher court had spoken.[167]

The grind of the grueling litigation campaign began to take its toll on Charles Houston and his marriage to Margaret. In 1936, newspapers began to inquire about the rumors that Houston was planning to leave the NAACP and had filed for a divorce.[168] With his domestic problems growing and the high-visibility national legal campaign gaining momentum, he felt compelled to make some form of public statement. In October of 1937, Charles Houston's divorce from Margaret became final.[169] Soon after, he remarried. His only public comment on the matter was "[a]ll parties made an agreement not to give any information and I would consider it ungentlemanly to do so. You can say I have introduced Henrietta Williams as Mrs. Houston."[170] The couple moved into the Dunbar Apartments in Harlem soon after they were married.[171]

Living in New York and newlywed, Houston still had many battles in front of him and not all in the area of education. During his time at the New York headquarters he filed discrimination cases against nearby Brighton Beach and Playland,[172] threatened legal action that resulted in job opportunities for Negroes in the New York railway transit system,[173] and negotiated job and management opportunities in Harlem retail stores.[174] On the national front, Houston lead an investigation of discriminatory practices at a federal Tennessee Valley Authority project in Knoxville[175] and scolded the insurance industry about discriminating against Negroes in risk assessment and pricing.[176]

Houston was a great admirer of prize fighting and was once called upon to give a prediction about the upcoming Joe Louis' heavyweight fight with Max Schmeling, "Louis will win because of his added experience and his great natural fighting ability."[177] On a social occasion Houston, his new bride, Thurgood Marshall and his wife along with many other guests, including Poet Langston Hughes, joined Joe Louis at a New York party hosted by NAACP head Walter White.[178] The cocktail event was to celebrate Louis's historic boxing victory as Houston had predicted a few days earlier.[179] Also among the guests was John W. Roxborough, Joe Louis's manager, who Houston would represent in the United States Supreme Court a few years later on charges related to the alleged operation of illegal lotteries in Michigan.[180]

An article in the *New York Amsterdam News* repeated speculation that Houston would return home to Washington, D.C., to his father's busy law office and be "compelled to give up at least part of his work with the N.A.A.C.P."[181] The strain on the practice in Washington was created by the growing success and recognized ability of its lawyers. Furthermore, his father William Houston had recently been appointed assistant attorney general of the United States[182] and Charles's cousin and a partner in the firm, William H. Hastie, had taken a position as a federal judge in the Virgin Islands.[183] While Charles did not refute that he might return to the District of Columbia, he made it clear that his important work with the civil rights organization would continue. In one press account Charles Houston made clear that he was doing "the most important work I have ever done...and that he would "not resign from my duties as counsel to it under any circumstances."[184]

What was lacking in his statement was whether he would remain as the first full-time special counsel in New York. On this point his statement was very non-committal. With recent changes in his personal life and the needs of his father's firm becoming obvious, he would continue to prepare Thurgood Marshall to take on more responsibility. Finally, in July of 1938, it was announced that Houston would leave the full-time position at the NAACP that he had created.[185] He would return to Washington and step back from full-time duty, but his work on behalf of the NAACP would be far from over. Although the civil rights organization provided a platform to begin his strategy to dismantle Jim Crow, he often felt that the political constraints within the organization bound him too much to make necessary progress. It was also recognized among the staff at the national office that Houston's new wife was encouraging him to leave New York to begin a more normal family life.[186] He also believed he needed to be free to strike when and where it was needed. He once reminded Thurgood Marshall, the "shock troops" do not occupy the city.[187]

Charles Houston was also concerned that the NAACP was focused too heavily on the needs of the middle class. The organization seemed to ignore the crisis of the truly needy among the black population, like the sharecroppers, the jobless and laborers calling the organization "top heavy with white collar interests and attitudes."[188] He was getting tired of the NAACP bureaucracy and became physically exhausted. In May 1938 in a handwritten note to Walter White after completing a Supreme Court brief, Charlie wrote, "completely exhausted. We've worked about 18–20 hours.... Quit at 2 a.m. this morning. Can't make it tomorrow going to get food, sleep."[189] He still loved the legal work and crafting case strategy, but he was content to leave the NAACP's day-to-day politics to his trusted understudy, Thurgood Marshall, who would now run the national legal machine. Houston would retain his role as chair of the National Legal Committee as well as select and work on cases of his own. He would soon return to his father's District of Columbia law office with Henrietta.

Justice Thurgood Marshall looking toward Charles Houston's portrait at Amherst Dedication in 1978.

COURTESY OF THE CHARLES H. HOUSTON, JR., FAMILY COLLECTION

Endnotes

1. "Under the Microscope," *Philadelphia Tribune*, May 10, 1934, p. 4.

2. Genna Rae McNeil, *Groundwork, Charles Hamilton Houston and the Struggle for Civil Rights* 131 (Philadelphia: University of Pennsylvania Press 1983).

3. D. G. Gibson, "Berkley," *Chicago Defender*, October 24, 1936, p. 9.

4. Ibid.

5. Ibid.

6. "Atty. Flays Segregation in Schools," *Chicago Defender*, February 8, 1936, p. 3.

7. Ibid.

8. Franklin Marshall Davis, "World in Review," *Chicago Defender*, February 13, 1936, p. 5.

9. Ibid.

10. "Memphis, NAACP Nearing Close of Membership Drive," *Pittsburgh Courier*, April 25, 1936, p. A8.

11. Ibid.

12. "Houston Urges Full Rights in Philly," *Baltimore Afro-American*, November 23, 1935, p. 4.

13.   Ron Cassie, "The Legacy of Thurgood Marshall," *Baltimore Magazine*, August 7, 2017, p. 5.

14.   Charles Houston to Atkins, May 15, 1935, NAACP Papers, Library of Congress, Box D-92.

15.   *Plessy v. Ferguson*, 163 U.S. 537 (1896).

16.   Ibid.

17.   Ibid.

18.   Ibid., at 538.

19.   Ibid.

20.   Leonard W. Levy, *Judicial Review and the Supreme Court* 34 (New York: Harper 1967).

21.   Ibid.

22.   Carl T. Rowan, *South of Freedom* 16 (New York: Alfred A. Knopf 1952).

23.   Harold Cruse, *Plural but Equal* 15–20 (New York: William Morrow 1987).

24.   Ibid.

25.   Anthony Lewis, *Portrait of a Decade: The Second American Revolution* 20 (New York: Random House 1964).

26.   Joel Spring, *The American School, 1642–1993* 174 (New York: McGraw-Hill 1994, Third Edition).

27.   Ibid., p. 175.

28.   Leon F. Litwack, *Trouble in Mind: Black Southerners in the Age of Jim Crow* 63 (New York: Knopf 1998).

29.   Nathan Margold, *Preliminary Report to the Joint Committee Supervising the Expenditure of the 1930 Appropriation by the American Fund for Public Service to the NAACP* 93 (1930).

30.   Charles H. Houston, "Letter to the Editor," *Washington Post*, September 22, 1934, p. 8.

31.   Ibid.

32.   Randall Kennedy, *Interracial Intimacies: Sex, Marriage, Identity and Adoption* 317 (New York: Random House 2012).

33.   Juan Williams, *Thurgood Marshall: American Revolutionary* 6 (New York: Random House 1998).

34.   Mark V. Tushnet, *Making Civil Rights Law: Thurgood Marshall and the Supreme Court, 1936–1961* 17 (Oxford 1994).

35.   Ibid.

36.   Charles H. Houston to Thurgood Marshall, June 25, 1936, NAACP Papers, Library of Congress.

37.   Thurgood Marshall to Charles H. Houston, March 1936, NAACP File Cases Supported - Baltimore County School case Oct. 1–31st., Library of Congress.

38.   Mark V. Tushnet, *Making Civil Rights Law*, p. 12.

39.   James T. Patterson, Brown v. Board of Education, *A Civil Rights Milestone and Its Troubled Legacy* 30 (Oxford University Press 2001).

40.   Mark V. Tushnet, *Making Civil Rights Law*, p. 18.

41.   Robert Goldman and David Gallen, Ed., *Thurgood Marshall: Justice for All* 26 (New York: Carroll & Graf Publishing 1992).

42. Carl T. Rowan, *Dream Makers, Dream Breakers: The World of Justice Thurgood Marshall* 46 (Boston: Little Brown & Co. 1993).

43. James D. Anderson, *The Education of Blacks in the South 1860–1935* 186 (Chapel Hill: University of North Carolina Press 1988).

44. Jerry Greshenhorn, "*Hocutt v. Wilson*, and Race Relations in Durham, North Carolina During the 1930s," *North Carolina Historical Review*, Vol. 78, No. 3 (July 2001) p. 275.

45. 182 A. 2d 590 (Md. 1936).

46. Richard Kluger, *Simple Justice: The History of* Brown v. Board of Education *and Black America's Struggle for Equality* 186 (New York: Alfred A. Knopf 1977). p. 186.

47. Donald Gaines Murray, Oral History Collection, Maryland Historical Society, OH 8319 G. Transcript, p. 1.

48. Richard Kluger, *Simple Justice*, p. 187.

49. Ibid., pp. 186–187.

50. "Personals," *Baltimore Afro-American*, July 9, 1932, p. 11.

51. José Felipé Anderson, "Perspectives on *Missouri v. Jenkins*: Abandoning the Unfinished Business of Public School Desegregation 'With All Deliberate Speed'" 39 *How. L. J.* 693, 699 (1996).

52. Ibid., pp. 699–700.

53. Ibid.

54. Ibid.

55. Ibid.

56. *See*, Gregory S. Parks, "Belford Vance Lawson, Jr., Life of a Civil Rights Litigator," 12 U. Md. L.J. *Race Relig. Gender & Class*, 320, 333–334 (2012).

57. Larry Gibson, *Young Thurgood: The Making of a Supreme Court Justice* 107 (New York: Prometheus Book 2012).

58. Ibid.

59. Richard Kluger, *Simple Justice*, p. 179.

60. Robert J. Brugger, *Maryland: A Middle Temperament* 419 (Baltimore: Johns Hopkins Press 1988).

61. Ralph L. Pearson, "The National Urban League Comes to Baltimore," pp. 523, 527 *Maryland Historical Magazine* Vol. 72 No. 4 (Winter 1977).

62. Ibid.

63. Bruce A. Thompson, *The Civil Rights Vanguard: The NAACP and the Black Community in Baltimore, 1931–1942*, Doctor of Philosophy Dissertation, (1996), p. 22.

64. Ibid.

65. Phillip L. Brown, *A Century of 'Separate but Equal': Education in Anne Arundel County* 101 (Baltimore: Gateway Press 1988).

66. Larry Gibson, *Young Thurgood*, p. 234.

67. Ibid.

68. Ibid.

69. Roger A. Fairfax, Jr., "Wielding the Double Edge Sword: Charles Hamilton Houston and Judicial Activism in the Age of Legal Realism," 14 *Harvard Black Letter Law Journal* 17, 41 (1998).

70. José F. Anderson, "Maryland Lawyers Who Helped Shape the Constitution – Father of Freedom, Charles Hamilton Houston," 44 *Maryland Bar Journal*, pp. 5, 6 (2011).

71. Stacy M. Brown, "Women's History Month: Juanita Jackson Mitchell," *The Baltimore Times*, March 2, 2020.

72. Charles H. Houston to Juanita Jackson, November 23, 1934, The Mitchell Family Collection, courtesy of Michael B. Mitchell.

73. "Christian Youth Plan to Organize," *Philadelphia Tribune*, March 4, 1937, p. 15.

74. Program Book, The Third Annual, The City-Wide Young People's Forum, April 27, 1934. The Mitchell Family Collection, courtesy of Michael B. Mitchell.

75. Ibid., p. 2.

76. Taunya Lovell Banks, "Setting the Record Straight: Maryland's First Black Women Law Graduates," 52 *Md. L. Rev.* 509 (2004).

77. Ibid.

78. William A. Elwood, Road to *Brown* Film Transcript, *California Newsreel*. A Presentation of the University of Virginia, p. 4 (1990).

79. John Carroll Byrnes, "In Memoriam: Juanita Jackson Mitchell," 52 *Md. L. Rev.* 522 (2004).

80. Larry Gibson, *Young Thurgood*, p. 276.

81. Carl T. Rowan, *Dream Makers, Dream Breakers: The World of Justice Thurgood Marshall* 51–52 (Boston: Little Brown & Co. 1993).

82. Stenographer's Record *Donald G. Murray vs. Raymond A. Pearson, et al*. In the Baltimore City Court Part III June 18, 1935, p. 32.

83. Ibid.

84. Ibid., 51. *See also*, "Admits Catch in Scholarship," *Baltimore Afro-American*, June 7, 1935, p. 7.

85. Stenographer's Record Donald G. Murray, pp. 28–29.

86. Stenographer's Record Donald G. Murray, p. 49.

87. Stenographer's Record Donald G. Murray, pp. 33–36.

88. "Barring of Negro by U. of MD. Argued," *Baltimore Sun*, November 6, 1935, p. 11.

89. H. L. Mencken, "An Ethiop Among the Aryans," *Baltimore Evening Sun*, September 23, 1935.

90. "Road to *Brown*," p. 4.

91. "Race Issue Sizzles at Maryland U.," *Chicago Defender*, October 5, 1935, p. 1.

92. Ibid., p. 593.

93. Ibid.

94. Ibid.

95. Ibid.

96. Proceedings at Testimonial Dinner on the Retirement of Eugene O'Dunne as Member of Supreme Bench, Gosnell Papers, Box 7A2, Thurgood Marshall Law Library University of Maryland School of Law (Reprinted from *The Daily Record*, Baltimore, November 5, 1945, p. 7–8.

97. Ibid.

98. Ibid.

99. Edward Kuebler, "The Desegregation of the University of Maryland," 71 *Maryland Hist. Mag.* 37, 46 (Vol. 1, Spring 1976). Rayford W. Logan to Thurgood Marshall,

January 15, 1936, NAACP Papers, Library of Congress (Discussing application process for Alpha Phi Alpha to provide Donald Gaines Murray a law school scholarship).

100. "No difficulties at Dixie School," *New York Amsterdam News*, March 14, 1936, p. 3.

101. "University of Maryland Applicant Gets Threatening Letter," June 29, 1935, *Baltimore Afro-American*, p. 7.

102. Ibid.

103. "Smash Ban on Race Students at University of Maryland," *Chicago Defender*, July 6, 1935, p. 12.

104. Charles H. Houston to President H. Curley Byrd, March 16, 1937, NAACP Papers, Manuscripts Division, Library of Congress.

105. Ibid.

106. H. C. Byrd to R. H. Wettach, 21 March 1933, Harry Clifton "Curley" Byrd Papers, Box 8, Folder: Negro Education, 1933–1935 Special Collections, University of Maryland at College Park Libraries, College Park, Maryland. H. C. Byrd to R. H. Wettach, 13 April 1933.

107. H. C. Byrd to Roger Howell, 16 July 1935, Records of the President's Office, Box 39,
Folder: Negro Students (including Murray papers).

108. William H. Murphy to the NAACP, September 7, 1939, NAACP Papers, Manuscripts Division, Library of Congress.

109. C. Fraser Smith, *Here Lies Jim Crow: Civil Rights in Maryland* 147 (Baltimore: Johns Hopkins University Press 2008).

110. Ibid.

111. *James v. State*, 65 A.2d 888 (1949).

112. *William v. Zimmerman*, 192 A. 353 (Md. 1937).

113. Ibid.

114. Ibid.

115. Ibid.

116. Ibid., p. 354.

117. Ibid.

118. Ibid., p. 355.

119. Ibid., p. 356.

120. W. Edward Orser, "Neither Separate Nor Equal: Foreshadowing *Brown* in Baltimore County," 92 *Maryland Historical Magazine* (Vol. Spring 1997) 5, pp. 11–12.

121. Ibid., 24.

122. Ibid., 25.

123. Juan Williams, *Thurgood Marshall*, pp. 63–64.

124. Ibid.

125. Ibid.

126. "Mass Action Seen Solution Negro Problem," May 23, 1935, *Philadelphia Tribune*, p. 2.

127. Ibid.

128. Ibid.

129. Ibid.

130. Mamie Clark, Columbia University Libraries Oral History Research Office, Transcriptp. 18. http://www.columbia.edu/cu/lweb/digital/collections/nny/clarkm/transcripts/clarkm_1_1_18.html. visited 5/22/2010.

131. Ibid.

132. Ibid.

133. Ibid.

134. Ibid.

135. "Houston Exposes More School Inequalities," April 24, 1937, *Baltimore Afro-American*, p. 7.

136. Ibid.

137. Ibid.

138. "South's Graduate School Limited," *Baltimore Afro-American*, April 24, 1937, p. 7.

139. *Missouri ex. rel. Gaines v. Canada*, 305 U.S. 337 (1938).

140. Ibid., p. 342.

141. Ibid., p. 343.

142. Robert L. Carter, *A Matter of Law* 128 (New York: The New Press 2005).

143. Ibid.

144. Gilbert Ware, *William Hastie: Grace Under Pressure* 188 (New York: Oxford University Press, 1984).

145. A. Leon Higginbotham, Jr., *Shades of Freedom* 159 (London: Oxford Press 1996).

146. Ibid.

147. Robert L. Carter, "The Long Road to Equality," *The Nation*, May 3, 2004, pp. 28–29.

148. Ibid.

149. Ibid., p. 350.

150. Ibid.

151. "Negroes Upheld in College Case," *Los Angeles Times*, December 13, 1938, p. 3.

152. *Sipuel v. Board of Regents of the University of Oklahoma*, 332 U.S. 631 (1948).

153. Ada's Day in Court, *Time*, January 19, 1948.

154. NAACP Press Release, "Still Unable to Find Lloyd Gaines," March 8, 1940. NAACP Papers, Manuscripts Division, Library of Congress.

155. David Stout, "A Supreme Triumph, Then into the Shadows," *New York Times*, July 11, 2009.

156. Phillip L. Brown, *A Century of 'Separate but Equal': Education in Anne Arundel County*, 69–70 (Baltimore: Gateway Press 1988).

157. Charles H. Houston to Oliver Hill, November 20, 1935, Group 1, Box C-203, Paper of the American Fund for Public Service, Library of Congress.

158. Margaret Edds, "The Letters of Oliver and Bernie Hill, 1934–36," 121 *Virginia Magazine of History and Biography* 211, 236 (Vol. I, 2013).

159. Ibid., p. 237.

160. Ibid.

161. Phillip L. Brown, *A Century of 'Separate but Equal'*, p. 70.

162. Ibid., p. 71–72.

163. *Mills v. Lowndes*, 26 F. Supp. 792 (Md. 1938).

164. Ibid.

165. William L. Marbury, *In the Catbird's Seat* 322 (Baltimore: Maryland Historical Society 1988).

166. Howard Ball, *Thurgood Marshall: A Defiant Life* 32 (New York: Crown Publishing 1998).

167. Ibid.

168. "Charles H. Houston to Seek Separation," February 15, 1936, *Chicago Defender*, p. 1.

169. "Houston Rewed After Divorce," *New York Amsterdam News*, October 2, 1937, p. 1.

170. Ibid.

171. "NAACP Attorney's Bride," *Baltimore Afro-American*, November 6, 1937, p. 3.

172. "Starts Crusades Against Beaches," *New York Amsterdam News*, August 24, 1935, p. 1.

173. "I.R.T. Plans, Use of Negro Station Men," *New York Amsterdam News*, July 16, 1938, p. 2.

174. "A & P Stores Assist in New Job Campaign," *New York Amsterdam News*, April 23, 1938, p. 1.

175. "Charges Negroes on T.V.A. Coerced," *The Kingsport Times*, August 18, 1938, p. 1.

176. "NAACP Demands Anti-Jim-Crow Insurance Law," *Philadelphia Tribune*, February 4, 1937, p. 11.

177. "Bomber Holds Edge in Local Opinion," *New York Amsterdam News*, June 18, 1938, p. 1.

178. "Round of Festivities," *New York Amsterdam News*, June 25, 1938, p. 8.

179. Ibid.

180. *See People v. Roxborough et al.*, 12 N.W.2d 466 (Mich.1943). *Roxborough v. People*, 64 S. Ct. 1287 (1944) (Charles H. Houston, counsel of record on unsuccessful petition for certiorari arguing race discrimination in jury selection).

181. "Houston Won't Quit N.A.A.C.P.," *New York Amsterdam News*, December 18, 1937, p. 7.

182. Ibid.

183. Ibid.

184. "Houston Won't Quit N.A.A.C.P.," *New York Amsterdam News*, December, 18, 1937, p. 7.

185. A. M. Wendell Malliet, "Story Behind Retirement of Houston Told," *New York Amsterdam News*, July 30, 1938, p. 3A.

186. Author Interview, Jack Greenberg, Washington, D.C., April 22, 2009.

187. Jack Greenberg, *Crusaders in the Courts: How a Band of Dedicated Lawyers Fought for the Civil Rights Revolution* 6 (New York: Harper Collins 1994).

188. Adam Fairclough, *Better Day Coming: Blacks and Equality 1890–2000* 147 (New York: Viking Press 2001).

189.   Charles Houston to Walter White, May 24, 1938, NAACP Papers, Manuscripts Division, Library of Congress. http;//www.loc.gov/exhibits/brown/images/br0033s.jpg, visited 1/25/2005.

ⅴ

Crime Stories

Scottsboro and Beyond

[W]hen a man is forced to lock horns with the authorities in attempting to help the poor and oppressed ... he loses a lot of his manners.

—Charles H. Houston, March 10, 1934

[C]onfidence in the law increases in proportion that the humble and insignificant know that their constitutional rights are just as well protected and their chances in court just as good as the rich and powerful.

—Charles H. Houston, *The Baltimore Sun*, September 25, 1948

One of the most interesting areas of Charles Houston's legal career was his fascination with the criminal justice system. His efforts, though little noted and often unsuccessful, spanned his entire career and serve as an interesting example of his visionary reform advocacy. In some ways, his interest in criminal cases makes perfect sense. In no area of the law during his lifetime were inequities based on race more pronounced. The history in the United States of the slave codes prior to the Civil War were a great indication of the widespread racial discrimination. Black codes imposed by many states after the Civil War further led to daunting statistical disparity in black incarceration and arrest rates.[1] What is noteworthy about Houston's activity in this arena were the often-horrific facts in many of the criminal cases in which he served as counsel.

In other areas of the law he was careful to avoid cases where legal precedent was hopelessly against him. In many of his criminal cases, however, he took a different approach, often handling cases that seemed impossible to win during the 1930s and 1940s. Interracial murders and allegations of rape were

Charles Houston's criminal cases of choice. Why would he choose to represent such difficult defendants? The decisions he made strongly suggest that in the criminal system black citizens were exposed to the greatest potential violation of constitutional due process. Furthermore, his concerns about lynching would not only lead him into court but into the streets with college students to participate in demonstrations.[2] As a result of those protests, hundreds of letters and telegrams were sent to President Franklin Delano Roosevelt urging him to back anti-lynching legislation then pending before Congress.[3]

The criminal court of the early twentieth century was very different from those operating today. Although the federal Constitution contained a Bill of Rights, those rights were largely meaningless for black people because of the lack of legal counsel for black defendants. The rights against illegal search and seizure and self-incrimination were substantially weaker at that time, allowing states more freedom to use questionable ways of obtaining and sharing evidence.[4]

Houston recognized that the disparities in the system suggested that more lawyers were needed to take on tough criminal cases. In a speech at Virginia State College in 1934, he pointed out the need.[5] He remarked that "there were only 57 black lawyers in Virginia to serve a population of almost 500,000 and only 4 in Alabama to serve a Negro population of over 700,000."[6] Black defendants in the 1930s were sometimes lynched before they could stand trial. Even if a black defendant made it to trial, the odds of his winning were remote. One Mississippi lawyer in 1940 pointed out that it was next to impossible "to convict even upon the strongest evidence any white man of a crime of violence upon the person of a Negro.... I have heard attorneys make the appeal to a jury that no white man should be punished for killing a Negro."[7]

In 1919, the NAACP published a report on lynching that covered about three decades, 1889–1918. During that period, of 3,224 persons that were lynched, only 61 were women, and 50 of those women were black and 11 were white.[8] During the same period of time when these reports were issued, young Charles Houston experienced first-hand the horrors of racial injustice during 1919 "Red Summer,"[9] shortly after the close of World War I. During that year, over 100 African Americans were lynched and about a thousand were injured during race riots across the nation.[10] Only about ten percent of the cases handled by his father, William Houston, were criminal.[11] One criminal case that William did accept was the defense of a man involved in a violent "Red Summer" shooting episode.

The client, William Laney, was convicted of manslaughter at his trial for the "killing of one Kenneth Crall, during a race riot in Washington on July 21,

1919."[12] While on his way to the theatre with his date, Laney was confronted by a mob that was yelling "catch the nigger" and "kill the nigger."[13] The men chased Laney from the 600 block of Massachusetts Avenue, where he allegedly pulled out a gun to stop the mob. According to Laney, his gun went off accidentally while he was trying to fix the safety.[14] Later, as the mob of more than 100 men pursued Laney, they fired shots at him, and Laney returned fire. Crall, a member of the mob, died from a wound to the head he suffered during the chase.[15] William Houston handled Laney's trial and appeal.[16]

William's involvements in the *Laney* case influenced Charles to become interested in criminal law early in his legal career. Writing his son at Harvard Law School during the trial, the elder Houston reported "[w]e had successfully fought to keep from the jury certain letters which the police had seized from Laney's room after his arrest.... It would have gratified you immensely if you could have seen the sympathetic interest the white members of the bar took in the case and how they came forward with helpful suggestions during the progress of the trial."[17]

Also key to Charles Houston's interest in criminal justice was the fact that during most of his career, black defendants were subject to criminal conviction by all-white juries. Charles represented defendants in Supreme Court cases to correct jury injustice. In the 1935 case *Hollins v. Oklahoma*, he served as co-counsel with his father.[18] The Houston legal team attacked the conviction of an Oklahoma man charged with rape. Because Negroes were excluded from jury pools in that county for a long period of time, the Supreme Court reversed the defendant's death sentence.[19] A few years later in *Hale v. Kentucky*, Charles Houston, representing Joe Hale, claimed Hale was denied equal protection because the jury commissioners excluded all African Americans from the jury pool.[20] Both of these cases reflect the decades-long battle to eliminate racist jury selection practices in the United States.

Prior to the Civil War, black Americans rarely served on criminal juries in America. During Reconstruction, however, federal "juries invariably consisted of white and black Republicans, with blacks sometimes outnumbering whites. White Southern Democrats interpreted the racial and political composition of federal juries as incontrovertible evidence of political persecution through judicial injustice."[21]

Hale was indicted for a murder in McCracken County, Kentucky. He moved to set aside the indictment upon the grounds that the jury commissioners had excluded from the list from which the grand jury was drawn all persons of African descent.[22] In support of his case, Hale presented an affidavit showing that the population of McCracken County was approximately 48,000, of which 8,000 were Negroes; that the assessor's books for the county contained the names of approximately 6,000 white persons and 700 Negroes who were qualified for jury service in accordance with certain Kentucky statutes.[23] The jury commissioners filled the wheel for jury service with between 500 and 600 names exclusively of white citizens. The Supreme Court agreed with the argument and invalidated the Kentucky practice.

One of Charles Houston's other efforts to attack the jury problem was his participation in the Supreme Court case *Nixon v. Condon* (1932).[24] In that case, he helped convince the Supreme Court to invalidate the Texas Democratic Party's practice of excluding Negroes from their primary elections. It was from these voter rolls that juries were often selected. In an opinion authored by Justice Benjamin Cardozo, the Court explained "[w]hile that mandate was in force, the negro was shut out from a share in primary elections, not in obedience to the will of the party . . ., but by the command of the state itself, speaking by the voice of its chosen representatives."[25] Twelve years later, Thurgood Marshall, relying on Houston's precedent in *Nixon v. Condon*, successfully argued *Smith v. Allwright*, where the Supreme Court finally did away with the "white primary" that excluded black citizens from voting.[26]

Another of Charles Houston's major contributions in criminal court would come in the early 1930s as a member of the NAACP's legal committee. The group of defendants known collectively as the "Scottsboro Boys" would provide an opportunity for his first collaborative criminal law work.[27] On March 25, 1931, a group of black and white men were traveling on a train passing through Scottsboro, Alabama, when a fight broke out. After some of the white youths complained to the stationmaster, a "posse" stopped the train in Paint Rock, Alabama, and arrested nine black youths.[28] Twelve days later they were on trial for rape. In four days, four different juries found eight of them guilty and sentenced seven of them to death.[29] The verdicts were assailed by national leaders of the Communist Party, and its legal arm, the International Labor Defense.[30]

From the start of the trial, many supporters of the Scottsboro defendants suspected that the white youths made their complaints to police because they lost the fight on the train. "Communist Party official said the charge was a frame up and the trials were a circus, nothing but a legal lynching: the women were prostitutes who had to be coerced to cry rape."[31] Thousands of white and black Northerners agreed and joined the Communists in protesting the convictions and death sentences.[32]

In April 1931, the Executive Committee of the ILD voted to defend the Scottsboro Boys and took over "the entire financial burden of the case."[33] The cases set the early tone between the relatively new NAACP Legal Committee and the Communist Party. The NAACP's Legal Committee was given the task of sorting out the problem of how to remain influential in the case without getting too entangled with the Communists.[34] Houston played a major role in all the NAACP discussions over the Scottsboro matter. The organization feared becoming associated with the Communists' larger anti-capitalist national agenda. On the other hand, it recognized that the Scottsboro Boys case was an injustice upon which the NAACP could build national credibility.[35]

Charles Houston encouraged executive secretary of the NAACP Walter White to remain cooperative with the ILD. The Communists were successful in getting the first Scottsboro trials overturned on appeal and retained famed criminal defense lawyer Samuel Liebowitz to represent the defendants in a new trial.[36] After Liebowitz entered the case, Houston advised Walter White "regardless of any division between the NAACP and the ILD…use of all the associations press contacts to guarantee that the third [Scottsboro] trial will be covered.… Get the branches to move, send telegrams, protests, etc.… It needs all the steam which the branches can raise to ensure publicity which will protect Liebowitz and the rest in…Alabama."[37]

In an effort to get the Scottsboro Boys exonerated, Houston participated in rallies where thousands of people gathered to hear evidence that the case was a "frame up."[38] As a special feature of one such rally, Houston introduced one of the Scottsboro female accusers, Ruby Bates, to the curious crowd.[39] Speaking in a Southern accent, she publicly recanted her rape testimony at Washington, D.C.'s Mt. Carmel Baptist Church. Bates explained that she was threatened during the first trial "by the bosses of the Southern counties" if she did not testify and her original accusations were because she "was only thinking about her own life, [not] the life of those innocent boys."[40]

Houston's contributions, behind the scenes in the Scottsboro cases, kept the loose confederation of lawyers from the ILD and other organizations working together until favorable results could be obtained. He even had Juanita Jackson, NAACP national youth director, pay a highly publicized visit to the "Boys" in Jefferson County Jail in Birmingham, Alabama, which became front-page news.[41] Without his coordination, a feud would likely have interfered with the case and its successful progress through the courts.[42] It would take several decades and many trips to the United States Supreme Court before the last of the Scottsboro Boys would be released or exonerated. Houston remained involved in advocating for the Scottsboro Boys until his death. He considered one of his prize possessions a poster that came from Europe calling for justice in the Scottsboro case.[43]

The *Crawford* Case

In the midst of the Scottsboro cases and during his final years as dean of Howard University's law school, Charles Houston also took on a high-profile death penalty case in Virginia. George Crawford was accused of killing two white women in Leesburg, Virginia. Walter White of the NAACP agreed to an arrangement with Howard's law school to allow Houston to use law students and law faculty to help defend the case.[44] This was an innovation in law school education at the time. His approach in Crawford was a forerunner to the modern legal clinics which are now a mainstay in almost all United States law schools.[45]

Among those students working on the case were Baltimorean Thurgood Marshall and Oliver Hill, a Virginia native. Years later, Hill would be elected as the first African American on the Richmond City Council.[46] Houston assembled a team that would be the first group of black lawyers to represent a defendant in a capital case. In the beginning of the case he and his colleagues had some practical difficulties representing Crawford. Initially, the prosecutors denied Houston and members of his legal team full access to Crawford while he was in jail before trial.

John Galleher, the Loudon County prosecutor, objected to what he called allowing "a flock of lawyers and others who we don't know to have access to this prisoner."[47] He ordered that only Houston, as lead counsel, be permitted access to Crawford. Complaining that this directive was limiting and "contrary to his understanding,"[48] Houston persuaded the prosecutor to change his mind and allow two other members of the defense team to have access to Crawford.[49] Galleher later explained the change in procedure stating that "we have no intention of embarrassing the defense in its preparation."[50]

While preparing for the trial Houston went on a national speaking campaign to raise awareness about the case.[51] At first, he made a national impact with the issue of the all-white jury that would decide Crawford's fate. Houston strongly suggested Crawford's innocence during many of those speeches.[52] When the case began, Houston challenged the Virginia jury selection process. He alleged racial discrimination occurred at each stage. His concerns were not without good reason. He summoned 45 Negroes from the Loudon County community to testify that they were qualified potential jurors but were never called to service.[53] He threatened to subpoena white jurors "as a basis of comparison with the negroes as their availability for grand jury service."[54] Houston also called as witnesses the clerk of the county court and Judge J.R.H. Alexander, who empaneled the grand jury that indicted Crawford.[55]

Houston argued that the "caste system" in Virginia prevented a fair jury selection process. He complained that "[i]nside the circle are White people. Outside are Black people. Black people cannot get inside."[56] Judge McLamore denied Houston's discrimination complaint. Surprisingly, the judge acknowledged in his remarks after the ruling that he was "perfectly conscious that the social caste is well marked in Virginia."[57] Later in the trial, Houston declared that Negroes had never "been permitted on trial juries in Loudon County."[58] While the case was being tried, mass meetings were held at churches like Washington, D.C.'s Nineteenth Street Baptist Church, where NAACP Executive Director Walter White would encourage donations for the defense team, noting that "Crawford's attorneys were serving without fee."[59]

The prosecution, perhaps fearful that the defense was gaining momentum, enlisted reinforcements. The Commonwealth retained Virginia State Senator Cecil Conner to assist them in presentation of the government's case.[60] The need to have another prosecutor available was also brought about by Houston's threats to call prosecutor Galleher to the stand as a potential witness.[61]

The courthouse scene in Loudon County was very tense as police were stationed at the exits and mingled among the crowd. "The defendant was guarded by 25 State and County police armed with rifles, clubs and tear gas guns. Six hundred spectators, half of whom were Negroes filled every available seat in the courtroom while scores of others milled about the courthouse."[62] In the midst of the case, however, information came to Houston's attention that suggested that Crawford may have actually been involved in the crime with another unknown man.[63] This might have been a fatal blow to a case for most lawyers, but Houston changed focus and was able to obtain a life sentence for Crawford rather than the death penalty.[64] He argued to the jury that executing Crawford might remove the only chance for law enforcement to find the other killer.[65] As Pulitzer Prize-winning historian David Levering Lewis noted, Houston shifted "gears seamlessly turning the Crawford trial into a plea for a guilty man but an opportunity for the state of Virginia to rise above judicial vindictiveness. Against all expectations, on December 16, 1933, the Loudon County jury declined to recommend the death penalty opting for a life sentence."[66]

This was the start of a career in criminal law that would be ultimately result in some Southern judges recognizing Houston's trial skill. One Virginia newspaper called the relationship between the *Crawford* trial judge and Houston a "Legal Love Fest."[67] One white bystander observing the trial commented that Houston really knew what he was doing "even if he is a nigger."[68] Houston did not appeal the case because the law at time would have permitted Crawford to be in jeopardy of execution again.

Not everyone praised the *Crawford* case outcome. Many members of the Communist Party and the International Labor Defense considered Houston's failure to appeal to be an unprincipled compromise. In an editorial which appeared in the *Nation* magazine, two ILD members wrote, "The precedent established in the Crawford case is, to the best of our belief, a new one in the history of the NAACP.... Is this policy to be exchanged for one of abject surrender? Has the NAACP decided on retreat?"[69]

Despite the complaints of some Communists over the decision to abandon Crawford's innocence claims, Crawford himself was grateful. In a statement given to the *Washington Post* he said "I am satisfied with what Dr. Houston did for me. I am satisfied with the trial. I am satisfied with the sentence. I am satisfied to stay here the rest of my life if they will just let me alone."[70] In a memorandum in early 1935, Charles Houston commented privately about the ILD criticism to NAACP head Walter White. "Don't pay any attention to the article,"[71] he said "and don't answer it. That is exactly what she wants. You couldn't convince her crowd no matter what you wrote; and you don't need to convince most of ours."[72] Rather than making the issue of dropping Crawford's appeal a public debate, Houston wrote that he would "prefer it to be personal, with me taking the whole responsibility."[73]

The fact that Crawford was allowed to stand trial at all was noteworthy, considering that the crime, allegedly killing two white women, might have typically qualified him for the intervention of a Southern lynch mob. During this time, it was not unheard of for elected officials to sanction lynching of a black man for even the alleged rape of a white woman. In 1892, for example, Governor Ben Tillman of South Carolina confessed that he "would lead a mob to lynch the Negro who ravishes a white woman."[74] U.S. Senator Theodore Bilbo of Mississippi commented during the mid-1900s that often the "only immediate and proper and suitable punishment" for a black who dishonored white womanhood was lynching.[75] During the case, Charles Houston's mother had occasion to observe him for the first time.[76] Carrying a cane, but not using it to support herself, she was worried about his lifestyle habits during trial. After a breakfast of eggs and milk before 7 a.m., he went "all day without food or rest."[77] He refused a lunch sandwich she had made for him and took aspirin at 4:30 p.m., about one hour before court adjourned.[78] He did not have supper until after the one and a half hour drive back to Washington.[79] She noted that when not trying a case he "eats heartily and raids the ice box at night."[80]

In the midst of the Crawford trial, trouble was brewing on a ferry boat ride from Virginia in Maryland. Racial unrest on the state's Eastern Shore led to a man being lynched. George Armwood had been taken by a mob from the jail in the town of Princess Anne.[81] As part of his NAACP responsibilities, Houston had been hastily called to Washington to testify before Congress on the lynching matter, along with the Attorney General of Maryland, William Preston Lane, and the United States Attorney for the District of Maryland, Simon E. Sobeloff.[82]

Maryland officials had arrested four men who allegedly were among those involved in the incident. The chair of the Senate Judiciary Committee, Frederick Van Nuys of Indiana, was beginning hearings on the Wagner-Costigan Federal Anti-Lynching bill. The Maryland Eastern Shore incident had suddenly become the centerpiece and a "case history" for the national lynching debate.[83]

In an editorial in the *Washington Post*, Houston explained the need for an anti-lynching bill. The "Federal Bureau of Investigation has no power of prosecution. What would you do with the facts after the Federal Bureau of Investigation has uncovered them?" he said.[84] Houston further informed Congress that less than "eight tenths of one percent of the 5,114 lynching's since 1882 were prosecuted."[85] He further explained, "[t]he trouble is not the facts" but how to "get prosecutions."[86]

Houston again became involved with the ILD and the Communist Party when he, along with Thurgood Marshall, decided to represent radical lawyer Bernard Ades in his disbarment proceedings in federal court in Maryland.[87] That matter resulted from a murder case in Berlin, Maryland, were a black man named Euel Lee, also known as "Orphan Jones," was represented by Ades. Lee was ultimately executed after several appeals of his case.[88]

The crime alleged was the murder of a farmer, his wife, and two daughters on October 13, 1931. The case generated great excitement and anger in the region and a "lawless element in the population attempted more than once to seized [Lee] and wreak vengeance upon him, and he was taken by the public authorities to a jail in Baltimore City for security."[89]

After his arrest, Lee "was for sixteen hours subjected to maltreatment by officials of Worcester County, and kept without food or drink; that on October

13, a mob of citizens of Worcester County prepared to lynch the prisoner.... Several other instances of civil unrest and attempted lynching on the shore led the court to conclude that "a fair trial in the county selected as the place for the trial of the charges against this man, and any defense he may make, is unlikely,... to attain the object of the Constitution and statues the case must be removed for trial to some other portion of the state."[90]

After Lee was convicted of the murders, in a trial that was removed to Baltimore County, the Maryland Court of Appeals overturned the conviction because the defendant established exclusion of Negroes as jurors through a "long-established custom in Baltimore County."[91] On Lee's third appeal, although he raised other jury selection issues, his convictions were finally affirmed.[92]

After Lee was executed, Maryland officials sought to have his attorney, Bernard Ades, disbarred for ethics violations. "Ades was charged with professional misconduct, malpractice, fraud, deceit, and conduct prejudicial to the administration of justice."[93] The most serious of the charges involved Ades' action, on the day before Lee's execution, "and without his request... visited him in the death house of the Maryland penitentiary, and caused him to execute a will, making Ades his beneficiary."[94] It was suggested that "Ades sought by legal proceedings... to secure the body of Lee in order that he might take it to New York and hold a memorial meeting in order to incite race prejudice."[95]

The disbarment charges were influenced by Ades' status as a member of the Communist Party and his affiliation with the International Labor Defense, its legal advocacy wing. Thurgood Marshall assisted Charles Houston in defending Ades.[96] Houston and Marshall succeeded in saving Ades' law license. In the disbarment opinion, the federal court explained that the International Labor Defense, "while not formally connected with the Communist Party, is offered by Communists, and within its scope, has like purpose and beliefs. It interests itself in cases in the courts which involve classes of persons whom it regards as victims of oppression or prejudice, and frequently offers its assistance when such persons are charged with crime."[97]

During the trial, the specter of the Communist-affiliated ILD directing the actions of attorney Ades was constantly raised by the prosecution. Eli Frank, Jr., argued that Judge Morris Soper should investigate the "ulterior motives of the organization to see whether its only purpose was to defend the accused, or to use a case for a purpose of spreading propaganda to advance political doctrine in which they believe."[98]

Houston countered the suggestion that the Communists dictated Ades' actions in the case by introducing letters that showed Ades had been severely reprimanded by Communist Party officials for refusing their instructions. Houston declared to the court, "Mr. Ades takes no orders from anybody."[99] To the claim that Ades injected himself into the *Lee* case, Houston asserted "as an officer of the court he had a perfect right to offer his services where he sees a miscarriage of justice about to be committed." In an argument that would become a credo of Houston's law reform philosophy, he explained, "a man like Ades at the bar who will point out ... error is beneficial to the whole system. He should be left as an effective prod to correct the legal machinery."[100]

According to Houston, the presence of lawyers like Ades "keeps the administrators on their guard to see there are few miscarriages of justice."[101] Responding to the claims that Ades' methods were aggressive and crude, Houston explained that "when a man is forced to lock horns with the authorities in attempting to help the poor and oppressed ... he loses a lot of his manners."[102] Houston made a final passionate plea in order to save Ades' right to practice law, asking the court to consider when balancing the interests in the case to "consider all the people, the poor and the rich, the black and the white. We are to decide whether we are to have Ades or the abuses to which the State of Maryland is subject."[103] Houston urged the judge to remember that in this mold of a lawyer you have an "unusual man."[104]

Looking at Ades' conduct as a whole and noting that he had even been physically beaten during his representation of Lee by an angry mob, the court explained its decision sparing Ades' law license:

> [T]he extreme punishment of disbarment should not be inflicted.... Taking into consideration the unquestioned service rendered in the *Lee* case, the injuries which the respondent suffered at the hands of lawless men while acting as counsel ... and the fact that he had already suffered a suspension from the bar ... for approximately five months, it is believed that a public reprimand will suffice.[105]

Ades had become an unpopular and controversial figure in Maryland with his aggressive defense of Euel Lee. Although avoiding further discipline from the practice of law would seem to be a victory, some members of the Communist Party did not feel that it was. Just as Houston had been criticized in the *Crawford* case, he again found himself subject to public attack by his so-called allies in litigation. There is no indication that Houston ever publicly responded to his critics on the matter. Instead, he respected the advocacy that Ades had provided to a black man who had a difficult criminal case and little or nothing in his favor. After Houston tried the Ades disbarment case, an admiring local lawyer who watched the trial wrote, "During ten years of practice I have never seen a cause so ably defended...every one of the numerous persons with whom I discussed the case agreed that your conduct of the case was faultless in every respect."[106]

The *Ades* case was the first time black lawyers represented a white lawyer in a disbarment proceeding in United States history. Houston stood by his decision to represent Ades and other suspected Communists throughout his career.[107]

The Strange Case of Samuel Legions

Houston returned to Virginia in 1942 to represent a black man named Samuel Legions in a bizarre rape case. He would take the case all the way to the Virginia Supreme Court. Legions was indicted on December 8, 1941, in Loudon County, Virginia, accused of the rape of Viola Miller, a white woman.[108] He was tried and found guilty by a jury and was given the death penalty and placed on death row pending his appeal.

Legions' conviction was based largely on the testimony of Mrs. Miller and her husband, who lived in a section of Leesburg, Virginia, "almost exclusively inhabited by Negroes." The two-room house of the alleged victim faced the street and was located "directly across the street from a Negro restaurant...near enough for loud talking in the house to be heard in the restaurant."[109] Mrs. Miller and her husband testified that at about eight o'clock on the evening of the alleged crime they were in bed. They were awakened at about ten o'clock by the falling of the window shade. According to the couple, they were sleeping together with their month-old child between them. The couple said that Legions entered the home and threatened to kill them.[110]

"They saw no weapon of any kind in his hands nor did [the defendant] say or pretend to have one." In a struggle the husband said he "struck the accused with a window shade and then pushed him into the window, breaking out the sash."[111] The defendant allegedly grabbed the victim and attempted to rape her in the bedroom but "eventually pulled her into the kitchen and accomplished his purpose across the table."[112]

Houston and his co-counsel, former student Oliver W. Hill, argued that the evidence was insufficient to sustain Legion's conviction for rape. The appellate court surprisingly agreed. The court concluded that the testimony of the Millers was not credible. The judge's opinion explained that "in light of the physical surroundings, and the absence of evidence that naturally ensue, is so contrary to human experience and so inherently incredible as to be totally insufficient to justify the verdict of guilty beyond a reasonable doubt."[113]

The appeal court appeared to chastise the jury for believing Mr. Miller's story. At one point in the opinion the court wrote, "Miller is forty-eight years old—almost in the prime of life. He was regularly engaged in manual labor.... In the presence of a tragedy that could mean nothing but disgrace and humiliation to [his] wife.... He was as servile as a slave."[114] Noting that the defendant and the alleged victim knew each other prior to the incident, the court concluded that the "whole thing does such shocking violence to any righteous conception of human conduct as to be unbelievable even to the most credulous and naïve."[115] The court made the curious statement "[w]hat we know as men we are not required to forget as judges."[116]

This case was a stunning victory for Houston and Hill. Only a few months before the decision, pleas were being made to the governor of Virginia by a former congressman to spare Legions' life from a pending execution. Loudon County Prosecutor Charles E. Harrison would announce that he would not press for any further trial.[117] While awaiting the outcome of his case Legions saw another condemned man, Odell Waller, go to the electric chair.[118]

What is remarkable about the *Legions* case is that Charles Houston persuaded a Southern appellate court to disbelieve a jury's verdict, in a rape case, were a white man and his white wife testified against a black man. The case defies all of the traditional criminal justice history and custom of its time.

The *Fisher* Case

Fisher v. United States (1946) was the most controversial criminal case Charles Houston ever argued in the United State Supreme Court.[119] Its content was unavoidably racial, the facts of the crime horrific and the behavior of the defendant seemingly inexplicable. With a white female victim as the centerpiece of the prosecution, the case would provide another enormous challenge on a national stage.

Fisher was charged with the murder of Catherine Reardon in the library building of the Cathedral of Saint Peter and Saint Paul in Washington, D.C., between 8:00 and 9:00 a.m., March 1, 1944. Fisher was employed as a maintenance worker in the cathedral.[120] The victim "complained to the Vicar a few days before about [Fisher's] care of the premises."[121] Fisher had given a statement that he killed Ms. Reardon "immediately following insulting words."[122]

The Supreme Court's opinion explained "[a]fter slapping her impulsively," he struck her with a stick of firewood and then "choked her to silence." When Reardon began screaming, Fisher "took out his knife and stuck her in the throat," and then dragged her body "into an adjoining pump pit, where it was found the next morning."[123] In addition to his written confession, Fisher provided inculpatory testimony at trial.[124] Houston presented evidence that suggested because of Fisher's mental abnormalities "[t]here was evidence that petitioner was unable, by reason of a deranged mental condition, to resist the impulse to kill Miss Reardon."[125] Despite Houston's efforts, Fisher lost the criminal trial, and his conviction was affirmed by the U.S. Court of Appeals for the District of Columbia.

In the Supreme Court Houston urged, "mental deficiency which does not show legal responsibility should be declared by this Court to be a reluctant factor in determining whether an accused is guilty of murder in the first or second degree."[126] That difference would be the key factor fixing Fisher's punishment as death. The Supreme Court, while acknowledging that "there are more possible classifications of mentality than the sane and insane," rejected making what it called "a radical departure from common law concepts [which is] more properly a subject for the exercise of legislative power."[127]

In a dissenting opinion, Houston's former Harvard professor, Justice Felix Frankfurter, observed that "[a] shocking crime puts law to its severest test." Recognizing that the trial may not have been entirely fair, Frankfurter said that an execution should not be authorized by society "without the most careful observance of its own safeguards against the misuse of capital punishment."[128] Unlike the majority's veiled reference to "insulting words," Frankfurter pointed out that Ms. Reardon was actually alleged to have called Fisher a "black nigger." After describing in greater detail Fisher's erratic behavior that day, Frankfurter concluded that the facts as presented at trial did not warrant a finding of premeditation.[129]

Frankfurter complained that the evidence of premeditation "was so tenuous that the jury ought not to have been left to founder and flounder within the dark emptiness of legal jargon."[130] Rather, the jury should have been given clear guidance through proper jury instructions directing their attention to the defendant's mental state defense. Justice Frankfurter suggested that men "ought not to go to their doom because this Court thinks that conflicting legal conclusions of an abstract nature seemed to have been 'nicely balanced' by the Court of Appeals for the District of Columbia."[131]

In another dissenting opinion, Justice Murphy wrote that "there are persons who, while not totally insane, possess such low mental powers as to be incapable of the deliberation and premeditation requisite to statutory first degree murder."[132] Justice Frank Murphy believed that the majority's conclusion required a jury to condemn persons of "low mental powers" to death "on the false premise that they possess the mental requirements of a first degree murderer or free them completely from criminal responsibility.... Common sense and logic recoil at such a rule."[133]

Justice Wiley Rutledge, in a third dissent, observed that "a revolting crime... requires unusual circumspection for its trial, so that dispassionate judgment may have sway over the inevitable tendency of the facts to introduce prejudice or passion into the judgment." He believed an instruction that would have provided Fisher his mental state defense was warranted.[134] Justice Rutledge explained, "[a] trial for a capital offense which falls short of that standard...does not give [Fisher] his due."[135]

Despite losing the case, Houston's strategy in *Fisher* was a remarkable prelude to the modern approaches of mental state defenses. The Supreme Court is still examining the same innovative issues Houston was attempting to establish in *Fisher*. His work in this case provided the legal foundations for innovations including diminished capacity and battered spouse syndrome.[136]

Famed writer Richard Wright, the author of the American classic *Native Son*, and Charles Houston corresponded with each other about the *Fisher* case and shared court records.[137] The material became the basis for a short story called, *The Man who Killed a Shadow*. Thanking Houston "profusely" for the material Wright commented, "[o]f course the women's scream is what set poor Fisher off.... A white women's scream to a Southern Negro is not just a scream...it's a scream of a woman calling the lynch mob." Wright thought so much of Houston that he paid tribute to him by making him an honorable lawyer character in a book he published in 1953 called *The Outsider*.[138]

The *Jones* Case

Houston would return to Maryland in the late 1940s to provide representation in a pair of murder cases that also had substantial constitutional issues entwined with gruesome facts. Such cases undoubtedly made his job of forging mental state defenses more difficult. In his typical fashion, he moved ahead with those defenses despite what appeared to be insurmountable odds.

In 1947, Houston represented Weldon Jones, Jr., an eighteen-year-old resident of Maryland's Eastern Shore, accused of the murder of I. Rayner Graham. On January 12, 1945, Graham's dead body was found in front of his packing house on Deal's Island. The keys to the house were in one hand and one of his pockets had been pulled out. Graham's automobile lights were on and its motor was still running.[139] Footprints at the scene led to the home of Weldon Jones and his younger brother, Holbrook Jones.[140] After searching the boys more thoroughly back at the station, the police found Graham's gasoline ration book in Weldon's possession.[141]

After keeping the Jones brothers in custody for about 30 minutes in the Salisbury police station, they decided to move them, this time all the way through Delaware to the police station in Harford County, Maryland, about 100 miles away.[142] They arrived at about 5:00 a.m. and both were then "quizzed by Sergeant Paul J. Randall in the presence of two other police officers and a stenographer." The sergeant said to Jones: "Your name has been mentioned in connection with the assault on two white women and the shooting of Mr. Rayner Graham." Weldon Jones thereafter allegedly confessed.[143]

On appeal, Houston challenged the voluntariness of the alleged Weldon Jones confession, contending that the fear of mob violence motivated his incriminating statements. Jones said that "after he was taken from his home at midnight, he was put in the automobile with the father of the girl he was suspected of having assaulted, and that he knew that mobs had lynched Negroes in the past when accused of having assaulted white women."[144] He asserted that he was a frightened "country boy, who had gone only as far as the sixth grade in school."[145]

Nonetheless, the Court of Appeals rejected Jones's claim that his confession was not voluntary and concluded that the evidence was sufficient to establish premeditation.

The *Jones* case reflects that Houston was concerned about the process of police interrogation. The overtones of possible mob violence and the police tactic of alleging unfounded instances of interracial sexual assault demonstrate the manner in which black Americans were subject to unfair prosecution during Houston's time. Extracting confessions in this manner was the very evil which the *Miranda v. Arizona*[146] opinion attempted to remedy in the middle 1960s.

Houston's concern for the integrity of the police evidence collection process in *Jones* is demonstrated in how he argued the confession issue before the Court. Although the appeal was unsuccessful, his approach highlighted the issues which today might constitute successful attacks on a police interrogation.

The *James* Case

Another criminal case handled by Houston in the Maryland courts was the murder prosecution of Eugene H. James. Noteworthy in this case were the other outstanding attorneys who participated. Along with Houston, as co-counsel, was an African American attorney named William H. Murphy whose family owned and operated the *Afro-American* newspaper.[147]

The prosecutors in the case also had outstanding legal careers. Anselm Sodaro, the state's attorney for Baltimore City, would become known to many as one of the fathers of forensic prosecution.[148] Alan Hamilton Murrell would later leave criminal prosecution for the defense bar. He would be known as one of the greatest criminal lawyers of all time and in 1971, became the founding attorney for the Maryland Public Defender's Office, one of the first state-wide public defender systems in the nation.[149]

The criminal case against James involved the July 6, 1948, killing of Marsha Brill, an eleven-year-old girl who was stabbed to death. There was no evidence of attempted rape or that her killer had ever seen her before.[150] Two of the victim's friends, who were riding their bicycles nearby, testified a man appeared and "pointed a large knife at Marsha."[151] The man followed and overtook Marsha, "who was found lying on the ground, stabbed and crying beside the road."[152] James was seen by another witness at about noon that day with a large knife in his hand near the crime scene.

The 31-year-old James was examined by four psychiatrists and one psychologist in preparation for the trial at Charles Houston's direction. One psychiatrist, Dr. Lerner, was of the opinion that James was "a mental defective belonging to a class of low-grade morons, and may be classified as a defective delinquent."[153] He was determined to have a mental age of about a ten-year-old, and testing revealed "some schizoid characteristics and evidence of hostility towards the immature female. Another doctor described James as "feeble-minded with an estimated I.Q. 60 to 65."[154]

On the day of the killing, the defendant was arrested at his house at 10:45 p.m. and taken by two police officers to the station. He was questioned until about 1:30 a.m. He was put into a line-up the next day about 3:30 p.m. and later taken by several detectives to a wooded section of Baltimore City near the crime scene. They removed him from his jail cell several times that day.[155] During one of his trips to the crime scene he allegedly confessed to the crime.[156]

Houston argued that, although there was no evidence of physical beating of James, the facts of how the police obtained the confession amounted to "psychological torture [that should render] the confession inadmissible."[157] Houston also argued that the facts of the case suggested that the evidence was not sufficient to convict James of premeditated murder.[158] Houston's court briefs described some of the facts that he believed favored James.

James "attended parochial school at St. Peter Claver's to the fourth grade....[159] The Defendant was examined by Doctors Guttmacher, Lerner, Cushing and Spear, as well as by Karl F. Schoenrich, a psychologist. All agreed that the Defendant was and is in the borderline group of mental defectives. All of the examiners agreed that the Defendant, although 32 years old chronologically, has a mental age between 8 years and 11 years.[160] James had never had regular employment for any length of time, and was usually employed, if at all, as a handy man or janitor."[161]

Houston noted that James was "questioned for several hours on the night of his arrest, and also for long intervals of time before the statement was finally taken at 8:45 P.M. on July 8, 1948, some fifty-five hours after he was taken into custody...the arresting officers took him to the Northern Police Station where he was booked for investigation and was placed in a regular cell. This cell had only a two-plank board as a bed, with an open toilet."[162] The judge admitted the confession over the strenuous objection of James' lawyers Houston and Murphy.[163]

The Court determined that the confession was voluntary because defendant was not legally insane.[164] As far as the sufficiency of the proof of premeditation, Houston's experts used the "Rorschach test" to show psychological features in an attempt to mitigate James's punishment; this was the earliest occasion on record that such a test was used in a murder trial.[165]

Despite the obstacles, the James defense team forged ahead. The young, brilliant Murphy attacked the confession and presented an alibi defense.[166] He offered the testimony of James' widowed mother and one of his sisters in his defense. His mother and sister had reported that when James was younger, he had been beaten nearly to death, and it had caused him headaches and other mental troubles during his life.[167] In the end, the defense was not enough to persuade the judge who rendered a verdict of guilty of first-degree murder, ultimately condemning James to a death sentence.[168]

At the announcement of the verdict, James was described as having his head "half bowed, his eyes half opened.... There was not a twinge of emotion."[169] Even in defeat, the advocacy of Houston was, in every way, exemplary. Indeed, the trial Judge H. Herman Moser commented in ruling against James that "Mr. Houston, as good counsel as this Court has ever had try cases before it, grasped the importance and significance [of the issues in the case]...that one can gather from the four corners of all the testimony."[170]

In rejecting James' appeal, Maryland's Supreme Court said that it would not "erect a medico-legal pseudo-science of [its] own to exclude this confession [to the murder]." The Court stated that to exclude a confession on the basis asserted by Houston "ha[d] no basis in existing law."[171] The case caused a national "media circus" as the trial judge tried to control press and media coverage, even attempting to hold media outlets in contempt for leaking information about the confession.[172]

This difficult case demonstrates Houston's interest in the prosecution of the mentally disabled, an issue that would decades later become a key factor in the Supreme Court's death penalty jurisprudence in the twenty-first century. Houston felt compelled to directly address his representation of James in a letter to the editor of the *Baltimore Sun*. After thanking the Baltimore press for what he described as "impartial coverage of the recent trial,"[173] he would explain his role in the case as an attorney was for the purpose of "seeing that James' constitutional rights were protected."[174]

Identifying himself in the letter as the chairman of the National Legal Committee of the N.A.A.C.P., he asserted that "it should not be necessary to say that as far as the crime itself is concerned, the N.A.A.C.P. condemns the crime without reservation, and publicly extends its deepest sympathy to the bereaved family."[175] He would remind the readers that the "N.A.A.C.P. constantly preaches respect for the law...and is just as opposed to anti-social conduct by negroes as anyone else."[176]

However, he noted that James was poor and mentally deficient and stated what he believed was the civil rights organization's position that "confidence in the law increases in proportion that the humble and insignificant know that their constitutional rights are just as well protected and their chances in court just as good as the rich and powerful."[177] He emphasized it was in "that spirit and to that end" that he and the organization associated itself with the James defense.[178]

His letter to the editor identifies some of the important values Houston thought should be part of a criminal trial. His use of the media here also reflects a certain savvy for balancing the social and political conversation with the important law reform work in the courtroom. His acknowledgement of the "resentment of the community" while advancing the important values of a fair legal system would become one of the great hallmarks of his legal career.

James did not help his own cause during the emotional trial. He sat before the court almost disinterested, with a shaggy beard which appeared not to have been shaved since his arrest. The 31-year-old janitor "seemed at times hardly listening" as the prosecution paraded dozens of witnesses to the stand.[179] The controversial *James* case demonstrated Houston's willingness to use a criminal case to point out issues that few others would tackle. Today, the Supreme Court forbids the execution of persons who are intellectually disabled as perhaps was James.[180] Houston showed great foresight on this issue, including his revolutionary use of the Rorschach ink blot test to establish a psychological profile. Again, such innovations demonstrated his genius for setting trends in the law.[181] Sadly, Eugene James was executed in a botched hanging in August of 1949. "The 32-year-old... who court psychiatrist said had the mentality of a child of 10, plunged screaming to his death... and groaned for eleven minutes as he slowly strangled to death."[182] Morphine had to be administered to end James' life after the "ghastly" execution.[183]

Toward the end of Houston's life, he was enlisted by the defense team for reputed spy Alger Hiss, a Harvard lawyer who had many famous friends like Houston's mentor Felix Frankfurter.[184] In the high-profile prosecution, Houston was unable to help establish that Hiss was not involved in espionage case for which he was on trial.[185]

Although he was less successful establishing case precedents in criminal law than in school integration, Houston left an impact on criminal law that would not be fully realized until decades later, during the Warren Court due process revolution of the late 1950s and 1960s.[186]

Endnotes

1. David Oshinsky, *Worse Than Slavery: Parchman Farm and the Ordeal of Jim Crow Justice* 22–23 (New York: Simon and Schuster 1997).

2. "U.S. Flag Half Mast on Campus: Dillard Univ., Howard and Other Schools Lead in Demonstrations Against Lynching Evil," *Pittsburgh Courier*, February 27, 1937, p. 10.

3. Ibid.

4. *Weeks v. United States*, 232 U.S. 383 (1914) (allowing state officials to turn over illegally seized evidence on a so-called "silver platter" to federal law enforcement).

5. "Alabama Has 4 Lawyers, Va. 57; Law for Those Who Like Fight," *Baltimore Afro-American*, April 21, 1934, p. 23

6. Ibid.

7. Arnold Rose, *The Negro in America* 180 n. 8 (New York: Harper and Brothers 1944) (collecting this and other stories of criminal trials in the South).

8. Nat'l Ass'n for the Advancement of Colored People, *Thirty Years of Lynching in the United States, 1889–1918* (1919) p. 7–8.

9. Howard Ball, *A Defiant Life: Thurgood Marshall and the Persistence of Racism in America* 25 (New York: Random House 1998).

10. Ibid.

11. Genna Rae McNeil, *Groundwork: Charles Hamilton Houston and the Struggle for Civil Rights* 231 (Philadelphia: University of Pennsylvania Press 1983).

12. *Laney v. United States*, 294 F. 412 (D.C.Cir.1923).

13. Ibid., at 413.

14. Ibid.

15. Ibid.

16. Ibid.

17. William L. Houston to Charles H. Houston, April 20, 1920, William LePre Houston Family Papers, Manuscripts Division, Library of Congress, p. 1–2. Box 19.

18. *Hollins v. Oklahoma*, 295 U.S. 394 (1935).

19. Ibid.

20. *Hale v. Kentucky*, 303 U.S. 613 (1938).

21. Robert J. Kaczorowski, "Federal Enforcement of Civil Rights During the First Reconstruction," 23 *Fordham Urb. L.J.* 155, 172 (1995).

22. *Hale v. Kentucky*, p. 613.

23. Ibid.

24. 286 U.S. 73 (1932).

25. Ibid.

26. 321 US 649 (1944).

27. James E. Goodman, *Stories of Scottsboro* xi (New York: Vintage Books 1994).

28. Ibid.

29. Ibid.

30. Ibid.

31. Ibid.

32. Ibid.

33. Ibid.

34. Ibid.

35. Ibid.

36. Ibid.

37. Charles H. Houston, Scottsboro NAACP Memo, November 21, 1935, NAACP Papers, Manuscripts Division, Library of Congress.

38. "Ruby Bates Tells Scottsboro Story," *Washington Post*, May 7, 1933, p. 10.

39. Ibid.

40. Ibid.

41. "Scottsboro Youths Being Interviewed by Miss Juanita Jackson," *The Savanna Tribune*, December 10, 1936 p. 1.

42. Dan T. Carter, *Scottsboro: A Tragedy of the American South* 315 (Baton Rouge: Louisiana State University Press 1969).

43. McNeil, *Groundwork*, p. 207.

44. Ibid., p. 90. (The NAACP's Walter White sought permission from President Mordecai Johnson for Howard law faculty and students to participate in the representation of Crawford).

45. *See generally*, Jane H. Aiken and Stephen Wizner, "Teaching and Doing: The Role of Law School Clinics in Enhancing Access to Justice" 75 *Fordham L. Rev.* 997 (2004).

46. "Oliver W. Hill, 100, Civil Rights Lawyer, Is Dead," *New York Times*, August 6, 2007, https://www.nytimes.com/2007/08/06/washington/06hill.html (visited July 5, 2020).

47. "Official Denies Crawford Kept from Counsel," *Washington Post*, October 31, 1933, p. 10.

48. Ibid.

49. Ibid.

50. Ibid.

51. "Crawford Case Aids Address Mass Meeting," *The Washington Post*, November 20, 1933, p. 13.

52. Charles H. Houston, "The Crawford Case," *The Chicago Defender*, July 14, 1934, p. 10.

53. "Crawford Defense Calls 45 Negroes in Jury Fitness Test," *Washington Post*, November 5, 1933, p. 1.

54. Ibid.

55. Ibid.

56. "Race Refuted as Crawford Jury Factor," *Washington Post*, November 8, 1933, p. 17.

57. Ibid.

58. "Crawford Defense to Demand Negroes on Death Jury Trial," *Washington Post*, November 19, 1933, p. 12.

59. Ibid.

60. "Conner to Aid in Ilsey Case," *Washington Post*, November 25, 1933, p. 10.

61. Ibid.

62. "Court to Rule on Crawford Defense Today," *Washington Post*, November 7, 1933, p. 1.

63. David Levering Lewis, *W. E. B. Du Bois, 1919–1963: The Fight for Equality and the American Century* 333 (New York: Henry Holt 1993).

64. Ibid.

65. Ibid.

66. Ibid.

67. *See*, Kenneth W. Mack, "Rethinking Civil Rights Lawyering and Politics in the Era Before *Brown*," 115 *Yale L.J.* 256, 296 (2005).

68. White, *A Man Called White* 155 (New York: Viking Press, 1948).

69. "Helen Boardman and Martha Gruening, Is the NAACP Retreating?" *The Nation*, June 27, 1934.

70. "Lifer Defends His Attorney from Criticism," *Washington Post*, March 1, 1935, p. 5.

71. Charles H. Houston to Walter White, January 15, 1935, Administrative File, Special Correspondences, NAACP Papers, Manuscripts Division, Library of Congress.

72. Ibid.

73. Ibid.

74. Randall Kennedy, *Race, Crime, and the Law* 45–46 (New York: Pantheon Books 1997).

75. Ibid.

76. "Mrs. Houston Sees Son Try Crawford Case," *Afro-American*, November 11, 1933, p. 1.

77. Ibid.

78. Ibid.

79. Ibid.

80. Ibid.

81. *See generally*, Sherrilyn Iffil, *On the Courthouse Lawn* 83–89 (New York: Beacon Press 2007).

82. "Senators Wait Princess Anne Lynching Story," *Washington Post*, February 20, 1934, p. 2.

83. Ibid.

84. Charles H. Houston, "Views on the Anti-Lynching Bill," *Washington Post*, January 20, 1938, p. X8.

85. Ibid.

86. Ibid.

87. *See*, Joseph E. Moore, *Murder on Maryland's Eastern Shore: Race, Politics and the Case of Orphan Jones* 212 (Charleston: History Press 2006).

88. Ibid., p. 212.

89. Ibid., pp. 13–14.

90. *See*, *Lee v. State*, 161 A. 284 (Md. 1932).

91. Ibid.

92. *See*, *Lee v. State*, 165 A. 614 (Md. 1933).

93. *In re Ades*, 6 F. Supp. 467, 468 (D. Md. 1934).

94. Ibid.

95. Ibid.

96. Thurgood Marshall to Charles H. Houston, December 15, 1933, Moorland-Spingarn Research Center, Howard University.

97. *In re: Ades*, 6 F. Supp. 467 (1934).

98. "Ades Painted as Idealist as Trial Closes," *Baltimore Afro-American*, March 10, 1934, p. 23.

99. Ibid.

100. Ibid.

101. Ibid.

102.   Ibid.

103.   Ibid.

104.   Ibid.

105.   *In re: Ades*, 6 F. Supp. 467, 483 (1934).

106.   Letter of Aaron Borden, Attorney at Law to Charles H. Houston, March 19, 1934, Houston Family Papers, Moorland Spingarn Research Center, Howard University.

107.   *See generally*, José Felipé Anderson, "Freedom of Association, the Communist Party and the Hollywood Ten: The Forgotten First Amendment Legacy of Charles Hamilton Houston," 40 *McGeorge L. Rev.* 25 (2009).

108.   *Legions v. Commonwealth*, 23 S.E. 2d. 764 (Va. 1943).

109.   23 S.E. 2d, p. 764.

110.   Ibid.

111.   23 S.E. 2d, p. 765.

112.   Ibid.

113.   Ibid.

114.   Ibid.

115.   Ibid.

116.   Ibid.

117.   "Suspect to Go Free After Year in Death Row," *Baltimore Afro-American*, June 26, 1943, p. 15.

118.   Ibid.

119.   328 U.S. 463 (1946).

120.   Ibid., pp. 464–465.

121.   Ibid.

122.   Ibid.

123.   Ibid

124.   Ibid., p. 466.

125.   Ibid.

126.   Ibid.

127.   Ibid., p. 467.

128.   Ibid., p. 477.

129.   Ibid., p. 487.

130.   Ibid., p. 486.

131.   Ibid., p. 489.

132.   Ibid., p. 492 (Murphy, J., dissenting).

133.   Ibid.

134.   Ibid., p. 494 (Rutledge, J., dissenting).

135.   Ibid., p. 495.

136.   David M. Siegel, "Felix Frankfurter, Charles Hamilton Houston and the N-Word: A Study in the Evolution of Judicial Attitudes Toward Race," 7 *S. Cal. Interdisc. L.J.* 317 (1998).

137.   Hazel Rowley, *Richard Wright: The Life and Times* 318– 319 (New York: Henry Holt 2001).

138.   Ibid., 576.

139. *Jones v. State*, 52 A.2d 484 (Md. 1947).

140. Ibid.

141. Ibid.

142. Ibid.

143. Ibid.

144. Ibid., p. 487.

145. Ibid.

146. *Miranda v. Arizona*, 384 U.S. 463 (1966).

147. "William H. Murphy, Sr.," *Baltimore Sun*, June 1, 2003, p. C4. *The Afro-American Newspaper*, About Us, http://www.afro.com/aboutus.htm (visited, Jan. 28, 2006).

148. "Anselm Sodaro, 91, Chief Judge and State's Attorney," *Baltimore Sun*, July 30, 2002, p. B5.

149. Rafael Alverez, "Alan Murrell, Lawyer for the Poor, Dies," *Baltimore Sun*, May 5, 1999, p. B1.

150. *James v. State*, 65 A.2d 888 (Md. 1949).

151. Ibid.

152. Ibid.

153. Ibid.

154. Ibid.

155. Ibid.

156. Ibid.

157. Ibid.

158. Ibid., pp. 888–889.

159. Petitioner's Appendix, Brief of Eugene James, p. 6.

160. Ibid.

161. Ibid.

162. Brief of Appellant Eugene James, pp. 2–3.

163. "Confession Admitted in James Trial," *Washington Post*, September 22, 1948, p. 1.

164. Ibid.

165. Brief of Appellant James, pp., 8–9.

166. Charles E. Davis, "James Found Guilty in Brill Murder Case," *Washington Post*, September 23, 1948, p. 1.

167. "James Calm Murder Day Family Says," *Washington Post*, July 11, 1948, p. M13.

168. Charles E. Davis, *Washington Post*, September 23, 1948, p. 1.

169. Ibid.

170. Appendix in *James v. State*, p. 9.

171. *James v. State*, 65 A. 2d, p. 894.

172. *Baltimore Radio Show v. State*, 193 Md. 300 (1949).

173. Charles H. Houston, "Letter to the Editor," *Baltimore Sun*, September 28, 1948, p. 8.

174. Ibid.

175. Ibid.

176. Ibid.

177. Ibid.

178. Ibid.

179. "Slain Child's Friend Points Out James," *Washington Post*, September 21, 1948, p. 1.

180. See, *Atkins v. Virginia*, 536 U.S. 304 (2002) (Striking down the death penalty for the mentally disabled).

181. The test, developed in 1921 by a Swiss psychologist, has been established in the twenty-first century as "one of the most popular personality tests in clinical psychology, still used in helping assess...the sanity of defendants in murder trial." Rosie Mestel, "Much Ink Being Spilled on Rorschach Test," *Baltimore Sun*, June 8, 2003.

182. "Noose Slips, Killer Strangles to Death," *Baltimore Afro-American*, August 20, 1949, p. 1.

183. Ibid.

184. Allen Weinstein, *Perjury: The Hiss-Chambers Case* 350 (New York: Random House 1997).

185. Mary Hornaday, "Two Supreme Court Justices Take Stand to Aid Hiss," *Christian Science Monitor*, June 22, 1949, p. 3.

186. Peter Arnella, "Rethinking the Functions of Criminal Procedure: The Warren and Burger Courts' Competing Ideologies," 72 *Geo. L.J.* 185, 202 (1983).

VI

Labor Wars

Porters and Presidents

The free choice of labor is fundamental to liberty and the pursuit of happiness. The whole structure of the system of free enterprise rests fundamentally on the right to sell one's labor in the open market.

— Charles H. Houston "The Highway," *Baltimore Afro-American*,
April 19, 1947

Part of the American dream for Charles Houston was the dignity and prosperity that comes from a hard day's work. He watched his parents as living examples of this idea during his lifetime. He also represented railroad workers who supported their families in one of the nation's largest, most important industries and observed the struggles they faced. Unequal treatment at work because of race was blatant in the United States during his lifetime. Legal action in court to resolve those wrongs became necessary. Charles Houston believed "[c]apital and wealth are nothing more than the accumulation of the product of labor and one of the surest ways to keep an individual or group suppressed is to put restrictions on their right to work."[1] He cautioned that Negroes "would never attain first-class citizenship in the United States until they have broken every barrier which prevents [them from] working in any capacity because of race."[2] His representation of businesses[3] and labor unions[4] early in his legal career at his father's firm informed his strategies when advocating for the rights of workers.

Prior to the twentieth century, most African Americans worked in the agricultural part of the economy or in domestic services. This lack of balance in the quality of job opportunities led Charles Houston during his NAACP special

113

counsel years to oppose President Franklin Roosevelt's New Deal Social Security Act. Before Congress he said: "The point that I am making is that in order to qualify for the old-age annuity there is a provision that taxes must be paid on behalf of this person prior to the day when he reaches 60 years."[5] He further testified, "Negro share croppers and cash tenants would be excluded. I take it that I do not need to argue to this committee the fact that of the Negro population and of the population of the country generally, your Negro share cropper and your Negro cash farm tenant are just about at the bottom of the economic scale."[6] Houston noted, Negroes in agriculture are not employed in the traditional sense, "[t]here is no relation necessarily of master and servant by whom he gets wages on which a tax could be levied. Therefore, this population is excluded from the entire benefits of the old-age annuity, and that represents approximately, according to the 1930 census, 490,000 Negroes."[7]

Houston pointed out that domestic servants would also be largely excluded from the protections of the act "because the system of employing domestic servants is so loose."[8] One could expect that Roosevelt was not pleased with Houston's opposition to his marquee "New Deal" legislation. This was not the first, nor would it be the last time that Charles Houston would be a source of irritation to a United States president. His constant participation on civil rights issues would lead him into many clashes over national policy regarding race, class and jobs.

The ever-changing labor situation in the early twentieth century had an overwhelming impact on national race policy. At the start of the century, the characteristics of the labor market in America were starting to change. During World War I, when the shortage of labor hit the Detroit manufacturing industry, about 1,000 black employees were on the payroll of the Packard automobile company.[9] The Ford Motor Company followed by hiring black workers for its factories, and other companies followed suit. By the 1920s, Ford had hired about 5,000 black employees out of a workforce of about 110,000. By the beginning of the 1940s, Ford had hired about 11,000 black workers, about two thirds of the black employees in the entire automobile manufacturing work force.[10]

This concentration of black workers ultimately lead to a need to addressed concerns raised by black workers. Legendary labor organizers like John L. Lewis were working for the rights of unskilled workers in the auto industry. There was, however, a great deal of discrimination within the labor unions.[11] The American Federation of Labor responded by establishing a committee to "look in to those charges."[12] Charles Houston's testimony during those committee investigations played a key role in documenting AFL discrimination. This historic inquiry would ultimately lead to Houston's decades-long fight for fairness in the activities of organized labor.[13]

Houston would write in an editorial that "working-class people are still plagued by unions which have the color bar or which set colored workers off into auxiliary lodges."[14] Houston's fight against workplace discrimination was multi-faceted. In the early 1940s, he complained that the capital transit company should hire more black bus operators. He talked about the problem at a mass meeting held at the Vermont Avenue Baptist Church in Washington, D.C., before an audience of many sympathizers including United States Supreme Court Justice Louis Brandeis, who with a number of other government officials, formed a committee to try to resolve the issue.[15] Houston complained about the racist hiring practices of other federal agencies like the Bureau of Engraving and Printing. He noted that the "bureau maintains Jim Crow locker and restrooms."[16] Suggesting that the agency must not recognize that the Civil War was over, he wrote that the next time someone hands you "a dollar bill take a good look at it. It was printed by 'whites only.'"[17]

Houston realized that a change of national policy was needed because litigating labor issues in court was an ineffective tool. He once commented that "the judicial process is too hazardous, too cumbersome and too slow to furnish adequate relief to workers, either white or black, from job discrimination."[18] Although Houston had long urged the federal government to increase access for minority workers,[19] there were also difficulties for Negroes getting jobs in the private sector supporting the World War II effort. Communications giants like Chesapeake and Potomac Telephone Company practiced discrimination in hiring. Women like Julia Newberry and Dorothy Alaba picketed outside the company's Baltimore headquarters, complaining that although qualified to be hired, they were refused jobs because of their race.[20] Both noted that they had relatives risking their live overseas. Mrs. Newberry had a husband and Mrs. Alaba had a brother fighting in North Africa at the time.[21]

Another area of focus for Houston was the policy of the federal government, which segregated federal recreation areas. He was the moving force behind the historic performance of Marian Anderson, the internationally known American singer, at the Lincoln Memorial. This issue reached the national spotlight because of the refusal of the Daughters of the American Revolution to allow her to perform in Constitution Hall because of her race. Houston's position was grounded in the belief that all recreation "areas belong to all the people all the time."[22] One of his consistent themes was that people need to feel included in order to prosper.

The Marion Anderson ordeal was particularly irritating to President Franklin Roosevelt because his wife Eleanor resigned from the DAR organization in protest and encouraged her supporters to find an alternative place for Ms. Anderson to sing by continuing to press government officials.[23] The matter was also important to Charles Houston because he was angered that a world-famous Negro could be so easily disrespected.[24] The great singer had other noteworthy friends to support her. When she visited New Jersey to perform, she stayed at the home of famed physicist Albert Einstein, an outspoken opponent of racial discrimination.[25] She could not stay at local hotels in Princeton.[26]

Houston succeeded in setting up her famous concert at the Lincoln Memorial, which was both a triumph for Anderson and an embarrassment to the United States government. After organizing the successful event, Marian Anderson wrote a note of gratitude for Charles on a copy of the original program.[27] Educator Mary McCloud Bethune also congratulated Houston on his effort on the concert. She wrote, "History may and will record it, but it will never be able to tell what happened in the hearts of the thousands who stood and listened yesterday afternoon."[28]

There were many important motivations fueling Charles Houston's interest in labor issues. None was more urgent than his desire to change the quality of life for his young son, Charles, Jr., who he called "Bo," born in 1944. After leaving the NAACP in the late 1930s and returning to private practice in Washington, D.C., his marriage to Henrietta Williams Houston[29] energized him. Between his busy courtroom activities, he spent the little free time that remained with his family. He took Henrietta and Charles, Jr., to parades, car trips, sightseeing across the country, and even the Preakness horse race at Pimlico racetrack in Baltimore.[30] He vacationed at Highland Beach near Annapolis, Maryland, a waterfront resort populated largely by black residents. Charles Houston one day hoped to also build a house near the beach and spend more time there with his family. During what turned out to be the final decade of his life, he believed there was much work to do before he would be able to realize his own American dream.

It is well documented that Houston's was most personally affected by racial discrimination in the United States military. He suffered discrimination and was forced to participate in discrimination against his fellow soldiers. Charles Houston's feelings about racial discrimination in the military directly influenced the priorities he addressed to each of the presidents of the United States who led the country at every juncture of his adult life. His relationship with each president had volatile moments. As early as 1939, a black employee organization urged President Franklin Roosevelt to appoint Charles Houston to the Supreme Court of United States. Pointing out that black Americans constituted one tenth of the total population of the country, the group urged the appointment of a black Justice to the court after the death of a Justice earlier that year.[31] As it would turn out, his clashes with Presidents Roosevelt and Truman would never put Houston in a position to be appointed to the Supreme Court. He had become far too controversial to ever be considered.

Charles, commenting on the discrimination he experienced during World War I, during the Woodrow Wilson administration, said that he was "damn glad he had not died for this country."[32] His lack of confidence in the nation's executive leadership was not without good reason. He decried the official policies that he suffered as a soldier during the war. "In 1917 the young Negro went to war with some hope that he was doing his part, to make the world safe for democracy. Instead of being encouraged in the service, he met only discrimination and abuse. Many white soldiers spent more time in France spreading lies about Negro troops then they did fighting the Germans."[33]

But even while thousands of Negro troops were fighting the Germans in France, their relatives were being lynched wholesale at home. He would argue that "if the war is supposed to preserve civil liberties and democracy, we can hardly preserve what we do not have."[34] Houston lamented the brutal treatment of black military members and black citizens during the painful episode in American history known as "Red Summer." After World War I, brutality, violence and racial unrest broke out across America because black troops returned home looking for jobs.[35]

He further observed, "[i]n the south the authorities squeeze Negroes off the relief rolls to force them into the cotton field at starvation wages. In addition to this, malicious propaganda is being spread in every direction over the country in an effort to vilify and misrepresent the Negro."[36] Houston deeply resented the anti-Negro policies of the army, navy and marine corps. He once complained, "If the general staff thinks that Negroes in the next war going to be content with peeling potatoes and washing dishes they have miscalculated the temper of the present-day Negro."[37]

Charles Houston once accused the Air Force of having "no blueprint for action"[38] to integrate in the 1940s, suggesting discussions being held were "pious hope but nothing concrete."[39] He believed the nation's war policy should reflect the view "that in most . . . industries, white and colored men work side-by-side in peace time; but the army finds it necessary to separate them in time of war for the defense of the country."[40] Houston complained that the "Army is actually introducing segregation into areas where segregation does not exist and where the people are now getting along perfectly on an integrated basis."[41] He would also comment that "[t]he Army insists on fastening the patterns of Mississippi and South Carolina on the entire country."[42]

Charles Houston's ideas about racial segregation were always evolving. He once wrote, "I confess that in 1940 I supported the idea of separate color combat divisions on the theory that was the only way to get a substantial number of colored combat officers.... I was wrong. We got our separate division.... They had the worst assignments, worst treatment and lowest morale of any color combat troops."[43] He did not argue for placing the colored soldier in any position they were not prepared for. All he asked was that they be given an unhampered chance to prove their worth; "the colored soldier is entitled to promotion on the basis of merit in any company, or he is not entitled to promotion at all."[44]

In another editorial, Houston expressed dismay that when he was on a train from Jacksonville, Florida, several Coast Guard members boarded the train and the black guardsman was asked to have his dinner behind a curtain separated from his colleagues. The next morning when the gentleman went to have breakfast, the white servicemen were seated right away and the black serviceman had to wait until the one table reserved for colored people was available. Houston lamented that "if you were good enough to wear the same uniform...this country should protect you from segregation and discrimination."[45] He urged people who were also offended by his story about the segregation of the service man to write the president of United States or their congressman and complain.[46]

He once called the commander of the United States Army, General Douglas MacArthur, "a liar" for suggesting that the military did not discriminate.[47]

Houston continued to be a "thorn in the side" of the federal government's discrimination in the military throughout World War II. When inequities were identified in the procedures for volunteering for military service, Houston retaliated by filing suit against the government. Robert B. Kelly of Washington, D.C.'s Armstrong High School had attempted to join the war effort.[48] He was informed that the "colored quota" had been met. Houston filed for an injunction prohibiting the local draft board from inducting anyone else until Kelly was permitted to enlist in the army.[49] The *Afro-American* newspaper questioned if any black Americans should fight if the government continued to practice such discrimination.[50]

Meetings with President Truman and the FEPC

Although the Pullman railroad company was the largest employer of Negro men during the 1930s and 1940s, constant disputes were a source of concern for the nation. In a private meeting with President Harry Truman about jobs, Houston asked quite directly "whether he [Truman] wanted to know how black people really felt in America."[51] That meeting with the president was organized by A. Phillip Randolph, the head of the largest black trade union, the Brotherhood of Sleeping Car Porters.

The meeting centered on the negative impact that the "Jim Crow" policies of the United States military were having on the spread of democracy abroad.[52] Houston wrote in his *Afro-American* column the week following the meeting that "Truman is afraid to move on the issue of segregation in the armed service." He explained that during the meeting, President Truman was told "colored people here would not be fooled by civil rights messages which float off in the air and are not backed up by action" and that they were "tired of always eating at the second table."[53]

Charles Houston was given a key role in many of the nation's race discrimination disputes when he was appointed by President Truman to the Fair Employment Practices Committee (F.E.P.C). The appointment led to a series of disappointments for Houston, resulting in his dramatic resignation from the F.E.P.C. This event caused great embarrassment to Truman, who is considered by many to have been a great civil rights proponent when he was president.[54] Houston did not feel that the D.C. Capital Transit Company should be permitted to discriminate while providing domestic transportation in the nation's capital during war time. On December 3, 1945, Charles Houston resigned in protest from Truman's Fair Employment Practices Committee. Standing up to Truman reflected how Charles Houston's principles matched his actions, and why others were so willing to follow his lead.[55] He explained, "the failure of the Government to enforce democratic practices and protect minorities in its own capital make its expressed concern for national minorities abroad specious."[56] As always, Houston was unrelenting when he believed government officials were not committed to civil rights.

Houston explain his decision, "The president's attitude in the Capital Transit case reflects a persistent course of conduct on the part of the administration to give lip service to the matter of eliminating discrimination in employment on account of race, creed, or color or national origin…. While doing nothing substantive to make the policy effective."[57] Houston's allies at the National Lawyers Guild sent a letter of protest to Truman, who accepted Houston's resignation from the FEPC. The Guild, through one of its officers, Jack B. Tate, wrote, that federal directives required that even the government transit companies "cease and desist" from engaging in discrimination.[58]

Houston's pressure on Truman did not let up even after the end of the war. Concerned that employment issues and employment discrimination would continue after World War II in the way that they did after World War I, Houston and other interested leaders again met with President Truman about the subject. During that meeting Truman reassured them that he understood the issue and would take "measures necessary to alleviate racial and religious employment bias…"[59]

On later occasions, Houston was critical of the direction Truman would take on other civil rights issues. "I get absolutely no sense of spiritual direction from the government these days. Pres. Truman's civil rights message made a big boom, but it looks as if the boom may be a bust. Both the Republicans and the Democrats are playing politics with civil rights on the Potomac while yelling about the Russians denying civil rights."[60]

Houston cared about all types of workers. He voiced great concern for California's poor whites, Mexicans and Filipinos. The large farms that hired migrant workers were big business, and he expressed concerns about potential exploitation. "Because this labor is unorganized, semi-literate and without permanent abode, living conditions are terrible, the children do not stay anywhere long enough to get an effective education. As agricultural workers, the adults are not covered by unemployment compensation laws, and between crops they seek out and existed along 'skid rows' and shantytowns."[61]

"Railroading" the Colored Employees

Charles Houston had great influence with the "Colored" railroad men. As a boy his father sent him personal letters from his Chicago law office on railroad union stationary. He had a close association with railroad union officials throughout his professional life. It is no surprise when they were confronted with one of the greatest unfair episodes of race discrimination in the Jim Crow era, Houston took on the fight. During the 1940s, the railroads were the major source of transportation and commerce in the industrialized world.

Houston noted that slaves were used to furnish the needed labor for railroads prior to the Civil War, often with the railroad actually owning the slaves that worked the old wood-burning locomotives. After emancipation of former slaves, many continued to work and were placed on the railroad's payroll.[62]

In late November of 1943, Charles Houston rose from counsel table in the Supreme Court of Alabama to make his argument on behalf of B.W. Steele, a black fireman working for the Louisville and Nashville Railroad. Steele was fighting both the railroad who employed him and the union who was supposed to protect him. The chief justice of the Alabama high court, Lucien D. Gardner, remarked that it was the first time in his 29 years of service on the bench that a colored person had argued a case before his court.[63] Justice Gardner's observation should not have come as a surprise. In a speech given by Houston in 1934, he would point out that in the "State of Alabama...there are only four colored lawyers, or only one to every 236,000 [of the] Colored population, in other words one lawyer to a radius of 12,999 square miles."[64] It was this lack of access to legal counsel that led him to Alabama.[65] He did find some local help. A courageous local lawyer named Arthur Shores, who had filed briefs but never argued in the Alabama Supreme Court, would be reliably at Houston's side throughout this railway labor war which would ultimately transform the nation's working conditions for all unionized employees.[66]

Houston argued to the court that it should stop the "secret fraudulent agreement" between the carrier and the union. He asked for financial "damages...for loss of wages, destruction of vested seniority preference rights and breach of its duty under the Railway Labor Act."[67] As was often the case during the "Jim Crow" years, black employees were given the worst jobs in the most difficult conditions. In the railroad business that job was known as "fireman."[68] It involved shoveling coal into the sweltering hot furnace of the railroad engine which powered the train's steam boiler. The high heat and close working conditions made this assignment life threatening each day. By the 1940s, the diesel engine was developed, which, suddenly and ironically, made the designation of fireman one of the most desirable jobs in the railroad industry because the fuel used to power the engines was no longer coal. Instead, the fireman job required only operation of a switch on the new diesel trains.[69]

When this change happened, white workers were given the fireman jobs and even black workers who were more senior were removed and given other less desirable assignments.[70] Houston argued that the Brotherhood of Locomotive Fireman and Engineers had been persistently disloyal and hostile to its black members, seeking to "drive them out of service." Houston alleged that the union even "refused to notify colored firemen of proposed actions adversely affecting their interests, to give them a chance to be heard or vote."[71] He further contended that the railroad had become a part of the union's conspiracy to deny colored men adequate representation and job assignments.[72]

The Steele Supreme Court Case

Steele, a locomotive fireman, sued on his own behalf and that of his fellow employees who were Negroes. On March 28, 1940, the Brotherhood, purporting to act as representative of the entire craft of firemen, without informing the Negro firemen or giving them opportunity to be heard, served a notice on respondent Railroad and on twenty other railroads operating principally in the southeastern part of the United States about the changes in job assignment.[73] The notice announced the Brotherhood's desire to amend the existing collective bargaining agreement in such manner as to exclude all Negro firemen from their jobs.[74]

The Brotherhood and the Railroad, acting under the agreement, disqualified all the Negro firemen and replaced them with white men, members of the Brotherhood, all junior in seniority to the Negro workers. As a consequence, Steele was personally deprived of employment for sixteen days and then was assigned to more arduous, longer, and less remunerative work in local freight service. In conformity to the agreement, he was later replaced by a Brotherhood member junior to him, and assigned work on a switch engine, which was still harder and paid less money, until January 3, 1942.[75]

The United States Supreme Court held that "The cloak of racism surrounding the actions of the Brotherhood in refusing membership to Negroes and in entering into and enforcing agreements discriminating against them, all under the guise of Congressional authority, still remains."[76] It further said, "[a] sound democracy cannot allow such discrimination to go unchallenged. Racism is far too virulent today to permit the slightest refusal, in the light of a Constitution that abhors it, to expose and condemn it wherever it appears in the course of a statutory interpretation."[77]

The Tunstall Supreme Court Case

In yet another railroad case Tom Tunstall, a Negro fireman, employed by the Norfolk & Southern Railway, brought suit with Charles Houston's help against the railway, the Brotherhood of Locomotive Firemen[78] and Enginemen and certain of its subsidiary lodges, and one of its officers, setting up, in all material respects, a cause of action like that alleged in the *Steele* case.[79] Tunstall complained "of the discriminatory application of the contract provisions to him and other Negro members of his craft in favor of 'promotable,' i.e., white, firemen, by which he has been deprived of his preexisting seniority rights, and then assigned to more difficult work with longer hours in yard service, his place in the passenger service being filled by a white fireman."[80]

Tunstall also complained "that the contract was signed and put into effect without notice to him or other Negro members of his craft, and without opportunity for them to be heard with respect to its terms."[81] Such a negotiation by the union was obviously harmful to the Negro workers. Houston argued that, "The day of the individual worker selling his labor for whatever he can get is over…labor unions now have such a hold on the economic life of a worker that he has no security even in an open shop except as a union member."[82]

Regarding the railroad labor cases, one of Charles Houston's co-counsel explained: "The reason that they have black firemen in the early days is 'cause that was the lousiest job you could have. You're stoking coal, and it was an ugly job, and it didn't pay much, but it—all of a sudden you get the diesel engine."[83] With the new trains "all a fireman has to do is pull this lever…sit and enjoy himself. Well, you can imagine…the whites, how quickly they went after those jobs. Well, Charlie Houston was a genius."[84]

Up until the end of his life he fought for the railroad workers. In a particularly nasty case in the Virginia federal courts, Houston fought for workers who were again replaced from favorable jobs by white workers.[85] The trial court held that the black railroad workers were not negotiating in good faith because they refused to apply for jobs that would require them to test for obsolete skills they would not need, but the white workers already had. On appeal to the Fourth Circuit in 1950, Houston challenged that result with the help of his protégées Oliver Hill and Thurgood Marshall. It would be the last time all three would appear on the brief in a case together.[86]

Overturning the lower court's conclusion, the Fourth Circuit wrote in 1951, "I cannot censure Negro firemen for going into court.… This is merely an act of self-defense on their part."[87] The appellate court also suggested that the award of counsel fees would be appropriate in the case, since "plaintiffs of small means have been subjected to discriminatory and oppressive conduct by a powerful labor organization which was required, as bargaining agent, to protect their interests."[88] Charles Houston's love for the black working people of the railroad was reflected in the time and energy he devoted to helping them.

Endnotes

1. Charles Houston, "The Highway," *Baltimore Afro-American*, April 19, 1947, p. 4.
2. Ibid.
3. Kenneth W. Mack, *Representing the Race* 56 (Cambridge: Harvard University Press 2012).
4. J. Clay Smith, *Emancipation: The Making of the Black Lawyers* 1844-1944 169 (Philadelphia: University of Pennsylvania Press 1993).
5. Excerpt from the Statement of Charles H. Houston, representing the NAACP, to the House Ways and Means Committee on the Economic Security Bill, February 1, 1935. Washington, D.C.
6. Ibid.
7. Ibid.
8. Ibid.
9. August Meier and Elliot Rudwick, *Black Detroit and the Rise of the UAW* 6-7 (Oxford, England: Oxford University Press 1981).
10. Ibid.
11. Ibid.
12. Ibid.
13. Ibid., p. 24.
14. Charles H. Houston, *Richmond Afro-American*, October 25, 1947, p. 4.
15. Carolyn Dixon, "Drive to Ban Jim Crow on Washington Buses," *New York Amsterdam News*, November 7, 1942, p. 2.
16. Charles H. Houston "Our Civil Rights," *Baltimore Afro-American*, February 19, 1949, p. 4.
17. Ibid.
18. Charles H. Houston, "The Union and the FEP," *Washington Post*, April 13, 1945, p. 8.
19. "Greater Efficiency Is Urged for Negroes in Industry," *New York Amsterdam News*, November 7, 1942, p. 2.
20. "They Picket Phone Co. for Jobs," *Baltimore Afro-American*, July 10, 1943, p. 9
21. Ibid.
22. Charles H. Houston, "Our Civil Rights," *Baltimore Afro-American*, July 16, 1949, p. 4.
23. Opinion, "The Marian Anderson Incident," *Baltimore Afro-American*, March 11, 1939, p. 24.
24. Constance McLaughlin Green, *Washington: A History of the Capital* 1800-1950 107 (New Jersey: Princeton University Press 1962).
25. Walter Isaacson, *Einstein, His Life and Universe* 445 (New York: Simon and Shuster 2007).
26. Ibid.
27. Marian Anderson, autographed program from 1939 concert at the Lincoln Memorial, Moorland-Spingarn Research Center, Charles Hamilton Houston, Box 163-1.
28. Brad Snyder, *Beyond the Shadow of the Senators* (McGraw-Hill 2003) p. 82 (Citing letter to Charles H. Houston from Mary McLeod Bethune April 10, 1989).

29. Louis Lautier, "Capital Spotlight," *Baltimore Afro-American*, March 25, 1944, p. 4.

30. "Saw Preakness," *Baltimore Afro-American*, May 22, 1948, p. 11.

31. "Negroes Ask Roosevelt Name Colored Supreme Court Justice," *Los Angeles Times*, November 20, 1939, p. 11.

32. Otto J. Lindenmeyer, *Black and Brave: The Black Soldier in America* 86 (New York: McGraw -Hill 1970) p. 86.

33. "NAACP Legal Advisor Demands Equality for Negroes in US Armed Forces in Peace Time," *Philadelphia Tribune*, April 11, 1940, p. 1.

34. Ibid.

35. See generally, Cameron McWhirter, *Red Summer: The Summer of 1919 and the Awakening of Black America* (New York: Henry Holt and Company 2011).

36. Charles H. Houston, "Pots, Pans Is Navy Policy," *Baltimore Afro-American*, March 19, 1938, p. 1.

37. Charles H. Houston, "Must Pass as White to Join the Marines," *New York Amsterdam News*, March 19, 1938, p. 15.

38. "Negroes Ban Advisory Unit for Military," *Washington Post*, April 27, 1948, p. 1.

39. Ibid.

40. Charles H. Houston, "Along the Highway," August 14, 1948, *Baltimore Afro-American*, p. 4.

41. Ibid.

42. Charles H. Houston, "Along the Highway," *Baltimore Afro-American*, May 8, 1948, p. 4.

43. Charles H. Houston, "The Highway," *Baltimore Afro-American*, November 15, 1947, p. 4.

44. Ibid.

45. Charles H. Houston, "The Highway," *Baltimore Afro-American*, August 9, 1947, p. 4.

46. Ibid.

47. Ibid.

48. Charles H. Houston, "For a Fifth Freedom," *Baltimore Afro-American*, September 24, 1946, p. 3.

49. Ibid.

50. Ibid.

51. Lyndon Baynes Johnson Library, Oral History Collection, Interview I., of A. Philip Randolph, October 29, 1969, by Thomas H. Baker, (regarding meeting March 1948 meeting with Harry Truman on race issues) p. 17.

52. Charles H. Houston, "The Highway," *Baltimore Afro-American*, April 3, 1948, p. 4.

53. Ibid.

54. Robert Shogan, *Harry Truman and the Struggle for Racial Justice* (University of Kansas Press 2013).

55. John H. Young III, "Houston Blasts Truman," *Pittsburgh Courier*, December 8, 1945, p. 1.

56. Ibid.

57. "Assailing Truman, Negro Quits FEPC," *New York Times*, December 4, 1945, p. 39.

58. "Lawyers Guild Assails Truman for FEPC Stand," *New York Amsterdam News*, January 5, 1946, p. 2.

59. "Negroes Chances for Postwar Jobs Good Says Truman," *New York Amsterdam News*, September 1, 1945, p. 14.

60. Charles H. Houston, "The Highway," *Baltimore Afro-American*, March 27, 1948, p. 4.

61. Charles H. Houston, "Along the Highway," *Baltimore Afro-American*, June 26, 1948, p. 4.

62. Charles H. Houston, "Our Civil Rights," *Baltimore Afro-American*, July 19, 1947, p. 4.

63. "Ala. High Court hears Dispute on Union Bar," *Baltimore Afro-American*, December 4, 1943, p. 13.

64. "Lawyers Can Help But Not Save Community," *Baltimore Afro-American*, December 8, 1934, p. 6.

65. Ibid.

66. "High Court to Review Cases of Two Locomotive Fireman," June 17, 1944, *Baltimore Afro- American*, p. 20.

67. "Ala. High Court Hears Dispute on Union Bar," *Baltimore Afro-American*, p. 13.

68. Ibid.

69. Ibid.

70. Ibid.

71. Ibid.

72. Ibid.

73. *Steele v. Louisville & N. R. Co. et al.*, 323 U.S. 192 (1944). On the same day the court issued an opinion in the companion case *Tunstall v. Brotherhood*, 323 U.S. 210 (1944). Charles Houston was counsel in both cases.

74. Ibid., p. 196.

75. Ibid.

76. Ibid., p. 209.

77. Ibid.

78. 323 U.S. 210 (1944).

79. Ibid., p. 212.

80. Ibid.

81. Ibid.

82. Charles H. Houston, "The Highway," *Baltimore Afro-American*, April 26, 1947, p. 4.

83. Interview of Joseph L. Rauh, Jr., *Road to Brown Transcript*, California Newsreel, A Presentation of the University of Virginia (William Elwood 1989), p. 6.

84. Ibid.

85. *Rolax et al. v. Atlantic Coast Line R. Co*, 91 F. Supp. 585 (E. D. Va. 1950).

86. *Rolax et al. v. Atlantic Coast Line R. Co, et al.*, 186 F. 2d 473 (4th Cir. 1951).

87. Ibid., p. 480.

88. Ibid., p. 481.

VII

A House Divided

Residential Discrimination

The [Shelley v. Kraemer case] will determine whether this country puts official sanction on ghettos or whether it will practice the democracy it preaches... if we lose now, we may have to wait twenty more years for another chance. Let us pray we win.

—Charles H. Houston, "The Highway," August 23, 1947,
Baltimore Afro-American

In the middle of the twentieth century, one of the great concerns for the African American family was finding a decent place to live. Black communities had been compressed into crowded areas in most major cities. Many white residents were unwilling to accept integration of their communities; such efforts were thought to lead to hostility and unrest. As one scholar observed, "increasing racial–ethnic diversity can add to inter-group tension and intensify conflict, especially in a society marked by a history of racial...oppression."[1] The lack of housing caused city ghettos to swell and resulted in poor living conditions and even life-threatening disease. In some cities, a high death rate from tuberculosis accompanied the overcrowding.[2] Although obtaining education at the graduate level, securing jobs in the railroad industry and obtaining fairness in the military were important priorities, Charles Houston knew that unless people could live together in diverse communities, the American dream could never be fully realized.[3]

Soldiers returning from World War II, as well the continuing "Great Migration"[4] of black people from the South, placed additional pressure on the swollen urban landscape. Intimidation of black farmers created an incentive for many to leave the South to try something new.[5] Legal restrictions in deeds known as "restrictive covenants" were the primary mechanism that deprived Negroes from the option to purchase in the new housing developments that were springing up in "suburbs" surrounding most major cities.[6] Some studies suggested that as many as "40 million homes throughout the country held ghetto covenants against Negroes, Jews, Mexicans and other minority groups."[7] Another thoughtful observer characterized the problem of racial ghettos as "self-perpetuating"[8] because often "where economic disadvantage is concentrated itself depresses disposable income, which makes departure more difficult."[9] Furthermore, reduced "housing supply led to higher rents and home prices in black neighborhoods than for similar accommodations in predominantly white ones."[10] Such housing issues also cause inappropriate cultural stereotypes regarding economically challenged people who want to live in decent neighborhoods.[11]

Charles Houston noted that these arrangements had "the same effect as racial zoning ordinances."[12] Because of these covenants "in every city and every area where the colored population has any significance, it is surrounded by an invisible wall which crowds it into a ghetto, just as tight as the walled ghetto of Warsaw."[13] Houston was particularly concerned about private racial restrictive covenants because, unlike legislation that prohibits people from living in certain locations, "a private covenant has no limits and can cover anything and everything to the end of time."[14] Toward the end of his remarkable legal career, the "Jim Crow" housing cases were Charles Houston's most ambitious and transformative legal work.[15]

Housing access was not a new issue in the long struggle for racial equality. Indeed, it was among the first discrimination matters the fledgling NAACP challenged in court.[16] In 1917 the organization successfully attacked a Louisville, Kentucky, racial zoning law that prevented white homeowners from selling homes to black buyers where the sale would change the racial balance of the city block in *Buchanan v. Warley*.[17] The court struck down a zoning plan that was originally created in 1910[18] in Baltimore that allowed sales of homes to be restricted because of the racial composition of a street as a "white block" or a "black block."[19]

However, another Supreme Court case decided less than ten years later, *Buckley v. Corrigan* (1926)[20] upheld the right of homeowners to contract privately with each other to exclude certain ethnic potential home buyers. The *Buckley* case permitted lawsuits to void the contracts of those who attempted to sell to minority buyers in a particular neighborhood. The *Buckley* decision was tempered somewhat in the late 1930s. *Hansberry v. Lee* (1940)[21] became the first "class action" case challenging those restrictive covenants. In that case, the Supreme Court concluded a black homeowner could not be excluded from his Washington Park, Chicago, neighborhood even though prior parties were successful in a lawsuit that upheld a restrictive covenant.[22] The court reasoned that to permit such an exclusion would violate due process of law, since the new Negro resident did not have their own opportunity to challenge the race-based exclusion.[23] Lorraine Hansberry, daughter of Carl Hansberry, the lead plaintiff in the case, authored the critically acclaimed Broadway play, *A Raisin in the Sun*, which was inspired by her family's experience in that court case.[24]

Even with this mixed record of court rulings, the limitations on housing access were still impacting the mobility and living options of the black family. With these concerns in mind, Charles Houston began planning to fight against residential "Jim Crow." The "restrictive covenant," usually contained in the deed of a property, was a clause that would exclude certain groups like "Jews," "Blacks" or other persons of color from being able to purchase a home in a particular neighborhood.[25] What made it so vicious is that these arrangements were enforced by state courts, making the taxpayer-funded legal system a partner in the discrimination. Houston decided that the NAACP needed to re-double its efforts to eliminate the restrictions. He began getting involved in cases around the country to test those laws. Furthermore, he believed that many of the ills of urban living could be cured by better economic and living conditions. He recognized that civil unrest among Negroes is often "caused by bad housing, inadequate recreation facilities and unemployment."[26]

The *Shelley v. Kraemer* Case

The legal challenge in the Supreme Court known as the *Shelley v. Kraemer* case began in Missouri and involved a neighborhood in the city of St. Louis. On February 16, 1911, thirty out of a total of thirty-nine owners of property fronting both sides of Labadie Avenue between Taylor Avenue and Cora Avenue, signed an agreement, which was subsequently recorded, providing in part:[27]

[T]he said property is hereby restricted to the use and occupancy for the term of Fifty (50) years from this date, so that it shall be a condition all the time and whether recited and referred to as [*sic*] not in subsequent conveyances and shall attach to the land, as a condition precedent to the sale of the same, that hereafter no part of said property or any portion thereof shall be, for said term of Fifty-years, occupied by any person not of the Caucasian race, it being intended hereby to restrict the use of said property for said period of time against the occupancy as owners or tenants of any portion of said property for resident or other purpose by people of the Negro or Mongolian Race.[28]

The entire district described in the agreement included fifty-seven parcels of land. The thirty owners who signed held title to forty-seven parcels, including the particular parcel involved in the *Shelley* case.[29] Ironically, at the time the agreement was signed, five of the parcels in the district were already owned by Negroes.[30] Indeed, one of those homes had been occupied by Negro families since 1882, nearly thirty years before the restrictive agreement was executed.[31] The trial court found that owners of seven out of nine homes on the south side of Labadie Avenue, within the restricted district and "in the immediate vicinity" of the premises in question, had failed to sign the restrictive agreement in 1911 at all.[32] At the time the court action was brought, four of the premises were occupied by Negroes and had been so occupied for periods ranging from twenty-three to sixty-three years.[33]

Such restrictions were common in the early 1900s, after the Supreme Court ruled that city governments could not pass municipal laws preventing black buyers from purchasing property in so-called "white" areas. However, a loophole in the Supreme Court's 1917 decision allowed private agreements, permitting property owners to engage in racial discrimination through community association agreements. For decades this formula created a sort of "residential apartheid."[34]

J.D. and Ethel Lee Shelley were migrants from the Deep South. They wanted to purchase a home in a tree shaded neighborhood.[35] Parents of six children, they were anxious to leave the crowded apartment in a crime ridden part of St. Louis in one of its notorious black ghettos.[36] Natives of Mississippi, they came to Missouri as part of the Great Migration that brought families to northern factories from the violence, depression and poverty of Southern "sharecropper" fields. They found a house where they could raise their family.[37] On August 11, 1945, the Shelley family purchased a deed to the parcel of disputed land. The Kraemer had no actual knowledge of the restrictive agreement at the time of the purchase.[38] The property which Shelley sought to purchase was held by a Mr. Bishop, a real estate agent and preacher, who placed the property in the name of Josephine Fitzgerald, a "straw purchaser." Bishop, who acted as agent for the Shelleys in the purchase, used this tactic to conceal the fact of his ownership since he was also a Negro.[39]

A few days after the purchase, Ethel was given a summons to come to court sent by a neighbor who lived ten blocks away to evict the family from their new home. The court claim, made by Fern Kraemer, was based on a 1911 recorded covenant that was placed in the land records that prohibited black families from occupying houses in the neighborhood.[40] The Marcus Avenue Improvement Association, founded in 1910 by white residents of the Grand Prairie neighborhood, assisted the Kraemer family with their complaint against the Shelley family.[41]

On October 9, 1945, the Kraemer family, as owners of other property allegedly subject to the terms of the restrictive covenant, brought suit in the Circuit Court of St. Louis, asking that the Shelleys be restrained from taking possession of the property and that judgment be entered divesting title from the Shelleys.[42] The trial court denied the requested relief made by the white property owners on the ground that the restrictive agreement had never become final since signatures of all the owners had never been obtained.[43] Tall and lanky, J. D. Shelley made decent money as a construction worker during World War II.[44] They pinched every penny from his earnings and from his wife's job as a maid to earn enough for a house with a yard.[45] It would take a team of lawyers across several states to give them that chance.

The strategy of Charles Houston and the NAACP was designed to force the Supreme Court to review several cases from different states, along with the *Shelley* case, before deciding about the discriminatory tactic. As predicted, most of the lower appellate courts rejected the equal protection arguments of the NAACP and their local cooperating lawyers.[46] The defeat in those lower court cases prompted a second conference on strategy regarding restrictive covenants, set up by Houston at Howard University in January 1947.[47]

Charles Houston had another practical problem. With so many cases from different states, it was important that a case with bad facts or a questionable legal theory not interfere with the possibility that the issue could be successful. The meeting of the lawyer group, "NAACP Lawyers and Consultants on Methods of Attacking Restrictive Covenants," were charged with building the strongest court case possible.[48]

However, not all of the lawyers agreed with that cautious approach of Houston and Thurgood Marshall.[49] George Vaughn, who actually represented Mr. and Mrs. Shelley in Missouri, did not attend the conference at Howard, because he did not agree with the direction the cases were taking. Rather than waiting for the NAACP, whose brief was expected to include testimony from economists and sociologist on the impact of racial covenants on racial tension,

Vaughn filed his case in the Supreme Court ahead of all the other appeals. Among Vaughn's arguments was an attempt to challenge the covenants as a violation of the Thirteenth Amendment's prohibition against slavery, an argument Houston desperately wanted to avoid.[50]

The NAACP, fearing that the Missouri case lacked the record needed for success, arranged to rush the other NAACP cases to court.[51] The work on the briefs for the case was assisted by Spottswood Robinson III, a recent Howard University law graduate. He provided great insight about the task and Charlie Houston's work ethic. He described one session where Houston edited his draft brief from 2:00 p.m. until 4 a.m.[52] Decades later, Robinson, who by then was a federal circuit judge in Richmond, would comment about Houston's high-quality work standards, "[t]horoughness was Charlie."[53]

In their most novel strategy, Marshall and Houston organized the preparation and filing of amicus curiae or "friend of the court" briefs by over a dozen organizations. Some of the briefs even argued the relevance of international human rights law to invalidate racially restrictive covenants.[54] Among the sixteen briefs debating the relevance of the U.N. Charter were the briefs of amicus curiae arguing that the United Nations Charter was binding on the Supreme Court.[55]

Another amicus brief, filed by lawyers including Alger Hiss, Asher Bob Lans, Philip Jessup, Joseph Proskauer, Myres McDougal, and Victor Elting for the American Association for the United Nations, detailed the "obligations of the United States" under the U.N. Charter. Those documents argued that the "domestic jurisdiction" did not reduce the obligations of the member states under the charter and thus, member states could not engage in discrimination.[56] The American Veterans Committee also filed in support of invalidating the covenants.[57] A few amicus briefs supported invalidation of the racial covenants but did not rely on the charter. Included among those taking that position were the American Jewish Congress, the American Indian League of California and the General Council of Congregational Christian Churches.

An amicus supporting the constitutionality of the racial covenants was filed by the Arlington Heights Property Owners Association. It argued that the charter either had no effect or, if it did, it violated states' rights.[58] Houston also expressed his personal view on the effect of racial covenants in an editorial during the late 1940s, writing:

> The device of racial covenants not only constricts colored people within urban ghettos, but is used to segregate and exclude other[s]...from decent housing. All minority groups such as Indians, Japanese-Americans, Orientals, Jews, Assyrians, etc., etc., are hit from time to time.[59]

One crucial supporter of the case was the United States Justice Department. In November 1947, U.S. Attorney General Tom Clark agreed to have the federal government file an amicus brief against the enforcement of restrictive covenants.[60] Clark's decision was heavily publicized, since it marked the first time in the action's history the Justice Department had ever intervened as "amicus curiae" in a civil rights case.[61] The decision of the government to file a brief in support of Houston's claims was the product of a complex set of factors. Political calculations regarding the upcoming presidential election, internal lobbying by officials in the Justice Department and the Indian Bureau (which opposed restrictive covenants against Native Americans), and the Report of the President's Committee on Civil Rights called for the banning of restrictive covenants.[62] In November of 1947, Attorney General Clark had been a speaker at the National Bar Association annual meeting in Washington, D.C., where many of the lawyers working on the restrictive covenant cases were in attendance.[63]

The Supreme Court ultimately ruled that by endorsing judicial enforcement of the restrictive agreements, the states would be denying the Shelleys equal protection of the law.[64] The Justices noted that freedom from discrimination by the states in the enjoyment of property rights was among the basic objectives sought to be effectuated by the framers of the Fourteenth Amendment.[65] The court reasoned that because of the race or color of these petitioners, they had been denied rights of ownership.[66] It concluded "the Fourteenth Amendment declares that all persons, whether colored or white, shall stand equal before the laws of the States, and . . . that no discrimination shall be made against them by law because of their color."[67]

The *Urciolo/Hurd* Cases

In a companion case the Supreme Court, on the same day, reached a similar conclusion. In what has become known as the *Urciolo/Hurd* cases the court made clear its intention to invalidate all forms of race restrictive property covenants. In *Hurd*, the petitioner purchased one of the restricted properties from the white owners.[68] In *Urciolo*, a white real estate dealer sold three of the restricted properties to the Negro petitioners Rowe, Savage, and Stewart.[69] Urciolo also owned three other lots in the block subject to the covenants. In both cases, the Negro petitioners were occupying the respective properties which had been conveyed to them.[70] Petitioner James M. Hurd maintained that he is not a Negro but a Mohawk Indian. Suits were instituted in the Federal district court by those who owned other property in the block subject to the terms of the covenants, requesting injunctive relief to enforce the terms of the restrictive agreement.[71] The trial court entered a judgment declaring null and void the deeds of the Negro petitioners and enjoining petitioners Urciolo and Ryan, the white property owners who sold the houses to the Negro petitioners, from leasing, selling or conveying the properties to any Negro or colored person, thus stopping Negroes from leasing or conveying the properties and directing those petitioners "to remove themselves and all of their personal belongings" from the premises within sixty days.[72]

The United States Court of Appeals for the District of Columbia, with one justice dissenting, affirmed the judgment of the district court. The majority of the court was of the opinion that the action of the district court was consistent with earlier decisions of the court of appeals.[73] The petitioners attacked the judicial enforcement of the restrictive covenants. Primary reliance was placed on the contention that such governmental action on the part of the courts of the District of Columbia is forbidden by the due process clause of the Fifth Amendment of the federal Constitution.[74]

Arguing the case as lead counsel in *Hurd v. Hodge*, Charles Houston maintained the primary stewardship of most of the briefs in the Supreme Court, ensuring some measure of consistency. The day the *Hurd v. Hodge* case was decided a former Charles Houston law student observed him walking from the Supreme Court building after getting a copy of the opinion in the case decided that day. As Houston crossed the street "he looked like he was walking on air, he was a pretty stern fellow, but he appeared to be very, very happy about something. I didn't know what the hell was going on.... I didn't know until that evening."[75]

Houston had been thinking about these issues a long time and had several litigation experiments pending around the country that did not end up in the Supreme Court, but were affected by the outcome of *Shelley*—for example, a Maryland test case filed before *Shelley* was decided was influenced by the decision.

Goetz v. Saunders (1948) involved the attempted enforcement of a restrictive covenant "against the sale, lease, transfer or permitted occupation of the respective properties mentioned to or by 'any negro, Chinaman, Japanese, or person of negro, Chinese or Japanese descent.'"[76] The properties were parts of a tract called Beachwood Forest, platted and subdivided in 1922, and were located on the Magothy River in Anne Arundel County, Maryland and sold to Negro buyers.[77]

The Maryland court ruled that it had no choice but to follow the precedent announced a few months before by the United States Supreme Court in *Shelley v. Kraemer*.[78] Despite some racist backlash, the restrictive covenant cases still stand as a hallmark to decency. Charles Houston revolutionized litigation by successfully using a so-called "Brandies Brief" in the Supreme Court.[79] In those briefs he combined aspects of sociology, psychology, law, religion and international relations to move America closer to the constitutional promise of equal protection of the law. That achievement, in some ways, was more technically well executed than the later effort in the *Brown v. Board of Education* cases. Houston placed the Supreme Court in a situation that it had little choice other than to agree with his well-crafted position. Indeed, several Justices had to recuse themselves from participating in the case because it was believed that they lived in neighborhoods that were subject to restrictive covenants.[80]

The case was a monumental victory for the lawyers, but a personal victory for the many working-class litigants who were involved. The Shelleys were humble, unassuming people who had made themselves available to transform a nation. J.D. Shelley concluded that "it was a good thing we done this case...when I bought the property, I didn't think there was going to be anything about it. But I knowed it was important. We was the first ones to live where they said colored can't live."[81] Ethel Shelley, who was deeply religious, said at the conclusion of the case "when she heard she could keep her house: My little soul is overjoyed. Wait till I get by myself. I will tell the Lord of my thankfulness."[82]

The Shelleys were the kind of people Charles Houston especially cared about. Their courage and struggle to live free from discrimination reflected the values Houston sought to protect. He also believed, without hesitation, that the *Shelley* cases would be ammunition for future civil rights battles. Months after the decision, Houston predicted, "[t]he general feeling about the Supreme Court decision in St. Louis, Chicago, Washington and Baltimore is that it gives great leverage to the fight against segregation in the Armed Forces, schools and other places because it establishes that Government cannot legally establish or enforce rules preventing white and colored people from living side by side."[83]

As the importance of this litigation became clear, Houston wanted to speak more broadly about the need for the nation to move toward racial integration. He appeared on the NBC national talk show *United America* hosted by legendary broadcast journalist David Brinkley. On the nation's airways he remarked that "on playgrounds...the children are separated so long as they are open officially and just as soon as the flags goes down, then all the children of the neighborhood come together and play."[84]

Charles Houston also cautioned that outlawing racial covenants alone would not make Negroes "welcome in new neighborhoods unless we demonstrate that we know how to conform to the highest standards of social conduct."[85] He further warned that the black community should get ready for the "tougher assignment to discipline and prepare ourselves for the enjoyment and preservation of our rights...[so it] does not catch us napping."[86] Soon after the *Shelley* decision, Houston provided some practical advice to those seeking to take advantage of the court victory and pursue home ownership. He would suggest "our people would be wise to sit down and do some straight figuring on the state of their finances."[87] He also encouraged people to pay off as much debt as possible and "keep six-months salary on hand, you may not be able to lick a depression, but you will give yourself a lot of precious time to keep the depression from licking you."[88]

However, Charles Houston was not finished being critical of government support for discrimination in future real estate development. He warned of a new segregation device on the horizon that created slums and ghettos, so-called "slum clearance" programs sponsored by the federal housing department.[89] He complained that such programs "too frequently means exclusion of colored people from new housing which public aid by way of tax exemption and land condemnation made possible."[90] He pointed out that everyone must chip in to compensate for the tax break given the developer.[91] Houston urged that such projects should be rejected "unless they have ironclad guarantees against racial, religious or national origin discrimination written into the plans before they get started."[92] Charles Houston's foresight on this issue anticipated a major urban development trend of the twenty-first century in most American cities.[93]

Not all people agreed that the elimination of restrictive covenants was a good idea. One housing developer stood in open defiance of the Supreme Court's ruling. William Levitt, the driving force behind the Long Island, New York's massive Levittown suburban home building project, published a statement in the community newspaper in 1949 declaring that his racial exclusion policy would remain unaltered despite the then-recent *Shelley* case decision. "Levittown has been and is now progressing as a private enterprise job, and it is entirely in the discretion and judgment of Levitt and Sons as to whom it will rent or sell."[94] The resistance of developers like Levitt would have enormous consequences for future decades since the federal government's support of housing loans in segregated housing developments would continue for years after the Supreme Court rulings.[95]

Even with all of the concerns expressed by Charlie Houston on the future of housing for Negroes, he felt encouraged and was grateful for the coalition he built to change the severely flawed legal precedents that *Shelley v. Kraemer* and its companion cases overturned. In one of his *Afro-American* columns he thanked not only the black members of the NAACP but also, "Jew, Gentiles, Catholics, Protestants, Conservatives and radicals, men and women, who had worked together."[96] Providing an optimistic perspective on the future, he proclaimed that the world should know "we have just begun to fight."[97]

Despite the resistance of developers and financers, Houston's litigation changed the way the nation thought about access to housing. Although the struggle for housing access would continue for decades after *Shelley*, the case would have a legal and social impact that transformed America forever.

Endnotes

1. Camille Z. Charles, *Won't You Be My Neighbor* 18 (New York: Russell Sage Foundation 2006).

2. Antero Pietila, *Not in My Neighborhood, How Bigotry Shaped a Great American City* 57 (Chicago: Ivan R. Dee 2010).

3. Charles H. Houston, "Along the Highway," *Baltimore Afro-American*, September 4, 1948, p. 4.

4. Nicholas Lemann, *The Promised Land: The Great Migration and How It Changed America* 6 (New York: Alfred K. Knopf 1991).

5. Cassandra Havard, "African-American Farmers and Fair Lending: Racializing Rural Economic Space," 12 *Stanford Law and Policy Rev.* 333 (2001).

6. W. Edward Orser, *Blockbusting in Baltimore: The Edmondson Village Story* 18–19 (Lexington: University of Kentucky Press 1994).

7. "Real Estate Notes," *New York New Amsterdam News*, May 4, 1948, p. 16.

8. Richard Rothstein, *The Color of Law: A Forgotten History of How Our Government Segregated America* 172 (New York: W.W. Norton & Co. 2017).

9. Ibid.

10. Ibid.

11. *See*, Jamie Alison Lee, "Poverty, Dignity and Public Housing," *Col. Hum. Rts. L. Rev.* 2 (2016) (discussing human dignity linked to housing choices).

12. Charles H. Houston, "The Highway," *Baltimore Afro-American*, June 21, 1947, p. 4.

13. Ibid.

14. Ibid.

15. Wendell E. Pritchett, "*Shelley v. Kraemer*: Radical Liberalism and the Supreme Court," 6 (Collected in *Civil Rights Stories*, Myriam E. Gilles and Risa L. Goluboff, Editors, New York: Foundation Press 2008).

16. Risa Lauren Goluboff, "Let Economic Equality Take Care of Itself: The NAACP, Labor Litigation, and the Making of Civil Rights in the 1940s," 52 *UCLA L. Rev.* 1393, 1477 n.379 (2005).

17. 245 U.S. 60 (1917).

18. Garrett Power, "Apartheid Baltimore Style: The Residential Segregation Ordinances of 1910–1913," 42 *Maryland L. Rev.* 289 (1983) (Discussing in detail the circumstances and origin of Baltimore, Maryland's racial zoning ordinance requiring city streets to have a designation by race).

19. Richard Rothstein, *The Color of Law*, p. 44.

20. 271 U.S.323 (1926).

21. 311 U.S. 32 (1940).

22. Ibid., p. 44.

23. Ibid.

24. Harold Cruse, *The Crisis of the Negro Intellectual*, 277 (New York: William Marrow 1967).

25. Charles H. Houston, "Along the Highway," *Baltimore Afro-American*, May 15, 1948, p. 4.

26. "Cooperation of Colored Groups Urged at Rally," August 14, 1940, *Washington Post*, p. 13.

27. *Shelley et ux. v. Kraemer et ux.*, 334 U.S. 1 (1948).

28. Ibid.

29. Ibid.

30. Ibid.

31. Ibid.

32. Ibid.

33. Ibid.

34. Ibid.

35. Peter Irons, *The Courage of Their Convictions* 66 (New York: The Free Press 1988).

36. Ibid.

37. Ibid.

38. Ibid.

39. Ibid.

40. Ibid.

41. Ibid.

42. Ibid.

43. Ibid.

44. "A House with a Yard," *Time* (National Affairs) May 17, 1948.

45. Ibid.

46. Ibid., p. 69.

47. Ibid., p. 69.

48. Genna Rae McNeil, *Groundwork: Charles Hamilton Houston and the Struggle for Civil Rights* 177 (Philadelphia: University of Pennsylvania Press 1983).

49. Irons, *Courage*, p. 70.

50. James Rawn, Jr., *Root and Branch: Charles Houston, Thurgood Marshall and the Struggle to End Segregation* 192–194 (Bloomsbury Press New York, 2010).

51. Ibid., p. 70.

52. McNeil, *Groundwork*, pp.178–179.

53. Ibid.

54. José Felipé Anderson, "The Viability of Multi-Party Litigation as a Tool for Social Engineering Six Decades After the Restrictive Covenant Case," 42 *McGeorge L. Rev.*786–787 (2011).

55. Brief of Amicus Curiae Civil Liberties Department of the Grand Lodge of Elks, L.B.P.O.E.W. at 7, (arguing that the charter prohibited such discrimination on the basis of race); Brief of Amicus Curiae St. Louis Civil Liberties Committee at 1, 16 (relying on the charter as evidence of United States' public policy); Brief of the American Civil Liberties Union at 27, reprinted in 46 *Landmark Briefs and Arguments of the Supreme Court of the United States: Constitutional Law* 393, Brief of the Congress of Industrial Organizations at 2, 4, reprinted in *Landmark Briefs*, at 505, 508, 510 (invoking both the charter and the need to fight fascism); and the Brief of the Non-Sectarian Anti-Nazi League to Champion Human Rights Inc. at 5 (arguing that covenants violate the treaty obligations of the charter).

56. *See* Brief for the American Ass'n for the United Nations as Amicus Curiae at 13–14, reprinted in *Landmark Briefs*, at 357, 374–75.

57. *See* Brief of Amicus Curiae American Veterans Committee at 2, n.1.

58. Brief of Amicus Curiae Arlington Heights Property Owners Ass'n at 26–31. Judith Resnik, "Law's Migration: American Exceptionalism, Silent Dialogues, and Federalism's Multiple Ports of Entry," 115 *Yale L. J.* 1564, 1601–02 n.168 (2006).

59. Charles H. Houston, "The Highway," *Baltimore Afro-American*, October 11, 1947.

60. Juan Williams, *Thurgood Marshall: American Revolutionary* 151 (Times Books: New York 1998).

61. Ibid.

62. Ibid., p. 43.

63. Agenda, National Bar Association November 28–30, 1947. Nicolas-Gosnell Collection, Thurgood Marshall Law Library, University of Maryland School of Law, Box A.

64. 334 U.S. 1 (1948).

65. Ibid.

66. Ibid., p. 21.

67. Ibid., p. 23.

68. *Hurd et al. v. Hodge et al.*, 334 U.S. 24 (1948).

69. Ibid.

70. Ibid.

71. Ibid.

72. Ibid., p. 28.

73. Ibid.

74. Ibid.

75. Hon. William B. Bryant, "A Symposium on Charles Hamilton Houston," 27 *New Eng. L. Rev.* 677, 680 (1993).

76. *Goetz v. Saunders*, 62 A. 2d. 602 (Md. 1948).

77. Ibid.

78. Ibid.

79. *See,* Garrett Power, "*Meade v. Dennistone*: The NAACP Test Case to Sue Jim Crow out of Maryland with the Fourteenth Amendment," 63 *Md. L. Rev.* 773, 807 (2004).

80. Leland B. Ware, "Invisible Walls, An Examination of the Legal Strategy of the Restrictive Covenant Cases," 67 *Wash. U.L.Q.* 737, 761 (1989).

81. Irons, *Courage*, p. 79.

82. *Time*, p. 42.

83. Charles H. Houston, "Along the Highway," *Baltimore Afro-American*, September 4, 1948, p. 4.

84. McNeil, *Groundwork*, p. 185.

85. Charles H. Houston, "The Highway," *Baltimore Afro-American*, November 8, 1947, p. 4.

86. Ibid.

87. Charles H. Houston, "Along the Highway," *Baltimore Afro-American*, September 18, 1948, p. 4.

88. Ibid.

89. Charles H. Houston, "Along the Highway," *Baltimore Afro-American*, October 23, 1948, p. 4.

90. Ibid.

91. Ibid.

92. Ibid.

93. Audrey McFarlane, "When Inclusion Leads to Exclusion: The Uncharted Terrain of Community Participation in Economic Development," 66 *Brooklyn L. Rev.* 863 (2001) (discussing the need for community participation in modern economic development).

94. Note, "Application of the Sherman Act to Housing Segregation," 63 *Yale L. J.* 1124, 1134 n.83. (1954).

95. Rothstein, *The Color of Law*, pp. 71–77.

96. Charles H. Houston, "Our Civil Rights," *Baltimore Afro-American*, Feb. 12, 1949, p. 4.

97. Ibid.

VIII

The Trials of the Hollywood Ten

Guardians of the First Amendment

The fact that one does not agree with the Communist party line does not require persecution or extermination of Communists. I had always thought that one of the most sacred rights in a democracy was the right to disagree.

—Charles Hamilton Houston, *Baltimore Afro-American*, April 12, 1947

Charles Houston's historic representation, at trial and on federal appeal, of a group of Hollywood, California, insiders known as the "Hollywood Ten" has received little attention. These individuals, mostly renowned screen writers, were vigorously pursued by the Federal Bureau of Investigation because of their alleged affiliation with the Communist Party.[1] Each of the defendants made a courageous decision to refuse to answer many of Congress' questions about their political associations. This led to their prosecutions for contempt of Congress at the end of the 1940s.[2]

This set of trials was part of a political focus in the United States in the middle of the twentieth century on the so-called "evils" of the Communist Party. Indeed, the idea that the Communist Party would have a negative effect on the nation began at least as far back as World War I. A revolution in Russia and labor unrest in the United States generated interest in communism as a political alternative to democracy.[3] Many men returning from the war believed this political threat needed to be suppressed. Congress passed various loyalty laws and many riots were touched off in major cities during that volatile period. In the 1920s, the Communist Party was a small but determined group that captured the interest of a few Americans but was never particularly large or influential in that decade.[4] However, during the 1930s and 1940s the Communist Party was perceived by many as the greatest enemy of democracy.[5]

Some people particularly feared the Communists in the summer of 1934, and law enforcement in San Francisco, California, permitted private raids of locations suspected of holding Communist meetings. Lawyers from the American Civil Liberties Union, among them Charles Houston, protested the police conduct. The *New York Times* reported the ACLU's signed protest as follows:

> On July 17, it was publicly known in San Francisco that certain private individuals contemplated raiding the meeting places of certain other private individuals. The police provided no protection. The National Guard, called out to preserve the peace, provided no protection. The police arrested not the raiders, but the victims of the raids. The police seized the papers of their prisoners. The police closed their meeting places. Three hundred of these men have been jailed.[6]

As a result of fears about Communists, exaggerated conclusions were reached concerning the size and influence of the movement. As historian Robert Murray observed, "[h]arassed by the rantings and ravings of a small group of radicals, buffeted by the dire warnings of business and employer organizations, and assaulted daily by the scare propaganda of the patriotic society and the general press, the national mind ultimately succumbed to the hysteria."[7] During the early 1930s, the party became more closely linked with the labor movement in the United States and began to attract the interest of a broader range of people. Although not many persons involved in the labor movement would ever actually join the Communist Party, they would accept the help of its organizers and activists in struggling for better wages and working conditions.[8] As one scholar has insightfully noted, "[t]he anti-communist persecution that followed the Bolshevik revolution was really a continuation and escalation of longstanding anti-labor sentiments and war-time suspicions of disloyalty, particularly directed against Jews and other recent immigrants."[9]

The Communists' interest in the economic change in the country was somewhat incompatible with Houston's own political views, but their view of fair treatment and due process mirrored his own values. It has been said that Charles Houston "sought the common ground on which radicals and the middle could come together. Principles were important to Houston, but they were not useful if all one did was polish them; they had to guide practical work."[10] Nothing was more practical than African Americans getting access to the opportunity to become part of the country they help to build. However, dealing with the Communists might provide a useful catalyst for change.

The entire country was affected by the economic collapse of the 1930s, but the African American community suffered more hardships than the rest of the nation during the Great Depression. With few private or government resources available to help anyone, black communities were in no position to turn help away from any group who offered it. The Communist Party found a way to help the black community, providing the legal defense of a few high-profile criminal cases like the "Scottsboro Boys."[11]

There is reason to believe that the Communists did not offer very many black members important leadership roles in the party. As one black FBI informant against the Communist Party explained, they were "completely dominated and controlled by white higher ups. This was the cause of no little dissatisfaction and dissension among Negro members. I was present at a number of meetings called for the purpose of determining ways to achieve equal status."[12]

Many politicians advanced the notion that communism was a threat to the United States, especially after the conclusion of World War II. In 1947, concern that Communists had infiltrated the American movie industry was also growing. The House Un-American Activities Committee (HUAC) subpoenaed dozens of Hollywood celebrities to question them about their alleged Communist activities. The famed "Hollywood Ten" members refused to answer these questions, claiming that such inquires violated their First Amendment rights to freedom of association and speech. "The congressional committee cited all ten of these industry professionals for contempt, fined them $1,000 and imposed a jail term on them of one year."[13]

The risks evident in being affiliated with the Communist Party at this time were highlighted by J. Edger Hoover, the longtime head of the Federal Bureau of Investigation's dogged pursuit of suspected Communists during the early twentieth century.[14] Hoover concluded that the party was engaged in an attempt to destroy American values and was the "most evil monstrous conspiracy against man since time began."[15] Hoover further demonstrated his rigor against the Communist movement by scrutinizing another organization that Houston was closely affiliated with, the ACLU. Hoover denied to the organization's leader, Roger Baldwin, that they were under scrutiny. Regardless, the FBI clearly pursued as much information as possible against the civil rights organization.[16] "The American Civil Liberties Union had been a subject of intensive investigation from almost the day it was founded."[17] Indeed, the depth of scrutiny into the organization's activities included recordings of speeches, examination of bank records and the placement of bugging devices.[18]

"Each member of the ACLU's national board rated a file. Several, such as those on [Roger] Baldwin and [Felix] Frankfurter, were sizable.... [Frankfurter] according to his Dossier was 'considered a dangerous man.' Helen Keller, the famed blind, deaf and mute author-lecturer, was to the Bureau 'a writer of radical subjects.'"[19] Frankfurter, who was a Harvard law professor at the time the FBI investigations began and later become an Associate Justice on the Supreme Court of the United States, was a teacher of Charles Houston. They both worked closely on many ACLU projects. Frankfurter also worked with Houston on projects for the National Association for the Advancement of Colored People's (NAACP) Legal Committee, which also was under intense FBI scrutiny.[20] While Communist activities on behalf of black defendants and alleged radical scholars and writers who seemed sympathetic to Communism drew the attention of the FBI, no group captured their investigative interest more than those persons affiliated with the motion picture industry.[21]

According to an early FBI report, the Bureau adopted the view of an unidentified informant that it is "becoming more and more clear that the Communists are using prominent sympathizers in the motion picture industry to further their policies." The informant stated that, using people of high standing and influence, "the Communist party hopes to cover up these individuals' real Communist connections."[22] Other information alleged that "a large percentage of this pro-Communist element was brought into Hollywood during the period of 1935 to 1944. Many of these individuals were European refugees who came to this country following the rise of Nazism in Europe and were employed in reliable positions in the fields of writing and directing."[23] Indeed, the FBI thought that some chapters of the NAACP in the South had been subject to this same infiltration. On the page of that part of the FBI file on the NAACP appears Charles Hamilton Houston's name along with other members of the legal committee.[24]

Hollywood writer and director John Howard Lawson and Dalton Trumbo had been identified in the FBI report as being key Communists, attempting to influence Americans through the movies. The FBI report stated, "the first real impetus to the infiltration of the motion picture industry was the sending by the Communist Party of John Howard Lawson to Hollywood in about 1941 for the purpose of promoting the party's influence in the motion picture industry."[25]

The report further noted that Dalton Trumbo was considered one of the members of the Hollywood community alleged to be "under Lawson's influence...other Hollywood actors were suspected of having ties with the Communist Party including Edward G. Robinson, Paul Robeson, and Gene Kelly."[26]

The scrutiny of Lawson was heightened because of his status as the first president of the Screen Writer's Guild. In the Bureau's view, that role played into the overall suspected infiltration scheme to turn the movie industry into a tool of Communist propaganda. According to an unnamed informant, "by mobilizing the Communist Party back of a particular picture which was to the liking of the Communists, management was to put on notice that it could expect tremendous support from the Communist Party in an effort to make the picture a success."[27]

It was also alleged that Communists were employed by top producers and studios but some motion picture producers and executives had "protected them whenever their names or reputations have been exposed."[28] It was these alleged protectors of "secret communists" in the motion picture industry that the Congress had become interested in investigating.

In October of 1947, the Committee on Un-American Activities of the House of Representatives called John Howard Lawson and Dalton Trumbo as witnesses in hearings it was conducting regarding Communist infiltration into the motion picture industry. The committee issued subpoenas for the two writers to appear.[29] Lawson was called to testify on October 27, 1947, and Trumbo testified the following day, on October 28, 1947. The single count indictment against Lawson charged him with refusing to answer the question whether or not "he was or had ever been a member of the communist Party?"[30] Trumbo's two count indictment charged him with failing to answer two questions. The first was "whether or not he was a member of the Screen Actors Guild and whether or not he had ever been a member of the Communist Party?"[31]

Many high-profile Hollywood actors of the time supported the screen writers during their ordeal, among them Humphrey Bogart, who said that the congressional committee "is not empowered to dictate what Americans can think."[32] During a "fly in" press conference among many autograph seekers, several celebrities voiced their concerns about the congressional probe.[33] Actress Judy Garland stated that she resented the House committee's actions.[34] Actress Myrna Loy questioned the right of congressmen "to abuse citizens in order to make headlines."[35] Famed comedian Lucille Ball read a portion of the Constitution to the gathered crowd.[36] Legendary film director John Huston noted that the only piece of legislation proposed by the House Un-American Activities Committee had been "rejected as unconstitutional by the United States Supreme Court along with a scathing denunciation."[37]

Despite the support of their Hollywood colleagues, the hearings did not go well. Before Congress, each man refused to answer the questions. Both men were tried by separate juries. Each was convicted of a violating 2 U.S.C.A. 192 and both received the maximum sentence of one-year imprisonment and a $1,000 fine.[38]

The federal appellate court actually consolidated the issues in deciding Lawson and Trumbo's case in a way that they were not presented in the briefs. Indeed, after announcing that it would proceed in this manner, the court explained that it "[i]n the few instances...where a particular claim is not raised by both, because of the different records on which these appeals are based, separate treatment will be given and will only relate to the appellant who made the claim."[39]

The court ruled that Congress had the power to make the inquiry. It explained "[n]o one can doubt in these chaotic times that the destiny of all nations hangs in the balance in the current ideological struggle between communistic thinking and democratic thinking people of the world."[40] The Court embraced the notion that "Congress nor any court is required to disregard the impact of world events." The court further asserted that "it is beyond dispute that the motion picture industry plays a critical role in the molding of public opinion and that motion pictures are, or are capable of being, a potent medium of propaganda dissemination which may influence the minds of millions of American people."[41]

Motion pictures were said to "vitally influence" and be "seen by millions."[42] The court finally reasoned that it would be "hard to envisage how there could be any more pertinent questions in these circumstances where the committee was investigating, pursuant to statutory authorization, 'the extent, character, and objects of un-American propaganda activities in the United States.'"[43] The court also rejected several other procedural objections raised by Houston on behalf of the screenwriters. Lawson and Trumbo both objected to certain instructions given in each of their cases as vague or misleading and certain limitations on their cross examination. Lawson's argument that the congressional sub-committee was not properly constituted was also rejected.

Both Lawson and Trumbo also claimed that their jury panels were not properly constituted because they were not impartially drawn from a fair cross section of the community.[44] Among those claims was the refusal to remove government employees from the jury.[45] Finally, through Charles Houston, Lawson and Trumbo urged the transfer of the case from the District of Columbia, because of the pressure against federal government workers who associated with Communists.[46]

After the two screenwriters lost in the court of appeals, they sought review in the Supreme Court of the United States. In two massive petitions for review, Lawson and Trumbo, under Charles Houston's guiding hand, set fourth an extraordinary assault on the government's tactics to ferret out alleged Communists. In Lawson's petition, Houston and his co-counsel asserted that "The Committee conducted its Hollywood investigations, determined the pertinence of questions, and otherwise proceed upon the basis that its authority was established by its own definition and application of the terms 'un-American propaganda activity' and 'subversive and un-American propaganda' that...attacked the principles of the form of government as guaranteed by our Constitution."[47]

Charles Houston further argued that what the committee believed to be "un-American" and "subversive" runs the gamut of what are often "progressive ideas in American life, from support of the New Deal to opposition to the Committee on Un-American Activities; from opposition to monopoly to defense of sit-down strikes."[48] The petition characterized the congressional committee as the "Grand Jury of America" building up "files containing names of more than a million individuals and more than a thousand organization accused of being subversive."[49] Houston asserted that Congress was acting as little more than a "vigilante committee" and a "'democratic' substitute for the 'Gestapo.'"[50] The petition asserted to the Supreme Court that there "is nothing in American motion pictures generally or in the motion pictures written by petitioner specifically which by any reasonable standard or definition could be considered subversive."[51] The petition also informed the Supreme Court that "as a matter of undeviating practice in the motion picture industry it is impossible for any screen writer to put anything into a motion picture to which the executive producers object."[52]

Trumbo argued that the broad assertion of authority to require compulsory disclosure would have a trickle-down effect on other government entities. "The determination of this issue is essential, for not only this agency of government claimed and exercised such power of compulsory disclosure, but the precedent set by the agency of government has sired a host of similar claims to like power throughout the length and breadth of the nation."[53] Suggesting that Congress was attempting to criminalize "dangerous thoughts,"[54] Houston posited that "no such power had ever been claimed by any agency of our government."

Further, Houston alleged, the Committee used this broad fear "…to censor the content of motion pictures and to purge from the motion picture industry alleged 'disbelievers' in 'Americanism' to which the members of the Committee subscribed."[55]

Houston's petition to the Supreme Court did not simply offer overtures to grand constitutional values, it also pointed out some serious practical consequences of Congress' broad assertion of power. The petition pointed out that "the Committee as an agency of government used its power to penalize individuals…because of their alleged beliefs and affiliations. The penalties imposed by such governmental actions included blacklisting, character assassination and incitement of public retribution."[56]

The government filed a brief in opposition, asserting that the house committee "was constitutionally authorized to investigate Communist infiltration of the motion picture industry."[57] The government suggested that the "conspiratorial nature of the Communist Party's infiltration" of the motion picture industry supported its argument for compelled disclosure of party affiliation.[58] The government asserted that although the First Amendment might embody a freedom to be silent generally, "it certainly does not accord a privilege to be silent when called before a lawful body of inquiry," reasoning that, "no investigation would be constitutional if that were the case."[59] The government further offered the position that if "the Committee transgressed the bounds of the power which was entrusted to the Committee by Congress, the remedy lies with Congress and, ultimately, with the voters."[60]

Giving short shrift to the issues raised by Charles Houston, the government concluded its brief; "[a]lthough the issue as to the Committee's authority to question petitioners as to their membership in the Communist Party is of great importance, it has been twice resolved against the petitioners' contentions by the court below."[61] When the petition for certiorari was denied, Lawson and Trumbo, through their counsel, filed a petition for rehearing. Ironically, the petition for rehearing was actually filed on April 24, 1950, two days after Houston's death.[62] Charles Houston's influence on this document was, however, very clear. It made powerful policy arguments and pointed out obvious contradictions in the government's position on First Amendment rights.

In that filing, Houston and his co-counsel asserted that the case involved not simply the First Amendment but the privilege against self-incrimination. The government's position was said to require that individuals be forced "to aid in their own prosecution," whether or not "a valid conviction can be obtained." It was argued that "[t]he privilege against self–incrimination was designed to protect the people precisely in situations such as this to prevent the use of governmental authority to compel witnesses to testify against themselves, where they might be prosecuted because of their alleged beliefs or associations."[63]

Noting that the film industry does business in California, the petitioners pointed out that the "Communist Party is a lawful political party in the state of California and electors of the State are free to affiliate with it." According to the law of California, "persons desiring to affiliate with that party may decline to publicly state whether they have or have not so affiliated."[64] The rehearing petition argued that Congress' action interfered with the political process of the state to conduct their elections. Petitioners noted that the "right to declare, or to decline to declare, political affiliation is no minor privilege."[65]

They further warned that "[t]he denial of certiorari in the cases here is a green light for the 'village tyrants' to pursue a course which recent history teaches us can have only disastrous results for our democratic institutions."[66] They feared that families "are now the prey of any governmental official who may with impunity pry into their private lives and subject them to the ostracism of the community with the stigma of disloyalty."[67] The petitioners predicted that, given "the uncertainty created by this court's action, the legal remedies afforded citizens against inroads into their liberties have become largely illusory."[68]

Many amicus briefs in the case called for review and "virtually every newspaper editor in the nation has assured the public that the questions of the Committee's power would be the subject of scrutiny by the Supreme Court of the United States."[69] Calling it the most significant issue to come before the Court in three decades, the petitioners repeated their "urgent request" for the Supreme Court to decide the controversy. They noted that "the conflicts between boards of regents and academic staffs over loyalty oaths rock campuses, as scientists in larger numbers leave their vocations in protest against political surveillance."[70]

The rehearing petition also addressed the international implications of the Supreme Court's failure to grant review, noting that these intrusive inquires "sanctioned by governmental agencies run afoul the international obligations solemnly undertaken by the Charter of the United Nations, of which the United States is a signatory."[71] In support of this assertion the petitioners cited Article 19 of the United Nations Declaration of Human Rights, passed on December 10, 1948, which provides that "[e]veryone has the right to freedom of opinion and expression. This right includes freedom to...impart information and ideas through any media."[72] Further, the Declaration of Human Rights also quite plainly stated "[e]veryone has right to peaceful assembly and association." The rehearing petition warned that the Supreme Court's failure to grant review "may be inexplicable to the peoples and the nations of the world and inconsistent with the positions taken by our representatives at home and abroad regarding universal respect for and observance of human rights."[73] The petitioners reasserted that the case was "ripe for review" and "no considerations…can outweigh the need for this Court to settle the constitutional question involved in these proceedings."[74] Without comment, the Supreme Court also declined the petition for rehearing.[75]

The House Committee on Un-American Activities was a source of deep personal irritation for Charles Houston because of its potential for government abuse. He was concerned that bringing the screen writers before Congress to answer questions about their political associations was nothing more than "a smear campaign to frighten the timid and drive all independence of thought from the screen."[76] Houston further explained that if the committee succeeded in controlling the content of movies "it will move on to radio, newspapers, and periodicals to books, to the Sunday pulpit, and even private conversations in the home."[77] Houston would insist that the courts would have to enter the fray to protect the freedom of association. He argued that "the courts have been the protection and refuge of the citizen against tyranny and usurpation by the legislature."[78]

Missed Opportunity

The Supreme Court's decision to affirm ruling of the Court of Appeals of the District of Columbia Circuit in the "Hollywood Ten" cases was a tragic decision for America. The Court's inaction made Congress bolder in its pursuit of alleged Communists and ushered in an intense period of First Amendment violations. It allowed politicians like Senator Joseph McCarthy to thrive in the "witch hunts" which followed the inquiries against Lawson and Trumbo and the rest of the Hollywood Ten in the decade after the Supreme Court declined review of the cases.[79] The real tragedy of this shameful of period of history is that so many lives were destroyed with so little justification. This important test case on the First Amendment and the legal theories it produced were the template for a host of rights which would be fought for in subsequent decades.

An analysis of the legal theories presented in the Hollywood Ten cases presents a mosaic of the personal liberties ideas that would ultimately dominate the "Warren Court" years.[80] By identifying the intersection between the First Amendment, the Fifth Amendment, and the right to privacy, Houston and his co-counsel identified the essence of what constitutes "fundamental freedom." As he had done in other collaborative litigation, Houston had combined legal theory and practical human need to develop a framework for building a safe haven for citizens. Although it would take many years for these rights to come to fruition, it was Houston's vision that would breathe full life into First Amendment freedom of association jurisprudence. He believed that the fact you disagree with someone's political beliefs "does not require either persecution or extermination."[81]

The Supreme Court set aside its responsibility to resolve this important issue when it passed up the opportunity to review the Hollywood Ten case. Perhaps the case came along at a time in history when the Court was unwilling to confront the obvious overreaching of Congress because of so-called "Cold War" concerns. Perhaps the civil rights issues working their way through the Supreme Court, largely at Houston's direction, created pressure on the Court such that it did not want to confront this additional "mega issue" at the same time.

Houston always encouraged activism and believed that the right to be a critic of the government was an essential American value. In the late 1940s he wrote: "What significance for us has the purge of Communists by the Federal Government?"[82] He always thought that one of the most "sacred rights in a democracy was the right to disagree."[83]

In later years, the Supreme Court would eventually extend more political protections to alleged Communists like Dalton Trumbo. There was still a cloud over Trumbo's career. Famed Hollywood movie actor Kirk Douglas would tell the story of how Trumbo won an Academy Award under an assumed name. Inspired by Trumbo's fight for freedom of association, Douglas risked his own career to support him. Douglas put Trumbo's name on the script for the movie *Spartacus* because he became angry that many people were using Trumbo to write but would leave his name off of scripts out of fear "because he was blacklisted."[84] Douglas believed that standing up for Trumbo in this manner helped break the blacklist.[85]

In the midst of the national controversy over Communism, another of Houston's famous acquaintances, and FBI target, became involved in a bitter debate over the United States' political role around the world. Paul Robeson, one of the world's most renowned singers and actors, made several public comments criticizing the United States and favorable to the Communist movement.[86] Houston and Robeson had occasionally corresponded with each other. In one letter, Houston wrote that he was unable to join Robeson for a lunch event in New York supporting an effort "to end government sponsored Jim Crow in Panama."[87]

When trouble broke out for Robeson, Charles Houston stood behind him. In a statement Houston, along with other black leaders, wrote in the press that although "many of us find ourselves in sharp disagreement" with public positions taken by Robeson, we are "united in affirming his inalienable right to speak and sing to all who wish to hear him."[88] Houston's work on behalf of the Hollywood Ten, although largely unnoticed, was his most historically significant work defending constitutional freedom of association under the First Amendment.

Endnotes

1. Office Memorandum, Federal Bureau of Investigation, Communist Infiltration-Motion Picture Industry (COMPIC) 6 (July 21, 1949).

2. Much of the material from this chapter is derived from my article: "Freedom of Association, the Communist Party, and the Hollywood Ten: The Forgotten First Amendment Legacy of Charles Hamilton Houston," 40 *McGeorge L. Rev.* 25, 26 (2009).

3. Ibid., p. 28.

4. Ibid., pp. 28–29.

5. Ibid.

6. "Lawyers Protest Raids on Radicals," *New York Times*, August 12, 1934, p. N1.

7. Robert K. Murray, *Red Scare: A Study of Hysteria, 1919–1920* 16 (Minneapolis: University of Minnesota Press 1955).

8. *See generally and compare*, Michael B. Hayes, "It's Now Persuasion, Not Coercion: Why Current Law on Labor Protest Violates 21st Century First Amendment Law," 47 *Hofstra L. Rev.* 526 (2019) (providing a thorough examination of free speech and labor union protest jurisprudence in the twentieth century).

9. Eric B. Easton, *Defending the Masses: A Progressive Lawyers Battle for Free Speech* 178 (Madison: University of Wisconsin Press 2018).

10. Kenneth Robert Janken, *White: The Biography of Walter White Mr. NAACP* 178 (New York: W.W. Norton 2003).

11. Harvard Sitkoff, *A New Deal for Blacks: The Emergence of Civil Rights as a National Issue, Volume 1: The Depression Decade* 149 (Oxford University Press 1978).

12. Julia Brown, *I Testify: My Years as an F.B.I. Undercover Agent* 11 (Western Island 1966).

13. *Lawson v. United States*, 176 F.2d 49 (D.C. Cir. 1949).

14. J. Edgar Hoover, *Masters of Deceit: The Story of Communism in America and How to Fight It* 70 (Holt, Reinhart & Co. 1958).

15. *See*, Curt Gentry, *J. Edgar Hoover: The Man and the Secrets* 80–81 (New York: W.W. Norton & Co. 1991).

16. Ibid.

17. Ibid.

18. Ibid.

19. Bruce Allen Murphy, *The Brandeis/Frankfurter Connection: The Secret Political Activities of Two Supreme Court Justices* 249 (Oxford University Press 1983).

20. Ibid.

21. Office Memorandum, Federal Bureau of Investigation, Communist Infiltration-Motion Picture Industry (COMPIC) 6 (July 21, 1949).

22. Ibid.

23. Ibid., p. 7.

24. Federal Bureau of Investigation report file number 100–662 Memphis, Tennessee, October 22, 1941, p. 2. NAACP summary BU file 61–3176.

25. Ibid., p. 79.

26. Ibid., pp. 79–80.

27. Ibid., p. 12.

28. Ibid., p. 79.

29. *Lawson v. United States*, 176 F.2d 49 (D.C. Cir. 1949).

30. Ibid.

31. Ibid., pp. 50–51.

32. "40 Film Folk Fly Here for Probe Protest," *Washington Post*, October 27, 1947, p. 1.

33. Ibid.

34. Ibid.

35. Ibid.

36. Ibid.

37. Ibid.

38. *Lawson v. United States*, 176 F.2d 49 (D.C. Cir. 1949).

39. Ibid.

40. Ibid.

41. Ibid.

42. Ibid.

43. Ibid.

44. Ibid.

45. Ibid.

46. Ibid.

47. Petition for Writ of Certiorari at 23–26, *Lawson*, 176 F.2d 49 (No. 248).

48. Ibid.

49. Ibid.

50. Ibid.

51. Ibid.

52. Ibid.

53. Ibid.

54. Ibid.

55. Ibid.

56. Ibid.

57. Brief for the United States in Opposition, *Lawson v. United States*, Nos. 248–249 (Oct. 1949).

58. Ibid.

59. Ibid.

60. Ibid.

61. Ibid.

62. Houston died April 22, 1950, after being confined to a hospital in Washington, D.C. He continued to consult in several legal matters right up until his death.

63. Petition for Rehearing, *Lawson v. United States*, Nos. 248–249 (Apr. 24, 1950).

64. Ibid.

65. Ibid.

66. Ibid.

67. Ibid.

68. Ibid.

69. Ibid.

70. Ibid.

71. Ibid.

72. Ibid.

73. Ibid.

74. Ibid.

75. *Lawson v. United States*, 339 U.S. 972 (1950) (Mem.); *Trumbo v. United States*, 339 U.S. 972 (1950) (Mem.). The rehearing was denied in May 1950. *See Lawson*, 339 U.S. 972; *Trumbo*, 339 U.S. 972.

76. Charles H. Houston, "The Highway," *Baltimore Afro-American*, November 1, 1947, p. 4.

77. Ibid.

78. Charles H. Houston, "The Highway," *Baltimore Afro-American*, November 29, 1947, p. 4.

79. See, David M. Oshinsky, *A Conspiracy So Immense: The World of Joe McCarthy* (New York: Free Press 1983).

80. *See*, Archibald Cox, *The Court and the Constitutions* (New York: Houghton-Miflin 1987).

81. Charles H. Houston, "The Highway," *Baltimore Afro-American*, April 12, 1947, p. 4.

82. Charles H. Houston, "The Highway," *Richmond Afro-American*, April 12, 1947, p. 4.

83. Charles H. Houston, "The Highway," *Baltimore Afro-American*, April 12, 1947, p. 4.

84. Kirk Douglas, *Climbing the Mountain: My Search for Meaning* 167 (New York: Simon and Schuster 1977).

85. Ibid.

86. *See generally*, Paul Robeson, *Here I Stand* 29–32 (New York: Beacon Press 1958).

87. Letter Robeson to Houston September 15, 1948, Moorland-Spingarn Research Center, Howard University Box 163-13 (Folder 1).

88. Martin Bauml Duberman, *Paul Robeson* 377 (New York: Knopf, 1988).

IX

Back to the Laboratory

Return to Maryland

As Maryland goes, so goes a large part of the nation.

—Charles H. Houston, Speech at Mount Vernon Methodist Church,
Baltimore, Maryland, January 1946

O f all the courts in which Charles Houston practiced law, the Maryland courts were his laboratory. He spent a great deal of time in Baltimore, Maryland's largest city. He married his first wife, Gladys Moran, in Baltimore in 1924.[1] He travelled to Baltimore by ferry as a child with his mother.[2] That ride included a trip to Harper's Ferry, Virginia, location of the John Brown raid, which his father described as "one of the great historical events in American history."[3] Although a native of Washington, D.C., Charles took many short drives and train trips to Maryland to do legal battle. In all, Houston was counsel in over a dozen cases in the Maryland trial and appellate courts.

He argued his first state appeal case in Maryland's highest court in *Murray v. Hurst*,[4] an estate matter which he won in 1932 with his co-counsel and cousin William Hastie assisting him with the brief.[5] He won his first civil rights case in Maryland when he triumphed in the *Pearson v. Murray* case in 1936.[6] He began a successful national campaign to equalize the salaries of colored teachers with their white counterparts in Maryland.[7] Houston operated with a high level of comfort in Maryland. He had many associates who corresponded with him about cases, and he enjoyed a great relationship with its nationally known *Afro-American Newspaper*, where he submitted a regular column.[8] During the 1940s, he was virtually a member of Maryland's Bar, being allowed to argue cases on the motion of local counsel, setting precedent after precedent in cases he used to test the limits of the Constitution's flexibility in extending

Office photo of Charles and William L. Houston, with Charles Jr. on the desk, in the mid-1940s.

COURTESY OF THE CHARLES H. HOUSTON, JR., FAMILY COLLECTION

civil rights. Maryland also had something that his native Washington, D.C., did not: "statehood" and a direct path to bring court challenges pursuant to the Fourteenth Amendment of the United States Constitution.

Since the District of Columbia was a federal territory and not a state, Houston could not provoke legal decisions that would apply to other parts of the country without the venue of the Maryland courts. His prior high-profile legal battles, fought while working closely with local lawyers, community groups, and churches on important civil rights issues, gave him a high level of credibility among the Maryland Bench and Bar. As the late Judge Harry A. Cole recalled, Charlie Houston told a group of young lawyers and law students in the 1940s to "commit yourself to excellence."[9] In 1977, Judge Cole became the first African American to sit on Maryland's highest court.[10] Cole remarked, Houston "was one of the most brilliant constitutional lawyers this country has ever produced...we sat at his feet."[11]

Baltimore also provided a convenient venue for litigation since the federal and state courthouses were located a short walk across the street from each other. Both were less than a one-mile taxicab ride from Baltimore's Pennsylvania Railroad Station and only about a one-hour train ride from the District of Columbia's Union Station. It became the perfect environment for the experimental work on the Constitution he was anxious to perform.

The Golf Course Cases

One of Houston's most aggressive challenges to public accommodations was the battle over the golf courses of Baltimore City. Maryland had a rather large middle-class community of black professionals who enjoyed golf but it was certainly considered a luxury for most people. There were those ready to sue the Baltimore City Department of Parks and Recreation to gain access to the city's several public courses.[12]

The story of the golf course cases begins with a group of black Baltimore professionals known as the Monumental Golf Club, which included several members of the Monumental Bar Association. "Monumental" was the name coined by both groups because of the numerous statues and monuments that were located throughout the city. The group included doctors, business persons and other prominent black Baltimoreans.[13] Like the battle over school desegregation that preceded it, the fight to desegregate the golf courses was long and bitter. Indeed, when black golfers first attempted to play golf on one of Baltimore's public courses, they had to have police protection from white protesters.[14]

The two most influential men behind the lawsuit were Arnett Murphy of the *Baltimore Afro-American* newspaper and William L. "Little Willie" Adams, a Baltimore businessman and alleged illegal numbers operator who loved golf and was willing to put up money for the legal fight to be able to play on any of Baltimore's public courses.[15] Adams frequently hosted former heavyweight boxing champion Joe Louis at Monumental golf events.[16] When Joe Louis came to Baltimore for golf, it would be front page news in the black press.[17] It was not simply the celebrity of the national hero coming to town that made attacking the segregated golf courses a priority for Monumental Golf Club members; like many white golfers, the club members had a true passion to excel and wanted to experience the game at the highest level. Adams himself had a "rabid enthusiasm for the game."[18] Adams not only played in Baltimore but travelled the country seeking a golfing challenge. He once went with Joe Lewis to California to play for 15 days, where he was also able to tee off with baseball legend Jackie Robinson.[19]

Not everyone was happy with pursuing the golf course cases. Baltimore NAACP leader Lillie Carrol Jackson rejected the case. She was not planning to use NAACP funds to focus on the golf course litigation, commenting, "if you fellows are wealthy enough to play golf together…you're wealthy enough to pay your lawyers yourself."[20] She did refer them to Charles Houston who had, by that time, returned to private practice in Washington, D.C.[21]

Adams took considerable pride, even decades later, that he had hired the great "Charlie Houston" to sue for his right to play golf on any public golf course.[22] Before the lawsuit, black golfers only had playing privileges on a nine-hole course known as Carroll Park in the southern part of Baltimore City, near the railroad freight lines.[23] By all measures, the Carroll Park course was inferior to the other courses owned by the city. It had greens made of sand rather than grass and it had no flags; only metal discs marked the holes.[24] There was no equipment for ball washing and no golf professional assigned to the course to provide instruction. During the early 1930s there were certain days when black golfers were given exclusive use at Carroll Park golf course.[25] The city's other courses were all eighteen holes, had longer fairways and were staffed with a golf professional to provide help for the players.[26]

One of the three courses reserved for white players was Mount Pleasant Golf Course, situated in the northeast section of the city. The 18-hole course with its "attractive surrounding landscape" occupied about 140 acres of ground and was more than 6,000 yards in length.[27] "Another 18-hole golf course maintained by the City was in Clifton Park."[28] This large tract of several hundred acres of land was originally the country estate of philanthropist Johns Hopkins, who made a gift of the land to the city.[29] Hopkins had earlier founded a prestigious university and hospital in downtown Baltimore.[30] Yet "another 18-hole golf course known as Hillsdale" was located in Forest Park in the northwest part of the city.[31] In 1942, in the case of *Durkee v. Murphy*,[32] "a Negro golfer brought a mandamus suit to require the Board of Park Commissioners to permit him to play on any of the three City golf courses reserved for white persons."[33] The golfers won at trial, but the case was reversed for errors in procedure on appeal.[34] In the opinion it was stated that for constitutional purposes, "golf should not be treated as a mere incident of recreational facilities, but a facility in itself from which Negroes cannot be excluded without having other substantially equal provision made for them." It was, however, further pointed out that it was "lawful and proper, in view of the general Maryland policy of segregation for the Board to provide separate golf courses for Negros and white persons, but if so the facilities for the colored race must be substantially equal to those afforded other classes."[35] It would still take almost six years for the Colored golfers to gain access.

The eighteen-hole city courses each had turf greens, and longer fairways. They also had "two alternating tees for each hole, whereas the Carroll Park course had [only] one."[36] The evidence showed "that of the rounds played on the four courses, 90 percent are by white players, 10 [percent] by Negro players."[37]

"The board apparently recognized the inadequacy of the Carroll Park golf course and, after what appears to have been an informal understanding with the Association of Colored Golfers who frequently used Carroll Park, the board agreed that substantial improvement would be made in the course and that until this was done Negro players would be permitted to use one or more of the other city courses." However, those arrangements were not suitable, and another suit had to be filed.[38]

The trial evidence in the new case showed that the courses for white patrons "has an adequate club house with accommodations for the two sexes."[39] "The other city courses had a golf professional but, while appointed by the board, the compensation is entirely from the patronage of those who use the courses."[40] "Bordered by an active industrial branch of the B. and O. Railroad and surrounded by commerce and industry rather than in a suburban or country district[, the Carroll Park course] had little attraction from the landscape point of view.[41] The land, while not completely level, has a comparatively uniform terrain."[42]

In its opinion finally granting access to the other Baltimore City courses, the Federal court pointed out, "[w]hile a beginner at golf might be satisfied with a 9-hole course located in a surrounding industrial section, the reasonably experienced golfer requires, for enjoyment of the game, conditions of play which contribute in other ways."[43] The Monumental members argued they had a personal constitutional right to substantially equal facilities. Indeed, during argument of the case Charles Houston suggested if Carroll Park was a separate but equal golf course he offered an exchange for the Mount Pleasant Golf Course, "a course so well appointed and maintained that the Professional Golf Association selected it to host professional tournaments."[44] The case was the first in the country where black Americans sued a governmental entity for equal recreational facilities.[45]

Using an analogy inspired by the *Plessy* case, the federal judge explained, "the superiority of the white golf courses over that at Carroll Park is roughly comparable, in the field of railroad transportation, to that of the Pullman car with the day coach."[46] The Baltimore City case later became helpful for the desegregation of public courses throughout the country.[47]

The Librarian Case

In another celebrated Charles Houston Maryland case, Louise Kerr, a young African American woman, was refused admission to a library training class conducted by the Enoch Pratt Free Library of Baltimore City. The program was to prepare persons for staff positions in the Central Library and its branches.[48] This case was particularly annoying to Houston. As one scholar noted "[t]o him it was clear that America was engaging in a tragic and depressing waste of human talent and squandering the genius of millions of citizens, solely because of race."[49]

In his court papers he argued "the library is performing a governmental function and that [Kerr] was rejected in conformity with the uniform policy of the library corporation to exclude all persons of the colored race from the training school." This action, done on behalf of the state of Maryland, deprived Kerr of the equal protection of the laws.[50] She asked for damages and a permanent injunction prohibiting the refusal of her application, and for a declaratory judgment to establish her right to have her application considered without discrimination because of her race and color.[51] Adding a new component to the lawsuit, her father became a plaintiff in the suit as a taxpayer. He argued that "if it be held that the library corporation is a private body not bound by the constitutional restraint upon state action, the Mayor and City Council of Baltimore be enjoined from making contributions to the support of the Library."[52]

The defendants in the suit were the library corporation, nine citizens of Baltimore who constitute its board of trustees, the librarian and the mayor and city council of Baltimore.[53] Each argued that the Library is a private corporation, controlled and managed by the board of trustees, and does not perform any public function as a representative of the state.[54] The federal district judge sustained all of the defenses and dismissed the suit.[55]

The training course was established by the library in 1928, primarily to prepare persons for the position of library assistant on the library staff.[56] There was no other training school for librarians in the state supported by public funds. Applicants were required to take a competitive entrance examination which, in view of the large number of applications for each class, was limited to fifteen or twenty persons who were selected by the director of the library and his assistants.[57] Members of the class were paid $50 monthly during training, since the practical work which they performed was equivalent to part-time employment. In return for the training given, the applicant was expected to work on the staff one year after graduation, provided a position was offered.[58] All competent graduates had been in fact appointed to the staff as library assistants during the prior two years before Louise Kerr's application.[59] During the existence of the school, more than two hundred applications have been received from Negroes.[60] All of them had been rejected.

Miss Kerr was a native and resident of Baltimore City, twenty-seven years of age. [61] She graduated with high averages from the public high schools of Baltimore, from a public teachers' training school in Baltimore, had taken courses for three summers at the University of Pennsylvania, and had taught in the elementary public schools of the City.[62] The court recognized that, "there can be no doubt that the applicant was excluded from the school because of her race."

She was refused consideration because the Training School is closed to Negroes, and it is closed to Negroes because, in the judgment of the Board, they are unfit to serve in predominantly white neighborhoods.[63]

The Federal appellate court concluded, the Library is an instrumentality of the State of Maryland.[64] It explained "if the state legislature should now set up and maintain a public library and should entrust its operation to a self-perpetuating board of trustees and authorize it to exclude Negroes from its benefits, the act would be unconstitutional."[65] A year later Kerr would integrate, without incident, the evening graduate school at the private Catholic-affiliated Loyola College of Maryland.[66] At the 100-year anniversary of the Pratt Library in 1986, Ms. Kerr-Hines was honored by the institution for her courage in filing suit with Charles Houston.[67]

The Leon Norris Art School Case

Leon A. Norris, a young Negro resident of Baltimore City and citizen of the state of Maryland, made application on September 11, 1946, to become a student at the Maryland Institute for the Promotion of the Mechanic Arts. At the time, the 32-year-old army veteran sought to have a career as a high school art teacher.[68] A native of West Baltimore, where the school was located, Norris was also a taxpayer. The institute declined his application on the ground that for fifty years past it had maintained a consistent policy and practice of admitting only white persons as students.[69] Indeed, the institute's registrar would not even see Norris when he visited the school.[70]

Norris was referred to a Jewish Baltimore attorney named Fred Weisgal by the local branch of the Maryland American Civil Liberties Union (ACLU), where he regularly had taken mostly pro bono (uncompensated) cases. Norris wanted to sue. Upon meeting Norris, he told Weisgal, "[m]y skin didn't prevent me from fighting for my country with a combat engineer unit in the South Pacific...now I want to study and teach art.... [T]he Maryland Institute is the only place I can get what I need."[71]

Wiesgal, a University of Baltimore law graduate, aware of his inexperience, sought the help of Charles Houston. He had come to admire Houston by watching his success on other discrimination cases, particularly the successful challenge to the Pratt Library on behalf of Louise Kerr. Weisgal travelled to Houston's D.C. office to make the request. He recalled Houston as a "brilliant man...[with] the unique ability to reach the heart of a problem, quickly and efficiently."[72] Houston agreed to become "counsel of record" and was able to secure some financial support from the local chapter of the NAACP for the case.[73] Houston was encouraged by the eagerness of Weisgal. He wanted to guarantee that he would remain part of the case until its conclusion. He wrote to the local NAACP chapter and insisted that he would only sign the complaint if Weisgal was designated as co-counsel.[74] The two men worked long hours on the case for months and became good friends as they prepared for trial. Weisgal remarked of Houston "that he was strong and honest and his love for mankind amazed me."[75]

Houston was concerned that if the Maryland Institute were able to discriminate and still receive public funds from the city and state government, they would have a "new device" for discrimination and thus would "abandon their public service and contract with private institutions serving whites only."[76]

The court rejected Norris's claim. Judge Chesnutt reasoned:

> Counsel for the plaintiff advances a new and far-reaching proposition not within the principle of the Pratt Library case. The contention is that whenever the State or Baltimore City as a municipal agency of the State, advances moneys to a private corporation of an educational nature in an appreciably substantial amount which thereby becomes mingled with other general funds of the institution, that action of the institution or City thereby becomes State action within the scope of the 14th Amendment. No authority is cited for this proposition and I know of none.[77]

Houston was very disappointed with the federal court's decision in the Maryland Institute case, complaining, "this country needs more education for whites and blacks instead of less."[78] Nonetheless, a decision had to be made whether to appeal. Houston suggested to Weisgal that the time for appeal "is not right." Ironically, on the day these two lawyers were trying to discuss the future of the discrimination case, they suffered their own episode of personal discrimination. They could not eat together in any restaurant in downtown Baltimore so they had to eat at the Baltimore train station.[79] Weisgal would lament how one of the nation's greatest constitutional lawyers could be treated in such a manner; "it burned me up" he said.[80] Houston explained to Weisgal the long-term plan and assured him the case was not a total loss: "the lower court cases provide an opportunity to test arguments and to gain insight to judges' thinking so that strategies could be developed for a 'big' case later."[81] Such cases served as a laboratory for future legal work. It was Charles Houston's belief that such hard court fights would mean that his son Charles Jr. would not have to be "subjected to the indignities which he was forced to suffer."[82]

Melvin Sykes, a Harvard law student at the time who worked in Weisgal office during the summer, helped prepare the *Norris* case. He remembered his time with Charles Houston fondly. He described the legendary attorney as extremely bright and pleasant with an understated sense of humor.[83] "I was proud to have been a gofer for him."[84] Influenced by Houston's example, Sykes had a long, outstanding career as one of Maryland's greatest appellate litigators.[85]

Weisgal would become one of the most noteworthy lawyers of his time, arguing several United States Supreme Court cases on civil liberties and defendant's rights.[86] He became active in the national movement to support the freedom riders demonstrating in the Deep South[87] and represented Vietnam War protesters known as the "Catonsville Nine."[88] In 1969, Weisgal would move his family to Israel to become a senior legal adviser to its attorney general.[89] Weisgal would comment during the 1960s "I owe to [Charles Houston] more than to any man, my love for the law."[90]

Chissell and the Highway Through Our Home

In 1948, Louis Rivers of the 1200 block of McCullough Street in Baltimore was struck and killed by a speeding taxi while crossing the street near his home in the middle of the day.[91] This was no ordinary accident. It was the touchstone for a mass meeting at Baltimore's Trinity Baptist Church. The guest speaker was Charles Houston. In his remarks he expressed concerns that action taken by Baltimore officials to convert two-way streets to one-way streets through the heart of the city's largest black middle-class community. Troubled that the city's plan would create a "deathway," the NAACP pointed out "that there are numerous schools on McCullough St., and Druid Hill Ave."[92] "The general feeling in the community is that these high-speed express-ways were designed for colored areas without any thought that the colored people themselves would resent and make an effort to protect themselves."[93]

The plaintiffs sued as citizens, residents and taxpayers who lived, and owned properties, on Druid Hill Avenue or McCulloh Street.[94] Making Druid Hill Avenue and McCulloh Street one-way streets was part of the general plan to improve traffic conditions for people driving from the suburbs into the city. The general plan had been carried out previously as to St. Paul and Calvert Streets and subsequently as to Charles and Cathedral Streets and Maryland Avenue.[95] An essential of the general plan and of the particular features mentioned was a substitution by Baltimore Transit Company of busses for street cars and changes in its routes.[96] To make Druid Hill Avenue and McCulloh Street more accessible for motor vehicle through traffic it was also deemed necessary to construct a "park boulevard" through the western edge of Druid Hill Park, running along Auchentoroly Terrace and also connecting Druid Hill Avenue and McCulloh Street with Reisterstown Road and Liberty Heights Avenue.[97]

In May 1945, Mr. Nathan L. Smith, then the city's chief engineer, made a report on traffic conditions and "present and post-war highway requirements," in which he suggested making Druid Hill Avenue and McCulloh Street one-way streets and construction of the Auchentoroly cut-off.[98] The Baltimore highway matter was a particular irritation to Charles Houston. The plaintiffs were the very middle-class black community members who had assisted him for years when he had made other assaults on discriminatory practices in the city. The change in the traffic patterns tore right through the heart of the neighborhood of Thurgood Marshall, NAACP President Lillie Carroll Jackson, and employees and leadership of the *Baltimore Afro-American* newspaper owners who had given him a media voice. Houston took the matter very personally. He assembled a case worthy of the issue of first impression he was attempting to create.

In what can be fairly characterized as the first environmental racism civil case in the nation, Houston would assemble an impressive group of engineers and other experts to explain how the city's procedures would unjustly destroy this important urban community. Press coverage of the case reported Houston's arguments that the "new driving one-way streets would create hazards to school children, depreciate property values, and worsen living conditions in the area."[99] One witness testified that on her street that had been already changed to one way "heavy trucks rumbling along…have caused the plaster in her home to crack."[100] Other witnesses said the increased traffic made it "impossible to sleep."[101] Some testified about the increase in dust, dirt and gasoline fumes.[102] Houston noted that about 1,000 homes in the black community would be effected on the two streets scheduled for the change.[103]

Noting the lack of recreational facilities in the area, Charles Houston "alleged that children now were required to play on the sidewalks."[104] Nine schools for the Negro community nearby "having a total enrollment of about 4,100 are located on or within two blocks of the two street arteries and many of the children have to cross the two streets."[105] To add insult to injury, before the traffic plan was announced, the property tax assessments for the Druid Hill neighborhood were increased and time had expired to complain about the tax increase.[106]

As the capstone of his attack on the process for obtaining approval of the highway, Houston called to the witness stand Baltimore's powerful mayor Thomas D'Alessandro.[107] A popular politician, he was a former congressman and father of six children from Baltimore's political stronghold known as Little

Italy.[108] Part of his rich political legacy was a son who would follow him as mayor of Baltimore and his youngest daughter, who decades later became the first woman to serve as Speaker of the United States House of Representatives, Nancy D'Alessandro Pelosi.[109] The mayor would be subject to Houston's most rigorous questioning during the trial. At one point, Mayor D'Alessandro would snap back during questioning saying, "I'm not that good Mr. Houston, for you to talk for a half hour and then answer your questions."[110]

The trial, which included many expert witnesses, testimony of neighbors and public officials was unsuccessful for the community. The trial court rejected Houston's claims, and Maryland's highest court did the same. In the appellate opinion, the court said that it did not have the legal authority to overturn the city's actions. "Courts are…without legal right or actual capacity to give effectual relief by any such usurpation of power."[111] The significance of the loss of the case would not resonate until decades later, when the neighborhood, scarred by the freeway, would lead to the loss in property value and produce the poverty that Charles Houston predicted. In 2015 some of the Druid Hill neighborhood would go up in flames as part of the unrest generated by the death of Freddie Grey while in police custody.[112]

Endnotes

1. Patricia Sullivan, *Lift Every Voice: The NAACP and the Making of the Civil Rights Movement* 160 (New York: The New Press 2009).

2. William L. Houston to Charles H. Houston, August 2, 1910, Box 19 William LePre Houston Family Papers, Manuscripts Division, Library of Congress.

3. Ibid.

4. *Murray v. Hurst*, 163 A. 183 (Md. 1932).

5. Ibid.

6. 182 A. 590 (Md. 1936).

7. John A. Kirk, "The NAACP Campaign for Teacher's Salary Equalization: African American Women Educators and the Civil Rights Struggle," *The Journal of African American History*, Vol. 94, No. 4 (Fall 2009) pp. 529–552.

8. During the late 1940s Charles Houston published columns in the *Baltimore Afro-American* newspaper under several titles including, "Our Civil Rights," The Highway" and "Along the Highway." His last offering appears to have been on August 13, 1949, where in a somewhat prophetic statement he wrote "Only by integrating scientific advancement with our ideas of justice can law remain a part of the living fiber of our civilization." Charles H. Houston, "Our Civil Rights," *Baltimore Afro-American*, August 13, 1949, p. 4.

9. Theodore W. Hendricks, "The Long Hard Road of Judge Cole," *Baltimore Sun*, December 12, 1977, p. B1.

10. Ibid.

11. Ibid.

12. "Players Under Guard as Park Course Opens," *Baltimore Afro-American*, September 8, 1934, p. 19.

13. Ibid.

14. Ibid.

15. "'Little Willie 'Taken in Raid," *Baltimore Afro-American*, November 26, 1949, p. A19.

16. Art Carter, "Champion Louis Thrills Baltimore Fans," *Baltimore Afro-American*, January 20, 1940, p. 20.

17. Ibid.

18. Mark R. Cheshire, *They Call Me Little Willie: The Life Story of William L. Adams* 90 (Ellison's Books 2016).

19. Ibid., p. 92.

20. Ibid., p. 89.

21. Ibid.

22. Ibid., pp. 87–88.

23. José Felipé Anderson, "Tiger Proves Meaning of Equal Access," *Baltimore Sun*, August 30, 2000, p. A21.

24. Ibid.

25. Ibid.

26. Ibid.

27. Ibid.

28. *Law v. Mayor and City Council of Baltimore*, 78 F. Supp. 346 (D. Md. 1948).

29. José Felipé Anderson, "Tiger Proves Meaning of Equal Access," *Baltimore Sun*, August 30, 2000, p. A21.

30. Ibid.

31. *Law v. Mayor and City Council of Baltimore*, 78 F. Supp. 346 (D. Md. 1948).

32. *Durkee et al. v. Murphy*, 29 A.2d 253, 255 (Md. 1943).

33. *Law v. Mayor and City Council of Baltimore*, 78 F. Supp. 346 (D. Md. 1948).

34. Ibid.

35. Ibid.

36. Ibid.

37. Ibid.

38. Ibid.

39. Ibid.

40. Ibid.

41. Ibid.

42. Ibid.

43. Ibid.

44. Mark R. Cheshire, *They Call Me Little Willie*, p. 88.

45. Ibid., p. 89.

46. *Law v. Mayor and City Council of Baltimore*, p. 349.

47. "Clevelanders Win Golf Suit," *Baltimore Afro-American*, February 4, 1950, p. 6.

48. *Kerr v. Enoch Pratt Free Library*, 149 F. 2d 211 (4th Cir. 1945).

49. Walter J. Leonard, "Charles Hamilton Houston and the Search for a Just Society," 22 *N.C. Cent. L.J.* 1,10 (1996).

50. *Kerr v. Enoch Pratt Free Library*, 149 F.2d 212 (4th Cir. 1945).

51. Ibid.

52. Ibid.

53. Ibid.

54. Ibid.

55. Ibid.

56.

57. Ibid.

58. Ibid.

59. Ibid.

60. Ibid.

61. Ibid.

62. Ibid.

63. Ibid.

64. Ibid.

65. Ibid.

66. Letter to the Editor, "Ed Young," *Baltimore Sun*, January 12, 1983, p. A8

67. Phillip Davis, "Pratt Honors Two Who Helped Knock Down Hiring Barrier," *Baltimore Sun*, March 10, 1986, p. 1D.

68. Barbara Mills, "*...And Justice for All*": *The Double Life of Fred Weisgal, Attorney & Musician* 71 (Baltimore: American Literary Press, Inc., 2000).

69. Ibid.

70. Ibid.

71. Ibid., p. 71.

72. Ibid.

73. Ibid.

74. Charles H. Houston to Robert L. Carter, March 26, 1947, NAACP Papers, Manuscripts Division, Library of Congress (Charles Houston making it clear, "I will not go into the case without Weisgal.)"

75. Ibid., p. 73.

76. Charles H. Houston, "Along the Highway," *Baltimore Afro-American*, July 17, 1948, p. 4.

77. *Norris v. Mayor and City Council of Baltimore et al.*, 76 F. Supp. 451 (Md. 1948).

78. Charles H. Houston, "Along the Highway," *Baltimore Afro-American*, July 17, 1948, p. 4.

79. Barbara Mills, '*...And Justice for All*,' p. 75.

80. Ibid.

81. Ibid.

82. Ibid.

83. Melvin Sykes, Author's Interview, March 12, 2009, Baltimore, Maryland.

84. C. Fraser Smith, *Here Lies Jim Crow: Civil Rights in Maryland* 244 (Baltimore: Johns Hopkins Press 2008).

85. Frederick N. Rasmussen, "Melvin J. Sykes, Attorney Who Left Mark on State Law and Generation of Young Lawyers," *Baltimore Sun*, May 25, 2017.

86. Obituary, Fred E. Weisgal, "Civil Rights Attorney, Israel Official, and Jazz Musician, Dies," *The Baltimore Sun*, June 18, 1991, p. 3D.

87. "Weisgal Seeks Johnson's Help," *Baltimore Sun*, June 20, 1964, p. 9.

88. Theodore W. Hendricks, "Illegal War Defense Plea Is Ruled Out," April 11, 1968, p. C24.

89. Fred E. Weisgal, Obituary, *Baltimore Sun*, p. 3D.

90. Barbara Mills, '...*And Justice for All*,' p. 73.

91. "Houston to Speak Against Proposal," *Baltimore Afro-American*, December 4, 1948, p. 1.

92. Ibid.

93. Ibid.

94. *Chissell v. Mayor and City Council of Baltimore*, 69 A.2d. 53, 55 (Md. 1949).

95. Ibid.

96. Ibid.

97. Ibid.

98. Ibid.

99. "One Way Street Conditions Are Called "Very Dangerous" *Baltimore Sun*, December 22, 1948, p. 9.

100. Ibid.

101. Ibid.

102. Ibid.

103. "Court Asked to Halt One-Way Plan for McCulloh, Druid Hill," *Baltimore Sun*, June 12, 1948, p. 4.

104. Ibid.

105. Ibid.

106. Ibid.

107. C. Fraser Smith, *Here Lies Jim Crow: Civil Rights in Maryland* 182 (Baltimore: Johns Hopkins Press 2008).

108. Colin Campbell, "The D'Alesandros: A Baltimore Political Powerhouse that Gave Us Two Mayors and House Speaker Nancy Pelosi," *Baltimore Sun*, October 20, 2019.

109. Ibid.

110. Stenographic Record, In the Circuit Court No. 2 of Baltimore City, *R. Garland Chissell, et al. v. The Mayor and City Council of Baltimore*, December 21, 1948, pp. 183–184.

111. *Chissell v. Mayor and City Council of Baltimore*, 69 A.2d. 53, 55 (Md. 1949).

112. Alec Mac Gillis, "The Tragedy of Baltimore," *New York Times*, (Feature) March 12, 2019.

Unfinished Business

The Final Days of Charles Hamilton Houston

Some of us have made up our minds we are willing to pay whatever price is necessary to make democracy work. If the result is to wipe out segregation and discrimination and set both white and black men free the price will be small.

— Charles H. Houston, "The Highway," *Baltimore Afro-American*,
June 12, 1948

I n the midst of all the legal battles during the late 1940s, Charles Houston had only a few opportunities to enjoy social activities. On one such occasion, he entertained famed jazz musician and composer Eubie Blake, who had become a national sensation with songs like "I'm Just Wild About Harry."[1] In appreciation, Blake wrote on January 28, 1949: "I just wanted to thank you for everything & all the kindness & help you gave my partner and me when I was in your city. Please give my respects to your family, and please if you and your family are ever in New York look me up and I will try my best to make it pleasant for you."[2] In the midst of these rare recreational outings, the battle against race discrimination raged on.

Even as progress was being made on many civil rights fronts, Houston pressed to address new discrimination challenges. He was concerned about an emerging mode of popular transportation, passenger air travel. He had worked on issues regarding common carriers like railroads and buses his entire career. The thought that the airports would take on permanent "Jim Crow" practices was something that he could not accept.[3] Houston commented, "[t]he only colored person in uniform around the airport are porters and 'sky-caps' hustling the passenger's luggage."[4] He also expressed concern that what he reasonably expected to be a lucrative and rewarding new industry had already began to exclude black pilots, as the military provided most airport-related training. Discrimination in the military had already placed blacks well behind their white counterparts in competing for skilled jobs. "The commercial pilots of the 20s were the Air Corps veterans of World War I,"[5] Houston proclaimed. "The latest developments in radar, electronics, navigation, aviation, metallurgics, [and] chemistry...are offered in the armed forces.... The question is how much of this training will our draftees and enlistees get?"[6]

Concessionaires at what is now known as Reagan National Airport on the Virginia/DC border, began excluding black patrons from the main cafeteria in the late 1940s. Houston argued that colored patrons should not be compelled to eat food from a "'hole in the wall' while it serves white patrons in an air conditioned dining room on the Terrace overlooking the landing field.'"[7] Houston further explained, "[f]ood is food regardless of where one has to eat it. Dining room food served from the kitchen will turn one's stomach from humiliation."[8]

The opportunity to challenge airport "Jim Crow" would come in a very personal way on September 9, 1948. Charlie Houston's longtime friend Dr. Sadie T. M. Alexander, a Philadelphia lawyer and member of the President's Committee on Civil Rights, was travelling through D.C.'s National Airport. Alexander was told that she would have to take the glass of milk she had purchased from the concessionaire's fountain counter and "drink it in the lobby, the ladies' room, or some other place."[9] Sadie's husband, another Philadelphia attorney, Raymond Pace Alexander, was a Harvard school mate of Charles Houston. The lawyer couple had a long friendship with Houston going back to his first marriage.[10] Charles Houston was particularly outraged regarding the airport food accommodations "because colored people had been served at the airport soda fountain as long as I can remember until this insult was offered to Dr. Alexander."[11]

Houston's firm filed suit against National Airport in late 1948 on behalf of Dr. Alexander and two other plaintiffs. January 5, 1949, the *Washington Post* reported that the airport had decided to end discrimination in its dining rooms.[12] Judge Albert V. Bryan held valid the order of the Civil Aeronautics Administration "banning segregation in airports dining rooms."[13] The change in the airport policy change was also assisted by a letter written by Mrs. Alexander to President Truman. She expressed to him that she did not believe, "the National Airport has the right to discriminate between interstate passengers on the ground of color."[14] She requested an opinion of the United States Attorney General Tom Clark on the matter. Ms. Alexander did not want money damages but wanted the racist practice ended. She explained, "I dislike legal action because our enemies abroad make capital out of court cases."[15] Acting on orders from the White House, the airport regulations were amended to read: "Operations of all facilities in the Washington National Airport shall be rendered without discrimination or segregation, regardless of race or color, or creed."[16]

Charles Houston indicated that his firm might be willing to drop the lawsuit if the segregation was actually banned at the airport, but he "would have to get the consent of his clients before taking such action."[17] Dr. Sadie Alexander dropped her suit, but one of the other plaintiffs, District of Columbia school teacher Helen Nash, with the assistance of different lawyers, filed a case in the Virginia federal court for damages.[18] Ms. Nash was partially successful.[19] However, even with this victory at the airport, more trouble was still looming, and more work needed to be done. Charles Houston started to feel his time was getting short.

As had been the case throughout his career, he pushed himself relentlessly to the end of the decade as his health began to fail. He had often suffered periods of fatigue from his hard driving style, but his weakened condition now required him to stop all work for periods of time until he could recover his strength. Thurgood Marshall was so concerned about his mentor's condition that he made an offer of assistance to the Houston law firm when informed Charlie was unable to work. On November 8, 1949, Thurgood wrote from the New York offices of the NAACP to Houston's law partner Joseph Waddy, that he wanted to make some "definite arrangements" to help handle some of the case load.[20] He made clear his commitment, "[t]he important thing is that Charlie not lose any money as a result of his illness and you can call on me to work with you on any case which you and Charlie have been handling and my services will be without charge."[21] So passionate was Marshall's concern, that he made clear help for "Charlie" should not be limited to cases the firm was handling for the NAACP. Indeed, Marshall explained, "[t]his goes not only for the school cases but any other case you think I can handle."[22]

The unfinished work of grade school educational inequality consumed Houston during this time of his most serious illness. His long-held sensitivity to the practice of placing inferior infrastructure near black communities and their schools resulted in additional battles. When Charles was a member of the

District of Columbia School Board in the 1930s, he complained about plans to put a junk yard near a Negro school, pointing out that the noise and trash would affect the quality of the students' education.[23] He felt his attack on Jim Crow education needed to accelerate if he was going to personally participate in its demise in the courts.

During the final decade of Charles Houston's life, labor cases, housing discrimination, military integration and the First Amendment activity had taken some of the focus away from the schools. Accordingly, the enemies of integrated education had continued to undermine the progress of some of Houston's earlier work. One of the great adversaries against integration efforts in higher education was Houston's old nemesis, University of Maryland's President Harry Clifton "Curly" Byrd. Byrd, had been named University president shortly after Raymond Pearson's embarrassing display on the witness stand when cross-examined by Houston in 1935 during the trial of the *Murray v. Pearson* case.

Byrd, like President Pearson before him, was a staunch segregationist. Born in Crisfield on Maryland's Eastern Shore, he was well acquainted and quite comfortable with segregation.[24] The Eastern Shore had been the site of much racial unrest and lynching, and a black population lived under the consequences of that regime for centuries.[25] The scars of its history extended racial biases well into the 1900s. It was out of this race-conscious culture that Byrd was nurtured. Houston was well aware of the Maryland's Eastern Shore history and once call it "as backward as the deep south."[26]

Byrd became a sports star as a student at the University of Maryland and later its football coach.[27] His action appealing the original court order desegregating its law school was consistent with Byrd's own personal segregationist philosophy.[28] As he made clear in the mid-1930s, "[w]e are going to battle the *Murray* case right down to the last ditch. Of course, your respect for the decision of the Court and all that it implies is fine, but the fact nevertheless remains that we cannot afford to have Negroes enter the University of Maryland. Perhaps I shall have to go to jail, but I think we have got to keep the Negroes out."[29]

Byrd was a leader in organizing the so-called "Southern Compact," a somewhat ingenious yet racist strategy to stem the tide of black students attempting to enter Southern graduate schools.[30] The compact would permit Southern states to pool resources to create graduate schools where black students could be sent to if they wanted professional education. The strategy was designed to keep Southern campuses "all white." President Byrd was attempting to stop the expansion of integration to other parts of all Southern universities. This confrontation with the University of Maryland continued the hostility between its President Byrd and Charles Houston which had begun after the *Murray* case. At that time President Byrd suggested in his legal briefs to the Maryland Supreme Court that if black students ever came to the College Park campus, it would make white women withdraw from attending.[31]

The University of Maryland and Byrd's discriminatory practices would once again become an aggravation to Charles Houston almost 15 years after he won the *Murray* case and his precedent-setting Supreme Court decision ten years before in *Gaines v. Missouri*.[32]

In fall of 1948, Byrd announced that because it would be "disastrous to have [Negroes] at College Park" he would implement a plan for what he described as "controlled segregation,"[33] providing few details about exactly what that term meant. NAACP leader Walter White had suspected President Byrd made some sort of deal with the Maryland legislature, that in exchange for some financial considerations in the state budget, he would keep Negro enrollment from expanding.[34] The fight against the admission of a Negro student to the graduate school at the university's flagship campus may have been an example of what President Byrd had in mind.

An ex-army officer from Salisbury, Maryland, named Wilmore B. Leonard was attempting to register in a graduate chemistry program.[35] He served with the famed Tuskegee Airmen of the 332nd Squadron during World War II and had been a school teacher.[36] He was heralded as a leader among the Tuskegee air corps unit during his service in Europe.[37] He was accepted to the university but when he showed up for classes he was refused admittance.[38] In July 1947, prior to his coming to campus to register, he had received a phone call from the director of admissions, E. F. Long, ordering him to "surrender his admission card." It had even been reported that a university official personally drove to Salisbury to get the admission card from Leonard after learning he was a Negro.[39]

Charles Houston, angered by this behavior, personally accompanied Leonard to the university at the College Park campus, where they were directed to Dean C.R. Appleman's office.[40] Dean Appleman explained that Leonard had only been admitted on a "provisional" basis and would not be permitted to register.[41] He was told that he had been sent a letter to that effect, questioning whether he had a "marginal" academic record in undergraduate school.[42] Although Leonard had not received that letter, according to Charles Houston, Dean Appleman "conveniently" had a carbon copy of the letter available on his desk when Leonard arrived on campus.[43]

Houston inquired about the process to determine if Leonard's credentials were adequate and was told that Dr. Nathan L. Drake of the Chemistry Department would usually review the transcripts to determine if the applicant's course work was sufficient.[44] Houston demanded that Dr. Drake make such a determination for Leonard that very day. That request was refused, and Houston was advised that it would be "useless."[45] Leonard and Houston were also told that if there were any course deficiencies he would not be able to make them up in the undergraduate school "because of crowded conditions."[46]

Interestingly, like the case of Donald Murray almost thirteen years before, it was the university officials and not the students who voiced major objections to Leonard's admission.[47] "Students at the university had already spoken out on the Leonard case, saying members of any minority group will be welcome on campus... [t]here was no untoward comment as Leonard and the attorney made their way across campus and students gave directions and assistance without a blink of the eye."[48] In his November 27, 1947, column in the *Baltimore Afro-American*, Charles Houston wrote "Dean Appleman was telling Wilmore B. Leonard, a World War II veteran, all the reasons, except one, why he could not admit him to the University of Maryland for graduate work in Chemistry. The reason he avoided because he did not want to expose the university to a lawsuit was that Leonard's skin was too dark for the lily-white campus of the State University."[49]

Houston revealed that the dean suggested Leonard would be "happier at a northern school."[50] Houston responded that the dean's position was "behind the times and reflected views of another day."[51] He pointed out that there were twenty colored students enrolled at the university's law school in downtown Baltimore in the prior academic year and "apparently nobody was unhappy."[52] Houston noted that "every student he came in contact with was courteous and cooperative."[53] He concluded his critique of university officials by saying "It is too bad the University officials were not drafted in the last war and sent to the far corners of the earth. Perhaps they could see farther than their noses."[54]

Leonard was never admitted to the graduate school at the College Park campus nor was a lawsuit filed on his behalf. The university responded that his undergraduate grade average at Hampton University was slightly below what was need to be admitted.[55] Soon after this sad episode in the desegregation battle, Leonard enrolled in dental school at Howard University. He would have a distinguished career and retire from the dental school faculty at Howard.[56]

McCready and the Professional School Student Cases

The Leonard rejection from College Park must have been extremely disappointing to Charles Houston. It strengthened his resolve to challenge the university's attempts to limit access to all University of Maryland departments that he had been planning since his victory in *Pearson v. Murray*.[57] Calling upon his former client Donald Gaines Murray, who was now as a practicing lawyer in Maryland, they began constructing a lawsuit. "There was a lovely symmetry there, Murray helping in a case nearly identical to his own, but the underlying message remained the same: Maryland was holding out to the end, giving ground grudgingly and only under pressure."[58] Prophetic of the approach later taken in the *Brown v. Board of Education* cases, it would be a multi-party challenge to the entire system by simultaneously suing with many plaintiffs applying for admission to several of university units.[59]

Marshall and Houston began to identify plaintiffs to sue for admission in multiple University of Maryland professional schools as they had done in the past.[60] Soon six plaintiffs would be identified to sue President Byrd and his interstate compact. The schools of dentistry, medicine, pharmacy and nursing were going to be drawn into court for a showdown.[61] The first case to be ready for trial turned out to be the nursing school case.

Quiet and poised, Esther McCready initiated the nursing school lawsuit on her own. When Charles Houston found out she had applied he telephoned her and interrogated her about her effort, asking "who put you up to this?"[62] When she told him "nobody," he replied that she was "very brave."[63] When the admissions office told her they were still reviewing her application after months of delay, she called the NAACP for help.[64] McCready's case would now become the first case to be tried among those Houston was assembling that would challenge Maryland's effort to join with many Southern states to export its Negro students out of state for graduate and professional education.[65]

In 1948 the State of Maryland and other southern states, without the consent of Congress under section 10 of Article I of the Constitution, entered into a regional[66] compact, which was subsequently amended and, as amended, is set out in and was ratified by Chapter 282 of the Acts of 1949, effective June 1, 1949, relating to the development and maintenance of regional educational services and schools in the southern states in the professional, technological, scientific, literary and other fields.[67] ... By arrangement pursuant to the regional compact the State of Maryland has sent a number of white students to study veterinary medicine in a school in another state and had sent, or was willing to send, Negro students for the same purpose to a different school in another state. No instruction in veterinary medicine is offered by the University of Maryland or any other state agency in Maryland.[68] Pursuant to the regional compact a contract for training in nursing education, dated July 19, 1949, was made between the Board of Control for Southern Regional Education, 'a joint agency' created by the regional compact, and the State of Maryland, relating to nursing education of three first year students from the State of Maryland to Meharry Medical College, School of Nursing, at Nashville, Tennessee.[69] Meharry Medical School and its school of nursing received [N]egro students only.[70] In August, 1949 the University of Maryland offered petitioner a course in nursing at Meharry Medical College at a total over-all cost to her, including living and traveling expenses, which would not exceed the cost to her of attending the school of nursing at the University of Maryland.[71] McCready declined the offer.[72]

There was an assertion that "educational facilities and living conditions at the nursing school at Meharry College [are] not only equal but superior to the University of Maryland nursing school."[73]

Thurgood Marshall decided to send Houston help from New York in his efforts on behalf of the nursing school litigation. Constance Baker Motley, who was then a recent Columbia University law graduate, begun to work with the NAACP in its national legal office.[74] Thurgood Marshall wanted Motley to "learn from the master," so he sent her to Maryland to assist Houston in the *McCready* case.[75] She was in awe of Houston's skill, his process of "writing out every question he wanted to ask in his trial notebook" and of positioning every exhibit carefully on the trial table.[76] Motley was allowed to sit at Houston's side for the entire trial, watching every move he made. Years later, after she had served for some time as the first African American woman in the nation to be appointed a federal trial judge, Motley wrote, "[t]o this day I have never seen a better prepared trial lawyer."[77]

Juanita Mitchell, who was present at the *McCready* hearing, described the effect of the case on Houston; he "was so perturbed he did something he never did, he argued with the judge."[78] The obvious reason for his anger was he believed he had established the law in the *Murray* case thirteen years before.[79]

The trial court rejected Houston's arguments.[80] Chief Judge Conwell Smith's ruling was so devastating "that it was believed to have sent...Houston to his sick bed."[81] The Maryland Supreme Court, however, agreed with Houston that the "regional compact" was in violation of law and ordered the University of Maryland to admit McCready.[82] By now Charles Houston, severely weakened by his heart condition, got the news from Esther McCready at his hospital bed-side.[83] A newspaper reported the victory was a "tonic" to Houston.[84] The legal battle, however, was taking a devastating physical toll on Charles Houston's health. He was weak, losing weight, his face drawn and his legendary patience waning. His anger at the University of Maryland cases made him anxious about his original goal to see the beginning of the desegregation of the grade schools. As for Miss McCready, she would encounter some resistance after she enrolled. A white supervising nurse told her, "If you don't pray to God you won't get out of here because no one is for you." But she replied, "If God does want me here no one can stop me."[85]

In his final days, Houston summoned Gardner Bishop to his bedside to plan for a discussion of the D.C. school desegregation case which would be the prede-cessor of *Brown v. Board of Education.* Bishop was the head of the Consolidated Parents Group Houston had supported. He told Bishop to take his case to Pro-fessor James N. Nabrit of Howard University to finish it. Bishop reluctantly did as Houston asked. William Houston was livid that Charlie was still thinking about these cases rather than resting in the hospital and "cursed out" Bishop.[86] William was anxious and worried for his son, knowing he had been working too hard. Charles replied, "Dad if it takes my life, I have to give it."[87] Years later, Bishop would express gratitude at the care Charlie Houston took with his case. "I knew Charlie Houston as a man, it's a little different.... He was a human being who could have feelings."[88] He fondly recalled the two of them going to a Christmas fundraiser sponsored by "Jack and Jill, Inc." to support the lawsuit. They would take a photo with a money tree the group had provided.[89]

Houston with Plaintiff Gardner Bishop at "Jack and Jill" fundraiser for legal campaign in the case which later became known as Bolling v. Sharpe, decided with Brown v. Board of Education.

COURTESY OF THE CHARLES H. HOUSTON, JR., FAMILY COLLECTION

Judge Joseph C. Waddy, one of Houston's last law partners, who was with Houston when he died. As a federal judge, Waddy was involved in matters regarding the Watergate defendants.
COURTESY OF THE JUDGE JOSEPH WADDY FAMILY COLLECTION

In a recorded statement shortly before his death, Charles Houston made a poignant declaration about his civil rights work. He said, "[T]here come times when it is possible to forecast the results of a contest, of a battle, of a lawsuit long before the final event has taken place. And, so far as our struggle for civil rights is concerned, the struggle for civil rights in America is won."[90] Charles died ten days after he learned of the *McCready* victory, in the presence of his doctor and his law partner Joseph Waddy.[91] Just before he passed away he had a visit from his aunt, Clotill Houston, who visited to pray for and with her nephew for encouragement. She left him a book written by an American Rabbi, Joshua Liebman, entitled *Peace of Mind.* On page 48 he wrote a note to his son Bo that said, among other things, that he "went down fighting that he might have better and broader opportunities...without prejudice or bias operating against him."[92] He asked his Aunt Clotill to make sure if he did not make it, his son would get the book because he had sent his beloved wife and son to Louisiana to stay with relatives during this phase of his illness.[93] His physician and friend Edward Mazique, who cared for Charlie

Dr. Donald Stewart, one of the last people Houston and Marshall represented together. They filed the lawsuit in 1949 that helped Stewart desegregate the University of Maryland Medical School.
COURTESY OF THE PHILIP STEWART FAMILY COLLECTION

throughout his last months, would recall how Charlie "was very proud of his victory over the University of Maryland" in the week before he died.[94]

Juanita Mitchell recalled at that time "there was just a sense of such a loss. And almost a sense of how could this have happened to a man who did so much good and whose life was still needed...and he literally...gave his life for the cause.... The doctors told him that he had to rest. And he said, 'I can't rest.'"[95] She described Charles Hamilton Houston as a "friend to man...[but while] saving the race he neglected himself."[96]

Houston's Final Farewell

Charles Houston's funeral services were held on May 6, 1950, at Rankin Chapel on the campus of Howard University, without his seeing the full magnitude of the legal reforms he had set in place. His funeral was attended by many dignitaries, including several Supreme Court Justices. Among the mourners was former senator and ex-Ku Klux Klansman Hugo Black, who Houston had helped transform into a civil rights giant through persistent conversation, even helping him gain the support of the N.A.A.C.P. for the high court appointment.[97]

Houston's longtime nemesis President Harry Truman even sent his condolences in a telegram, honoring Houston as "a man of great achievement and unselfish service to the cause of democracy"[98] The president further commented his "strength of conviction and integrity made his counsel invaluable to me."[99] A *Washington Post* editorial commented "[f]ormidable statutory barriers of discrimination on grounds of race crumbled under the skill and stubbornness of his onslaught."[100] Herman Edelesburg, director of the Anti-Defamation League of B'nai B'rith wrote of Houston, "we will longest remember the prophetic quality of his dedication to the cause of freedom and equality."[101]

A eulogy given by Reverend A. F. Elmes noted Houston's devotion to "unpopular causes" and his "unending struggle to break down walls."[102] An editorial writer for the *Baltimore Afro-American*, Dr. Marshall Shepard, noted that Houston had worked so "indefatigably for human justice and fair play for the people farthest down." Making a comparison to the example of Christ, the writer, quoting Scripture, pointed out "whosoever will lose his life for my sake shall find it."[103]

Dr. Louis T. Wright, chairman of the NAACP board, commented that Charles Houston was "an advocate and legal technician without peer, he will be remembered as the inspirational genius for...the equality of man—that all men are equal before the law." [104] "I'm sure it was the *McCready* case...that really knocked Charlie off his feet." Thurgood would explain after the funeral, "during his illness all of us were more interested in getting him back on his feet than anything else. Whatever credit is given him is not enough."[105]

Marshall would recall that Charlie built such a "perfect" record in *McCready* that "anyone could have won the appeal."[106] Thurgood was devastated by Houston's death. Gardner Bishop would later explain that Marshall "grieved for Charlie as if he were a brother.... He had lost the man who had been as important in his life as his father had been."[107] University of Maryland's resistance and the fact that his great mentor had to get out of his sick-bed to try the *McCready* case was a possible reason that Thurgood Marshall would not return to the University of Maryland for the dedication of its law library in his name decades later.[108]

A *Washington Post* editorial would declare that both white and black people should mourn his death because he was a "crusader for a principle that lies at the heart of American Democracy."[109] Later that year, Charles Houston would be posthumously awarded the Spingarn Medal, the NAACPs highest honor. Dean Erwin Griswold of the Harvard Law School would make the presentation of the medal to Houston's son. He commented at the event that "[I]t is doubtful that there has been a single important case involving civil rights in the last fifteen years in which Charles Houston has not participated directly or by consultation of advice."[110] He "was a tower of strength...an inspiration to all freedom loving people—a great man."[111] At the ceremony with his mother and Thurgood Marshall at his side, Charles Jr. commented "Thank you for the Spingarn Award and I hope I will be half as good as my daddy was."[112]

James Nabrit, who would later win Gardner Bishop's Supreme Court case,[113] which outlawed Jim Crow in schools in the nation's capital, would say Houston was "a man of great imagination and creativeness in the highest sense of the law."[114] Comparing Houston to the great football coach Vince Lombardi, "he was a tough excellent technician who drove you to produce to the limit of your ability."[115] Years later Nobel Peace Prize winner Dr. Martin Luther King Jr. would call Houston a "defender of great renown,"[116] noting that he "had an immutable commitment to the philosophy that, with all of its uncertainty and weakness, the law is majestic and the judicial process supreme."[117]

Supreme Court Justice Felix Frankfurter, Charlie Houston's former professor, mentor and friend was broken hearted about Charlie Houston's passing. He commented a few days after his funeral, "[f]or Charlie...to be struck down in mid-career came to me as a heavy blow...when he argued before this court I took pride in the excellence of his advocacy."[118] Supreme Court Justice and former attorney general of the United States Tom C. Clark called him an "eminent" American whose "record as a scholar and a leader of men is unparalleled."[119] Nobel prize winner Dr. Ralph Bunche wrote that "Charlie's untimely death was a tremendous loss."[120]

Walter White, head of the national NAACP, reflected on Charlie's concerns that perhaps he prophetically knew his time was running out, "there is so much to do and so little time."[121] At a memorial service held in Baltimore at Bethel AME Church about two years after his death, Charles' cousin William Hastie would once again point out his uniqueness. "He had a genius for inspiring people. The ability to communicate zeal, and inner fire to other people—to make them as ambitious as he was."[122] Characterizing Charlie as "God's angry man,"[123] Hastie called him a true pioneer in that he "willingly undertook new enterprises that other people shunned."[124]

About three years after Charles Houston's death, his father William passed away after sixty years practicing law, at the age of eighty-three. He had been gravely ill for three months prior to his death, and his life ended in the same place as his son's, Freedman's Hospital in Washington, D.C.[125] The bulk of William Houston's estate, conservatively valued at $60,000, was left to his grandson, Charles Houston Jr., in trust for his "proper education, care and maintenance."[126] The elder Houston's brother, physician Ulysses Houston, was named the executor.[127] When Charles Jr., reached the age of 25 the accumulated income from the trust was to be distributed to him.[128] Years after his death, famed journalist Louis Lautier would characterized Charlie Houston as the most fascinating man he had ever met, describing him as "a rare creature—intelligent, courageous, selfless, yet he never lost the common touch."[129]

Charles H. Houston's wife, Henrietta Houston, and son, Charles H. Houston, Jr. ("Bo"), with Houston's portrait photo at their home Christmas tree.

COURTESY OF THE CHARLES H. HOUSTON, JR., FAMILY COLLECTION

Endnotes

1. David A. Jassen, *A Century of Popular Music* 99 (New York: Routlegde Publishing 2013).

2. Eubie Blake to Charles H. Houston, January 28, 1949, Houston Family Papers, Moorland-Spingarn Research Center, Howard University.

3. Charles H. Houston, "The Highway," *Baltimore Afro-American*, December 6, 1947, p. 4.

4. Charles H. Houston, "Along the Highway," *Baltimore Afro-American*, July 3, 1948, p. 4.

5. Ibid.

6. Ibid.

7. Ibid.

8. Ibid.

9. Charles H. Houston, "Along the Highway," *Baltimore Afro American*, October 30, 1948, p. 4.

10. Sadie Tanner Moore Alexander to Charles H. Houston, August 21, 1929, William LePre Houston Family Papers, Manuscripts Division, Library of Congress.

11. *Baltimore Afro American*, October 30, 1948, p. 4.

12. Richard L. Lyons, "Segregation Ended at Airports; Restaurant Equality Prevails," *Washington Post*, January 5, 1949, p. 5.

13. Ibid.

14. "Truman Opens Airport to All," *Baltimore Afro American*, January 1, 1949, p. 1.

15. Ibid.

16. Ibid.

17. Ibid.

18. Anke Orlepp, *Jim Crow Terminals: The Desegregation of American Airports* 66 (Athens: University of Georgia Press 2017).

19. *Nash v. Air Terminal Services*, 85 F. Supp. 545 (E.D. Va. 1949).

20. Thurgood Marshall to Joseph F. Waddy, Esquire, November 8, 1949, NAACP Papers, Manuscripts Division, Library of Congress.

21. Ibid.

22. Ibid.

23. "Citizens Protest Junk Pile Near the Bell School," *Baltimore Afro-American*, May 19, 1934, p. 20.

24. "Dr. H.C. Byrd, UM Founder, Ex-President, Is Dead at 81," *Baltimore Sun*, October 3, 1970, p. 1.

25. *See generally*, Sherrilyn Iffil, *On the Courthouse Lawn* 8–9 (New York: Beacon Press 2007).

26. Charles H. Houston, "Saving the World for Democracy," *Pittsburgh Courier*, August 10, 1940, p. 13.

27. "Dr. H.C. Byrd, UM Founder, Ex-President, Is Dead at 81," *Baltimore Sun*.

28. H.C. Byrd to Roger Howell, 16 July 1935, Records of the President's Office, Box 39, Folder: Negro Students (including Murray papers).

29. Ibid.

30. Charles H. Houston, "Along the Highway," *Baltimore Afro-American*, November 6, 1948, p. 4.

31. "Race Issue Sizzles at Maryland U.," *Chicago Defender*, October 5, 1935, p. 1.

32. 305 U.S. 337, (1938).

33. "Maryland Prexy Mysterious About His New Type of Jim Crow," *Washington Post*, November 27, 1948, p. 1.

34. John Jasper, "Can't Duplicate H.U.'s Plant for Less Than 20 Million," *Baltimore Afro-American*, March 13, 1948, p. M5.

35. U. of M. Rejects "Admitted Vet," *Baltimore Afro-American*, September 20, 1947, p. 1.

36. Ibid.

37. Ibid.

38. Ibid.

39. Ibid.

40. Ibid.

41. Ibid.

42. Ibid.

43. Ibid.

44. Ibid.

45. Ibid.

46. Ibid.

47. Ibid.

48. Ibid.

49. Charles H. Houston, "The Highway," *Baltimore Afro American*, September 27, 1947, p. 4.

50. Ibid.

51. Ibid.

52. Ibid.

53. Ibid.

54. Ibid.

55. "NAACP Will Back Vet at U of Md.," *Baltimore Afro-American*, August 23, 1947, p. 14.

56. "W.B. Leonard, Dentist-Professor, Dies, *Washington Post*, April 5, 1978, p. C5.

57. 182 A. 590 (Md. 1936).

58. C. Fraser Smith, *Here Lies Jim Crow* 147 (Baltimore: Johns Hopkins University Press 2008).

59. "Suit Filed Against U. of Md., 6 Pending," *Baltimore Afro American*, October 30, 1948, p. 4.

60. Charles H. Houston to President H. Curley Byrd, March 16, 1937, NAACP Papers, Manuscript Division, Library of Congress.

61. "6 Spurn Offer to Withdraw Suits Against U. of Md.: Will Continue Effort to Enter," *Baltimore Afro-American*, August 27, 1949, p. 7.

62. Ibid., p. 133.

63. Ibid.

64. Ibid.

65. Pauli Murray, Editor, *States' Law on Race and Color* 201–205 (Athens: Women's Division of Christian Service, 1950).

66. *McCready v. Byrd*, 73 A.2d. 8, 9 (Md. 1950).

67. Ibid.

68. Ibid., p. 9.

69. Ibid.

70. Ibid.

71. Ibid.

72. Ibid.

73. Ibid.

74. Roger Goldman and David Gallen, *Thurgood Marshall: Justice for All* 161 (New York: Carroll and Graf 1993).

75. Ibid.

76. Ibid., p. 163.

77. Ibid., p. 162.

78. Juanita Jackson Mitchell, University of Virginia Library, William A. Elwood Civil Rights Project, Oral History, video recording, September 1, 1988.

79. Ibid.

80. "Nursing School Bid by Negro Rejected," *Washington Post*, October 11, 1949, p. 3.

81. "Open U. of Md., Court of Appeals Reverses City Judge," *Baltimore Afro-American*, April 22, 1950, p. 12.

82. *McCready v. Byrd*, 73 A.2d 8 (Md. 1950).

83. Phineas Smith, "Victory over U. of Md. Held Tonic for Houston," *Baltimore Afro-American*, April 22, 1950, p. 6.

84. Ibid.

85. Ibid., p. 134.

86. Richard Kluger, *Simple Justice: The History of* Brown v. Board of Education *and Black America's Struggle for Equality* 517 (New York: Alfred A. Knopf 1977).

87. Geraldine R. Segal, *In Any Fight Some Fall* 74 (Rockville: Mercury Press 1975).

88. University of Virginia Library, William A. Elwood Civil Rights Project, Oral History, Gardner L. Bishop, video recording, July 15, 1987.

89. Genna Rae McNeil, *Groundwork: Charles Hamilton Houston and the Struggle for Civil Rights* 190–191 (Philadelphia: University of Pennsylvania Press 1983).

90. William A. Elwood, *Road to* Brown, Transcript, California Newsreel, University of Virginia, p. 10.

91. Rawn James, Jr., *Root and Branch: Charles Hamilton Houston, Thurgood Marshall and the Struggle to End Segregation* 216 (New York: Bloomsbury Press 2010).

92. Geraldine R. Segal, *In Any Fight Some Fall* 75 (Rockville: Mercury Press 1975).

93. Genna Rae McNeil, *Groundwork*, p. 210.

94. Edward Mazique, University of Virginia Library, William A. Elwood Civil Rights Project, Oral History, video recording, December 11, 1985.

95. Juanita Jackson Mitchell, University of Virginia Library, William A. Elwood Civil Rights Project, Oral History, video recording, September 1, 1988.

96. Ibid.

97. "Black Won't Talk, Silent on Klan Issue," *Baltimore Afro-American*, August 21, 1937, p. 1.

98. "Truman, Noted Jurists Mourn Charles Houston," *The Chicago Defender*, May 6, 1950, p. 1.

99. "High U.S. Officials Join Last Tribute to Houston," *Baltimore Afro-American*, May 6, 1950, p. 7.

100. "Charles H. Houston," Editorial, *Washington Post*, April 25, 1950, p. 8.

101. Herman Edelsberg, "Charles H. Houston," Letter to the Editor, *Washington Post*, May 1, 1950, p. 8.

102. "High U.S. Officials Join Last Tribute to Houston," *Afro-American*, May 6, 1950, p. 7.

103. Dr. Marshall Shepard, "The Church," May 13, 1950, *Baltimore Afro-American*, p. 4.

104. "NAACP Board Grieve over Chas. Houston," *Baltimore Afro-American*, May 6, 1950.

105. Ibid.

106. Ibid.

107. Hunter and Clark, *Thurgood Marshall: Warrior at the Bar, Rebel on the Bench* 120 (New York: Birch Lane Press 1992).

108. Justice Thurgood Marshall to University of Maryland President John Toll, March 29, 1979, University of Maryland School of Law Special Collection.

109. Obituary, Charles H. Houston, *Washington Post*, April 25, 1950.

110. "Race Prejudice Held Hurting U.S. Abroad," *New York Times*, June 26, 1950 p. 31.

111. "Honor Paid to Houston," *Baltimore Afro-American*, July 1, 1950, p. 1.

112. Ibid.

113. *Bolling v. Sharpe*, 347 U.S. 497 (1954).

114. "Services Honor Late Civil Rights Lawyer," *Baltimore Afro-American*, May 9, 1953, p. 14.

115. Richard Kluger, *Simple Justice*, pp. 278–79.

116. Dr. Martin Luther King, Jr., "The Law Is Majestic," *New York Amsterdam News*, July 31, 1965, p. 16.

117. Ibid.

118. Felix Frankfurter to Donald G. Murray, Esq., May 11, 1950, Juanita Jackson Mitchell Family Collection, courtesy of Michael Bowen Mitchell.

119. Justice Tom C. Clark to Donald Gaines Murray, Esquire, May 12, 1950, Juanita Jackson Mitchell Family Collection, courtesy of Michael Bowen Mitchell.

120. Ralph Bunche, Director, United Nations to Donald Gaines Murray, Esquire, May 19, 1950, Mitchell Family Collection, courtesy of Michael Bowen Mitchell.

121. Walter White, "Houston Helped Close the Gap Between Talk and Implementation of Democracy," *The Chicago Defender*, May 13, 1950, p. 7.

122. "Judge Hastie Extols Dr. Houston's Militancy," *Baltimore Afro-American*, May 3, 1952, p. 22I.

123. Ibid.

124. Ibid.

125. "Bulk of Estate Left to Grandson in Trust," *Baltimore-Afro American*, October 10, 1953, p. 20.

126. Ibid.

127. Ibid.

128. Ibid.

129. Louis Lautier, "Most Fascinating Man and Woman I Have Ever Met," *Baltimore Afro-American*, February 4, 1956, p. 20F.

Epilogue

"We Shall Not Be Content": The Legacy of Charles Hamilton Houston

---

Great movements of conscience sweep the imagination when men are willing to suffer for what they believe.

—Charles H. Houston, "Our Civil Rights," April 30, 1949,
Baltimore Afro-American

Charles Hamilton Houston's legacy continues in the people he personally influenced. His only son Charles Hamilton Houston Jr., given the nick named "Bo," for many years taught the American history that his father made as a member of the faculty at Morgan State University in Baltimore City.[1] It was an appropriate venue, considering that it was in Baltimore that his father had his first great civil rights victory in the *Murray* case as special counsel of the NAACP.[2] The son of a legendary father passed away after a long battle with Parkinson's disease on July 15, 2018.[3] A pleasant and soft-spoken man, he told me that he had a difficult adjustment throughout his life because of his father's legacy. He candidly recalled the difficulty his mother suffered in losing her husband after only about a dozen years of marriage.[4] She experienced debilitating depression until the end of her days, particularly on the anniversary of her husband's death.[5]

Charles Houston's grandson, Charles Hamilton Houston III, graduated from the University of Texas Law School at Austin, that his grandfather helped to desegregate. Tall, elegant, with his Granddad's quiet, persuasive eyes, he presents himself with the calm dignity worthy of the Houston legacy. He is a commercial lawyer who represents businesses like his great-grandfather

William LePré Houston. In October of 2019, his wife gave birth to Charles "Hamilton" Houston IV.[6]

Charlie Houston's granddaughter Karyn Houston-Mendes is a physician in a medical practice with her husband in Sacramento, California. Kamali Houston, Charlie Houston's great-granddaughter, graduated in May 2020 form Howard University School of Law, making a fourth generation of the Houston family to pursue a career in the law. She is to start her legal career with the law firm Davis, Polk, & Wardwell. Ironically, its iconic late named partner, John W. Davis, was defeated by Thurgood Marshall in the school desegregation cases of 1954 with the strategy developed by Charles Houston.[7]

When I first met Charles Houston, Jr., in December of 2003, he shared with me the circumstances of how he ended up in Baltimore in the early 1980s after his mother's death. Describing himself at the time as "sad and depressed," he returned to the home of one of his father's oldest allies, Juanita Jackson Mitchell, who as a teenager worked on the early NAACP campaigns with Houston. Noting that Charles Jr. needed encouragement, she pulled a picture from a box. It was of his father standing in the pulpit of a large Baltimore church with several hundred people packed tightly in the sanctuary.

She explained that she had great sympathy for him losing his father at such a young age. She wanted him know how much he meant to so many people. "No matter what the problem or issue, when he was needed, Charlie always came to help."[8] She had watched Houston, Marshall and William Gosnell desegregate the University of Maryland School of Law in the 1930s as a teenager. Juanita Mitchell enrolled in Maryland's law school at Charlie Houston's urging and graduated in 1950.

Working by the side of her husband Clarence Mitchell, Jr., the NAACPs chief lobbyist, the couple would help shape the nation's civil rights agenda for three decades following Charlie Houston's death. Clarence would credit Houston's contributions as game changing because of his integrity and legal genius.[9] Mitchell helped President Lyndon Johnson pass important civil rights legislation during the 1960s,[10] following many of Charles Houston's priorities.[11] The Baltimore City Courthouse in which Houston had tried many great cases would be named for Clarence M. Mitchell, Jr. in the 1980s.[12]

Charles Houston Jr., also shared with me during our early meetings that he felt somewhat responsible for why his father was not better known. The difficulty of sifting through his father's papers and writings had always taken an emotional toll. He had limited contact with prior biographers and chroniclers of his father's work. He greatly admired historian Genna Rae McNeil, who had done in a prior biography, but even in his later years he admitted he could only work briefly reconstructing his father's legacy before deep sadness would set in. He also recalled that his late mother had always desired to chronicle her husband's life, but mental health issues were a stumbling block.

During the celebration of the fiftieth anniversary of the *Brown v. Board of Education* case,[13] however, a renewed interest in his father's work stirred a quiet courage in Charles Houston Jr. to recapture what history he could, so that his father's story would be told. He accepted most invitations to celebrate his father's legacy in order to keep his memory alive.[14] He helped to launch a program to encourage minority students to attend law school in his father's name at the University of Baltimore School of Law.[15] He provided museums and archives material from his family collection related to his father's work. Charles Houston Jr.'s concern, that he was somehow responsible for his father's low visibility is, in my view, misplaced. It is worth examining the issue in some detail. Charles H. Houston's character traits, displayed during his legal career, contributed to his relative anonymity.

First, he was a man of great humility.[16] Although he was supremely confident as a courtroom advocate, he did not seek the "spotlight" for its own sake. Second, the quality of his work defied description. Like Michelangelo or Einstein, Charlie Houston's genius cannot adequately be defined with traditional measurements alone. Scholars are still discovering the innovations in his legal strategies. Many judges who he appeared before commented that his skill was unsurpassed. The sheer volume of his productivity is phenomenal. In a world without computers and other modern document producing technology, he filed expertly crafted, exhaustive briefs in scores of cases breaking new legal ground, often in a manner that judges did not understand.

Over one hundred appeals and trials he personally handled in dozens of states, he completed often through exhaustion and illness. All of this work produced during a legal career that spanned a little more than a quarter century. It also boggles the mind the amount of documented consulting he was able to provide on cases handled by others, as reflected in the mass of legal correspondences that have been collected in many archives. He wrote extensively in newspapers and made dozens of public appearances each year. Like most true geniuses, it often takes decades, perhaps a century to comprehend their greatness.

Even trying to digest Charles Houston's law school notebooks is a daunting task. Reading his analysis and the complexity of his thinking, even as a student, reflects the depth of the operation of his mind. After over three decades of my own experiences in litigation, research and law teaching, I stand in awe of even his student notes that were made a century ago. Charles, Jr., gave me the unique privilege to review most of them privately. Those notes reflect a vision of the power, majesty and potential of the law as a tool for reform and insight, that far exceeded his years and experience at the time. No matter the subject, each notebook reflects a depth of understanding that would humble most legal thinkers today. I have no doubt that my conclusions in this regard will be supported if the family ever makes all the notebooks publicly available for further scholarly review.

Second, Houston permanently established the foundational work for at least three great American institutions in his relatively brief career. He developed a law school at Howard University that is a model of current legal education, with clinical and simulation components.

He designed the NAACP legal campaign, establishing the model for the advocacy groups which now dominate our modern era of law reform. That organization combines lobbying, litigation and community involvement as tools of social change. This approach should not be mistaken for simply inviting courts to engage in judicial activism. Houston's legal theories required respect for the entire constitutional scheme. He not only required the use of the Bill of Rights and precedent, but also sought to establish community consensus before any court action he proposed. He also helped build the foundation of the modern ACLU.

Third, it might also be fair to say that one of Houston's greatest contributions to American law were those he mentored. His star pupil, Thurgood Marshall, was at his side during the development of much of the dynamic legal doctrine that was developed to kill Jim Crow. He placed Marshall in position to lead the NAACP Legal Defense and Education Fund and developed the model for advocacy litigation organizations around the world. He assisted Marshall with all the important civil rights litigation that the NAACP pursued until his untimely death. Marshall would become a member of the United States Court of Appeals for the Second Circuit and later was appointed solicitor general of the United States, representing the federal government before the Supreme Court of the United States.[17]

In Marshall's long career on the Supreme Court from 1967–1991 he was an unashamed advocate for civil rights in many of his judicial opinions. Often joining Chief Justice Earl Warren and his best friend on the Court, Justice William Brennan, Marshall would help mold the court's so-called "liberal wing" during the Warren Court era.[18] In all those years he continued to pay respect and give credit to his mentor and teacher.[19]

In the early 1980s the University of Maryland, which Marshall had fought so hard against, desired to name its law school library for him upon a request by student leaders Emerson Dorsey and later, André Davis. Justice Marshall responded that he would not attend the event to dedicate the building because of continuing racial unrest and the treatment of African American students at the university at that time.[20] His friend Justice Brennan would help dedicate the building on his behalf.[21] Many observers of the Marshall "snub" were perplexed.

Indeed, Marshall had come to other Maryland locations in person for other dedications. He was in attendance when the Baltimore City Courthouse was named for his friend and NAACP civil rights ally Clarence M. Mitchell, Jr.[22] He also attended the unveiling of his statute near the federal courthouse in Baltimore only blocks away from the law school.[23] Why would Marshall pass up the opportunity to be present when the school that would not have accepted him as a student attempted to engage in the ultimate repentance?

When I was a student at Maryland's law school, shortly after the Marshall Library opened, there was a great deal of folklore surrounding Thurgood Marshall's failure to attend the dedication. Among the things that were rumored was that Justice Marshall had told people he would never "knowingly" step foot on any property owned by the University of Maryland.[24] The library had only been open less than a year, and much of the publicity at the time centered on how Thurgood had been denied admission to the law school. However, there is no evidence that he had actually ever applied.[25]

The fact that Charles Houston fought the university for two decades and had to leave his sick bed to try the *McCready* case was likely part of Marshall's anger against the university.[26] Certainly his love for his mentor and the tragedy of having lost him at the peak of his career added to Marshall's grief. The school's stubborn resistance to integration, forcing Houston to return over and over against to take it to court, left a sore spot with Marshall that may have never healed.[27] The relentless resistance by long-time President "Curley" Byrd was an open part of Marshall's anger.[28] In a 1985 interview during the dedication of the Mitchell courthouse in Baltimore, Marshall was asked about how he felt returning to Baltimore for the occasion. He responded somewhat sarcastically, "'I joined millions of other people who…were born in Baltimore, were raised in Baltimore, but were not going to die in Baltimore'…he would not elaborate."[29]

Marshall continued the fight he and Houston started together. I speculate that his unwillingness to return to any university activity was directly attributable to his anger over the death of his mentor, who literally gave his life in litigation with the university. Marshall had made harsh public criticism of Byrd shortly after Houston's death.[30]

The opportunity for Marshall to vindicate Houston came in the person of a soft spoken but brilliant Morgan College student named Donald W. Stewart, who had been one of the original plaintiffs in the matter that became the *McCready* case.[31] It was the last successful school desegregation case for Houston and Marshall before Houston's death. Stewart decided to change from aspirations of being a dentist to becoming a doctor. The decision pleased Marshall and allowed him to open the floodgates to the rest of the University of Maryland by a final barrage of lawsuits that ultimately broke the University Maryland's will to resist integration and fulfilled one of Charles Houston's final purposes.[32] The final barrier to the admission at the university crumbled in January 1951, when Hiram T. Whittle became the first Negro accepted to the University of Maryland, College Park as an undergraduate engineering student with plans to live in a college dormitory.[33] The Maryland Attorney General Hall Hammond finally directed President Harry "Curley" Byrd not only to provide Whittle dormitory space, but allow him to use, "any other facilities which the State supplies the university for the use of students."[34]

Marshall's anger with the University of Maryland lasted well into his last years on the Supreme Court. A former assistant dean from the University of Baltimore School of Law, Thomas Corey, recalls his efforts to get a portrait of the Justice signed for the school's law library in the late 1980s. When he contacted Justice Marshall's chambers about the request, he remembers overhearing Marshall in the background of the call say "he was not signing anything for the University of Maryland, including his own portrait."[35] When the dean of students assured Marshall's chamber's staff that the University of *Baltimore* was not the University of *Maryland* he agreed to sign the picture.[36] That portrait, offered as a gift by the black law students of the University of Baltimore, hangs in the school's moot courtroom today.

Fourth, Houston's career ended with his death just prior to the onset of broadcast television, an age he would have surely dominated. Instead, he left his handsome understudy, Thurgood Marshall, to use the electronic media to become the first lawyer to be the face of civil rights movement. With his glib sense of humor and easygoing manner, Marshall was the perfect national voice for the coast-to-coast legal campaigns that would follow in the television age. One wonders whether the prophetic Houston knew of Marshall's suitability for this task as early as when he first encountered him as a student.

He Influenced Many

William I. Gosnell, co-counsel in *Murray*, would become one of the most successful lawyers in Baltimore of any race. He would develop a thriving estate practice. Included among his clients was the owner of Baltimore's Negro League Baseball team.[37] Gosnell would continue to occasionally engage in civil rights work after Houston's death. Among his activities fighting discrimination were his efforts to aid three black Methodist ministers gaining access to a public library in 1952, when a Calvert County, Maryland, judge would remark that "[a] Negro will never set foot in that library as long as I have anything to do with it."[38] Gosnell would also successfully represent a mentally challenged man in a death penalty case.[39] Gosnell's primary fortunes would be linked to his mother-in-law's beauty supply business that would make national news and even lead to the purchase of a large hotel in Atlantic City, New Jersey.[40]

Two legendary Baltimore lawyers, Milton B. Allen and Robert B. Watts, who law clerked for Charles Houston during the late 1940s, graduated from the University of Maryland School of Law to be founding partners of what would become the most important African American law firm in Maryland history, Brown, Allen, Watts, Murphy & Russell.[41] The firm was the first to have a downtown Baltimore office in a federally financed skyscraper and the first to integrate by hiring Stephen E. Harris, a white attorney in the early 1960s.[42]

Watts worked on many important cases for the NAACP, including the landmark United States Supreme Court case *Bell v. Maryland* in 1963.[43] In that case Robert Mack Bell, a freshman at Morgan State University, would be arrested in a protest at a downtown Baltimore restaurant that would not serve black patrons. Years later in 1996, that civil rights protestor was elevated by Maryland Governor Parris Glendenning to the office of chief judge of Maryland's highest court.[44]

Milton B. Allen would become a legendary trial lawyer. He was honored by the Maryland State Bar Association in 1994 as the first African American to win its prestigious Thomas Heeney Award for lifetime achievement in criminal justice.[45] In 1970, Allen became the first black chief prosecutor of a major American city when he was elected state's attorney for Baltimore.[46]

Years later Allen would describe Houston "as an unusually gifted man whose fertile brain gave birth to the...civil rights cases that have been filed in the last [several decades]." Judge Allen would recall that he "spent a whole summer preparing a case based on the theory that the...taking of that property for the purpose of building a road was taking that property without due process of law and denied equal protection of the laws. We lost that case...."

That was one of Charles Houston's theories, that running a super highway through black neighborhoods was a form of racial discrimination."[47] Allen, in a prophetic statement, concluded, "It might prove right before long, I do not know. But at that time the court wasn't ready for it."[48]

Allen would later join Robert Watts as a member of the Supreme Bench of Baltimore City, were each would serve many years. Commenting on the same Druid Hill highway case, Robert Watts would say, "Charlie Houston...felt it unfair to run this highway through the black community in our best neighborhood simply to bring whites from the suburbs into the downtown areas."[49] This was yet another of Houston's "ahead of his times" innovations,[50] a first-of-its-kind environmental racism case.[51]

The next African American to serve as state's attorney for Baltimore City was a Baltimore native named Kurt L. Schmoke, a graduate from Harvard Law School who grew up in the very neighborhood that Charles Houston had fought to make safer in the 1940s. Schmoke would later serve several terms as mayor of Baltimore City and would later be appointed dean of Houston's beloved Howard University School of Law.[52] In 2014 he was named president of the University of Baltimore in his hometown, his office only yards away from the Pennsylvania Railroad Station that Houston would regularly use to travel to litigate in Baltimore.

Houston's work still influences the Supreme Court today. Much of his most enduring legal theories came to life during the Warren court years. When Earl Warren became Chief Justice of the United States the balance of power on the Supreme Court began to make a shift toward greater recognition of the rights of individuals. As the 1950s proceeded, the Supreme Court began to re-examine the Constitution in much the same way as Houston had envisioned in his litigation during the 1930s and 1940s.[53]

Houston's Influence on the Modern Supreme Court

Houston's work has influenced several Supreme Court trends. Almost a third of all tax money goes to education.[54] Houston recognized that education was also the most valued resource for people of color to change their circumstances. His first advances were against the separate but equal doctrine. The precedent he set in the Supreme Court in *Gaines v. Missouri*[55] required states to take responsibility for the racism they championed and come to grips with the notion that equality requires attention to circumstances and not merely suggesting that "some" equality is good enough.

With little money, few lawyers and in the midst of the Great Depression he used the hypocritical separate but equal doctrine first against Maryland, then Missouri, to begin the road to what became *Brown v. Board of Education*.[56] Whatever one may think of the *Brown* decision, no one can deny it transformed America. It stands as the moral hallmark of our constitutional law. The *Brown* decision is often referred to as the most influential decision in the history of the court.[57] The cases that followed *Brown* also expanded judicial power to enforce civil rights. When Thurgood Marshall argued cases like *Cooper v. Aarons*,[58] in the late 1950s to require states to comply with federal desegregation orders, even President Dwight Eisenhower felt compelled to use the power of the United States' military to enforce the Court's power to require compliance with a constitutional mandate.[59] The *Brown* decision was then used by the Supreme Court to summarily eliminate Jim Crow in all other types of public places of service, recreation and transportation.[60]

In Baltimore, where the battle to desegregate education first achieved a court victory, the school system immediately ordered the desegregation under the leadership of School Board President Walter Sondheim. Charles Houston's former courtroom adversary, Mayor Thomas D'Alesandro, Sr., when informed by Sondheim of the decision in *Brown* reportedly said, "I don't know if you did the right thing...but the priests say you did, so I guess you did."[61] Despite some public outcry and political opposition to integration, Mayor D'Alessandro left the Baltimore School Board's decision to immediately desegregate undisturbed.[62] After his decision Sondheim would have a cross burned on his lawn and even received a racist letter from a former judge, but he pressed on to oversee school desegregation even when many other Maryland school districts and Southern and Northern states refused.[63]

Houston inspired lawyers like Alabama's Fred Gray, who represented Rosa Parks and Martin Luther King Jr., during the 1950s and 1960s. Gray commented decades after Houston's death that the reform lawyers of his time won most of their civil rights court cases because they "were carefully working on precedents that had been laid by...Charles Hamilton Houston."[64]

Houston changed labor law by fighting for the black union members in the *Steele* case.[65] If he could improve the conditions of the workers in that important industry, he would score an important victory for all workers who were potentially exploited. By advancing before the Supreme Court fair practices for railroad workers he sent a message to both labor leadership and industry that fairness is an important value. The labor cases he won in the 1940s are still the law of the land.

Restrictive Covenants Eliminated

The restrictive covenant cases are also an important statement in the history of American justice. To remove the enforcement power of the courts to protect racist policies in housing in *Shelley v. Kraemer* is, in some ways, more important that the equality that was achieved in *Brown*. Everyone must live somewhere. When one is limited in those choices by racial, ethnic or religious discrimination, there is a feeling of dehumanization. Houston's work in these cases rescued America from an ugly tradition of government-imposed racial superiority and racial inferiority in dwelling spaces.

The Jury Selection Cases and the Criminal System

The bright glare of *Brown* and its importance in American history often eclipses the importance of Houston's other contributions. This is particularly true in the area of criminal justice, where Houston accomplished many important benchmarks. Although many of his cases in the area of criminal procedure generated mixed results, viewed as a collection, those cases represent a body of important and visionary work in American law. Several of the principles that he established through successful litigation still have a permanent impact. His ground-breaking work in jury selection, starting in the1930s, laid the foundation for the so-called "*Batson* doctrine,"[66] which now controls not only the criminal justice system, but also the civil litigation jury selection landscape by prohibiting racial and gender bias in jury trials.[67] His emphasis on the fairness of an inclusive jury almost eighty years ago still provides the basis for establishing that right today.

Houston's early work on capital punishment with the NAACP demonstrates an insight into unfair punishment which still guides the contemporary capital punishment debate. Concepts like arbitrariness and the absence of guided discretion are a direct result of the impact of cases like the *Crawford* case in Virginia, where very serious allegations subjected a black defendant to a harsh criminal justice system with little mercy. His concern for fair trials and his disdain for violence visited against black individuals by lynch mobs, while they were awaiting trial, made his work on difficult murder and rape cases a career-long pursuit.

In *James v. State*,[68] Houston used the latest techniques from psychiatry in order to attempt demonstrate that a "feeble minded," low-I.Q. defendant made an unreliable statement, which was coerced by the police. In another Maryland case, *Jones v. State*,[69] Houston tested the boundaries of what makes a confession voluntary. Removing a defendant to a distant location and questioning him in a manner which suggested that officials would turn him over to a mob where the crime had occurred demonstrates his concern for the integrity of police investigative practices.

The eighteen-year-old Jones and his fourteen-year-old brother were handled in a manner inconsistent with the interrogation practices that are approved by courts today. Both the *James* and *Jones* cases raised concerns hauntingly similar to those finally addressed by the Supreme Court in *Miranda v. Arizona*,[70] which now sets the standard for voluntary confessions throughout the nation. It is clear that by focusing attention on the practices of the local police in obtaining statements from the defendants,[71] Houston was attempting to draw attention to the problem of intimidation of suspects by local police. Houston also emphasized the absence of legal counsel during the ordeals in each of these cases as a factor making the confessions questionable.[72] His arguments illustrated the "best practices" embraced by thoughtful twenty-first century legal scholars.[73]

It would be about two decades before Houston's suggestion that counsel is critical in these circumstances would be adopted as the law of the land. In 1963, the Supreme Court announced its opinion in *Gideon v. Wainwright*,[74] which established the right to counsel for nearly all criminally accused. Later in the 1960s and 1970s, the Court expanded those rights to the early stages of the criminal investigation process. In his most controversial criminal case in the Supreme Court of the United States, Houston represented Julius Fisher, who killed a white librarian in the Washington Cathedral.[75] Such shocking facts might have resulted in an uninspired defense. Such was not the case. The complex psychiatric approach he developed at trial and advanced through each stage of the appeal was an innovation for its time.[76] Houston argued that Fisher was suffering from a complex mental disorder that, although not rising to the level of insanity, still warranted a mitigating effect on his criminal responsibility. Three Justices of the Supreme Court agreed with him. Although this type of defense is still controversial under the modern headings of "diminished capacity" or mental "syndrome" defenses, it has become the modern trend in many courts around the country.[77] Additionally, his work preceded modern capital punishment jurisprudence regarding death penalty prohibition for juveniles and mentally disabled individuals.[78]

First Amendment

Charles Hamilton Houston's long and complex relationship with the Communist Party spanned almost two decades, from the early days of the Scottsboro cases to his final federal and state court litigation defending suspected Communists and other government critics. He was always a passionate advocate for First Amendment freedoms. His involvement with alleged subversives during his legal career was a shining example of principled advocacy of the freedom of association and expression. Nevertheless, Houston's devotion to the democratic ideal of freedom of association could not reasonably be questioned. He served honorably in the United States military and followed the constitutional principles of democracy and the rule of law his entire life. Clearly, he believed the Constitution could withstand even rigorous dissent.

His First Amendment advocacy came at a critical time in American history when the country was struggling with freedom of speech and association, while at the same time becoming fearful of its enemies abroad. Houston took courageous steps to strike that balance in the nation's courts. He fought against Congress, the Federal Bureau of Investigation and the national paranoia that dominated pre- and post-World War II America.

His efforts would not return dividends until years after his death. The foundation he laid for stronger protections for those who would voice protest against the government became another key part of the historic Warren Court's due process revolution. His work helped confirm the notion that the right to associate, free from government interference, is cherished.[79] History should recognize Houston's forgotten contribution to this effort. Houston's attempt to expand and clarify First Amendment protections could have a profound effect on contemporary issues faced by the United States. In the post-9/11 world America has faced challenges about how it may protect itself from what it believes are its unseen enemies while at the same time preserving its valued freedoms.[80]

Up until the last days of his life Houston engaged in extensive litigation for those considered at the time subversive and radical. In the case of *Lawson v. United States*,[81] Houston mounted an attack on the power of Congress or any government entity to punish thought, speech or political preference. His representation of those accused of being Communists at such a critical stage in American history reflected his great insight into a true danger against American democracy: the suppression of dissent.[82] Houston believed the, "test of justice is not whether we deal fairly with our friends, but whether we deal fairly with those persons we disagree with."[83]

Although he died before the abuses of Senator Joseph McCarthy on the House Un-American Activities Committee[84] would reach their apex, history should recognize that Houston's commitment to challenge Congress for its investigative activities was appropriate and indispensable. His advocacy led him to suspect that he was also being followed by government officials, have him noted in Federal Bureau of Investigation files and likely cost him many opportunities to serve in appointed public office.[85]

Finally, Charles Houston's philosophy of justice was pointing toward visions of a world community where international human rights should be recognized. His editorial writings and the shape of the litigation he was filing late in his career clearly establishes that his concern went beyond domestic justice and embraced global justice. The best evidence of this evolution is reflected in his *Afro-American* newspaper columns, where he often wrote about international affairs toward the end of his life. He wrote "that segregation has no place in a democracy, and that if the United States had any chance to retain its position in world affairs it must conquer the race problem at home."[86]

Some of his views were prophetic. He would complain in the 1940s "[t]here will be no complete freedom in this country as long as there is a color barrier in South Africa or any other part of the African continent."[87] He made this statement almost four decades before apartheid would be ended in South Africa. Years before Martin Luther King, Jr. would apply the non-violent protest principles of Mahatma Gandhi, Houston would note that Gandhi's movement in India was an "irresistible...spiritual movement toward freedom, [that] gives hope and heart to all the peoples who lack guns and atom bombs, but are still determined to be free."[88] Houston argued that race relations around the world were complicated "partly because the U.S. has never learned to treat people of another color and culture as human beings and equals."[89] He hoped America "would learn before it is too late."[90]

During his life he expressed a keen interest in the issues surrounding the Middle East, and he expressed a strong advocacy for the plight of persecuted Jews, writing that the United States, during the late 1940s, should demonstrate "our appreciation of freedom... [by] broadening admission of Jewish refugees from Europe."[91]

At the end of his life Houston, in a tape-recorded message, declared that in some battles it was possible to forecast victory before the battle was over. He urged that people should "not be content" with the present victories over discrimination.[92] He provided more raw material for that vision to come true than any other attorney before or since. The evidence of Charles Hamilton

Houston's contribution clearly establishes him as a worthy candidate to be considered the most influential lawyer of the twentieth century. His influence reaches well into this century in ways well known and lesser known.

Notably, he was recognized in a speech by President Barak Obama at the 100th anniversary of the NAACP.[93] The president commented, "Houston was optimistic enough to believe that America could have a black president in the future."[94] In 2008 a United States postage stamp baring Houston's image along with Walter White was issued.[95] Although many honors have been bestowed on Charles Houston, one which has alluded him has been the Presidential Medal of Freedom, the nation's highest civilian honor. Curiously, many of the persons he mentored have received the medal, including Thurgood Marshall.[96] Always outspoken about the dangers of capital punishment, Houston's unfinished civil rights work has provided inspiration. A state legislator sought Houston's motivation in the midst of his own twenty-first century battle to abolish the penalty in Maryland. Samuel I. ("Sandy") Rosenberg shared the distinction with Charles Houston, Sr., of being an Amherst College alumnus. A long-time advocate for civil rights, Rosenberg had been heavily influenced by Houston's legacy through fellow Marylander Juanita Jackson Mitchell and other civil rights pioneers who Houston mentored.

Rosenberg was on the Amherst campus the day he learned that the death penalty repeal legislation he sponsored failed in the Maryland House of Delegates. In need of motivation, Rosenberg thought that if he could find Houston's portrait on campus he could be energized to prepare for the uphill fight that he faced when he returned home to the General Assembly. The Jewish politician walked to Johnson Chapel, where the portraits of the college's presidents are hung. There was also the portrait of Charles Hamilton Houston in the chapel. He touched the frame of the portrait, to make the connection between Houston's legal work against the death penalty and his own.[97] Miraculously, the death penalty abolition bill was revived in the days that followed with the help of the NAACP and was signed into law in 2013.[98]

In an unanticipated final recognition of Houston's reach into this century, an organic student movement at the University of Maryland, College Park in 2015 succeeded in having the university Regents remove the late Clifton "Curley" Byrd's name from the university's football stadium because of his blatant segregationist views. The university's president, Wallace Loh, stated, "[c]ontinuing the Byrd Stadium name divides us at a time when we need unity more than ever. We must accept the full truth of our past and the responsibility of our future."[99]

Recognizing the great impact lawyer Charlie Houston had on us all, he would want us to remember a number of things if he were able to tell us. In the words of his only son:

"White flight to the suburbs and ever-widening economic disparities have confined many black students to largely segregated, generally inferior school districts, a stark reminder of the chasm separating *Brown's* opportunity and reality."[100] "*Brown* was a milestone on a journey that was not over, *Brown* was a stop along the way. Celebrate *Brown*...yes, but include a long moment of silence on a job not yet finished." "When we shout for *Brown* we should shout for an equal measure of joy and indignation."[101]

Charles Houston's work may be unfinished, but his genius that transformed American law is part of what Albert Einstein described when he said, "[i]magination is more important than knowledge."[102] When genius Ben Franklin invented the battery, he noted the parallels between its sparks and lightning and wrote in his journal, "Let the experiment be made,"[103] He explored nature of lightning with a kite to ultimately invent the lightning rod. Charles Houston applied similar principals to use the courts to bend the arc of the incomplete Constitution closer toward justice. He dared to believe that we could live together in true equality when few thought it even possible to try. German Philosopher Arthur Schopenhaur reminds us, "[t]alent hits a target that no one else can hit.... Genius hits a target that no one else can see."[104] May Charles Hamilton Houston's restlessness with injustice help move us toward his own stated goal to make the system that ultimately survives in the United States one "which guarantees justice and freedom for everyone."[105]

Endnotes

1. Frederick N. Rasmussen, "Charles H. Houston Jr., Retired Morgan Lecturer Who Founded Scholars Program at University of Baltimore, Dies," *Baltimore Sun*, August 3, 2018.

2. *Pearson v. Murray*, 169 Md. 478 (1936).

3. Rasmussen, *Baltimore Sun*, note 1.

4. The reflections on Charles H. Houston, Jr., reflect my interviews with him over the course of the first year we met, beginning in December 2003 in preparation for the *Brown v. Board* Symposium held at the University of Baltimore School of Law in February of 2004. Our regular interactions spanned from late 2003 until June 2018, two months before his death.

5. In the Foreword to this book Charles Houston, Jr. mentions his mother being distraught over her husband's death. *See*, Foreword, Charles H. Houston, Jr., *supra*. He reported to me that this continued until her death on January 4, 1979. She desired to

personally complete her husband's biography but was unable to complete the work. Author's Interview, Charles H. Houston, Jr. June 10, 2011.

6. Charles Hamilton Houston IV, born October 10, 2019.

7. "South Carolina Hired Davis to Match Thurgood Marshall," *Baltimore Afro-American*, December 20, 1952, p. 6.

8. Juanita Mitchell's passion was also expressed by Charles H. Houston, Sr.'s, own words toward the end of his life when he wrote that our society "cannot tolerate injustice for a single day," Charles H. Houston, "Our Civil Rights," May 14, 1949, p. 4.

9. Denton L. Watson, *Lion in the Lobby: Clarence Mitchell, Jr.'s Struggle for the Passage of Civil Rights Laws* 151 (New York: William Morrow & Company 1990).

10. Ibid., p. 13.

11. Ibid.

12. Ethel Payne, "Remembering Clarence Mitchell, Jr. Alive and Well at the Courthouse," *Baltimore Afro-American*, July 12, 1986, p. 5.

13. *Brown v. Board*, 347 U.S. 483 (1954).

14. Rasmussen, *Charles H. Houston, Jr.*

15. Ibid.

16. Juanita Jackson Mitchell, University of Virginia Library, William A. Elwood Civil Rights Project, Oral History, video recording September 1, 1988.

17. Susan Low Bloch, "Thurgood Marshall" in *The Oxford Companion to the Supreme Court of the United States* 611 (Kermit L. Hall 2nd ed. 2005).

18. Ibid.

19. Carl T. Rowen, *Dream Makers, Dream Breakers: The World of Justice Thurgood Marshall* 52 (Boston: Little, Brown 1993).

20. Andre Davis to Dr. B. Herbert Brown, February 17, 1978, University of Maryland School of Law, Thurgood Marshall Library Collection.

21. Justice William J. Brennan, Jr. to Dean J. Michael Kelly, June 2, 1980, University of Maryland School of Law, Thurgood Marshall Library Collection.

22. David Margolick, "A Courthouse in Baltimore Renamed for Black Leader," *New York Times*, March 9, 1985, p. 6.

23. Thurgood Marshall, "Civil Rights Lawyer," *Baltimore Sun*, February 26, 2007.

24. Judge Andre Davis, author's interview, Thursday, September 21, 2017, Baltimore, Maryland.

25. Larry Gibson, *Young Thurgood: The Making of a Supreme Court Justice* 107 (New York: Prometheus Book 2012).

26. David Michael Ettlin, "Justice Skips Dedication of New UM Law Library," *Baltimore Sun*, October 18, 1980, p. C3.

27. Bettye Moss, "If You Ask Me," *Baltimore Afro-American*, October 17, 1970, p. 5.

28. 20 H.C. Byrd to R.H. Wettach, 21 March 1933, Harry Clifton "Curley" Byrd Papers, Box 8, Folder: Negro Education, 1933–1935 Special Collections, University of Maryland at College Park Libraries, College Park, Maryland. H.C. Byrd to R.H. Wettach, 13 April 1933.

29. David Margolick, "A Courthouse in Baltimore Renamed for Black Leader," *New York Times*, March 9, 1985 p. 6.

30. "Lane, Byrd Criticized: Thurgood Marshall Speaking at NAACP Meeting," *Baltimore Afro-American*, March 5, 1949, p. 5

31. *McCready v. Byrd*, 73 A. 2d 8 (1950).

32. Donald W. Stewart, "Doctors of Distinction," *University of Maryland School of Medicine Bulletin*, Winter 2004–2005, p. 9. Donald Stewart was joined in medical school by Roderick E. Charles as the first two black medical students in 1951.

33. "Negro Is Given Dormitory Room, *Baltimore Sun*, February 1, 1951.

34. Ibid.

35. Thomas Corey, Esquire, Author's interview, February 1, 2011, Baltimore, Maryland.

36. Ibid.

37. "Baseball Owner's Mother Sues to Share Estate with Wife," *Baltimore Afro-American*, November 19, 1944, p. 13.

38. "Reactionary White Judge Bars Library in Md. County," *Baltimore Afro-American*, May 31, 1952, p. 14.

39. *Farrell v. State*, 131 A.2d 863 (Md. 1957).

40. "Resort Hotel Purchased by Mrs. Sara Washington," *Baltimore Afro-American*, September 16, 1944, p. 1.

41. *Celebrating a Century of Service: The Clarence M. Mitchell, Jr. Courthouse 1900–2000* 44, 76 (Baltimore: Maryland Centennial Celebration Committee, 2000).

42. Opinion, "Farewell to Stephen E. Harris," *Baltimore Daily Record*, April 30, 1994.

43. *Bell v. State*, 227 Md. 302, 176 A.2d 771 (1962); *See generally*, William L. Reynolds, "Foreword: The Legal History of the Great Sit-In Case of *Bell v. Maryland*," 61 *Md. L. Rev.* 761 (2002).

44. William L. Reynolds, "The Life and Times of Chief Judge Robert Bell," 72 *Md. L. Rev.* 1077 (2013).

45. Maryland State Bar Association, Section Council of Criminal Law and Practice, Robert C. Heeney Award Winner Roster, 2019.

46. David Michael Ettlin, "Milton Allen, City State's Attorney Dies at 85," *Baltimore Sun*, February, 13, 2003.

47. Milton Allen, oral history interview OH 8138, McKeldin-Jackson Oral History, Maryland Historical Society (1976).

48. Ibid.

49. Robert B. Watts, oral history interview OH 8102, McKeldin-Jackson Oral History, Maryland Historical Society (1976).

50. Ibid.

51. Rachil D. Godsill, "Remedying Environmental Racism," 90 *Mich. L. Rev.* 394 (1991).

52. David Michael Ettlin, "Milton Allen, City State's Attorney Dies at 85," *Baltimore Sun*, February 13, 2003.

53. *See*, Bob Woodward and Scott Armstrong, *The Brethren: Inside the Supreme Court* (New York: Simon & Schuster 1979) (Describing the liberal leaning of the Warren Court).

54. José Felipé Anderson, "Perspectives on *Missouri v. Jenkins*: Abandoning the Unfinished Business of Public School Desegregation 'With All Deliberate Speed,'" 39 *Howard L. J.* 693 (1996).

55. 305 U.S. 337 (1938).

56. *Brown v. Board*, 347 U.S. 483 (1954).

57. *See, Ramos v. Louisiana*, 140 S. St. 1390 (2020) (Justice Cavanaugh concurring) (The lengthy and extraordinary list of landmark cases that overruled precedent includes the single most important and greatest decision in this Court's history, *Brown v. Board of Education*, which repudiated the separate but equal doctrine of *Plessy v. Ferguson*, 163 U.S. 537, 16 S. Ct. 1138, 41 L. Ed. 256 (1896).

58. 358 U.S. 1 (1958)

59. See, José Felipé Anderson, "'Law Is Coercion,' Revisiting Judicial Power to Provide Equality in Public Education," 68 *Arkansas L. Rev.* 83 (2015).

60. *See e.g., Cooper v. Aaron*, 358 U.S. 1 (1958).

61. C. Fraser Smith, *Here Lies Jim Crow* 183 (Baltimore: Johns Hopkins University Press 2008).

62. Ibid.

63. Ibid., p. 184.

64. Fred Gray, *Bus Ride to Justice: Changing the System by the System* 353 (Montgomery: New South 1995).

65. *Steele v. Louisville & Nashville Railway Co.*, 323 U.S. 192 (1944).

66. *Batson v. Kentucky*, 476 U.S. 79 (1986).

67. José Felipé Anderson, "Catch Me If You Can! Resolving the Ethical Tragedies in the Brave New World of Jury Selection" (Winter 1998). 32 *New Engl. L. Rev.* 343 (1998).

68. *James v. State*, 65 A.2d 888 (Md. 1949).

69. *Jones v. State*, 52 A.2d 484 (Md. 1947).

70. *Miranda v. Arizona*, 384 U.S. 436 (1966).

71. Ibid.

72. Stephen P. Grossman, "Separate but Equal, *Miranda's* Right of Silence and Counsel," 96 *Marquette L. Rev.* 151 (2012).

73. Ibid.

74. *Gideon v. Wainwright*, 372 U.S. 335 (1963).

75. *Fisher v. United States*, 328 U.S. 463 (1946).

76. David M. Siegel, "Felix Frankfurter, Charles Hamilton Houston and the N-Word: A Study in the Evolution of Judicial Attitudes Toward Race," 7 *S. Cal. Interdisc. L.J.* 317 (1998).

77. Ibid.

78. Amy Dillard, "And Death Shall Have No Dominion: How to Achieve the Categorical Exemption of Mentally Retarded Defendants from Execution," 45 *Richmond L. Rev.* 961 (2011).

79. *See,* José Felipé Anderson, "Freedom of Association, the Communist Party, and the Hollywood Ten: The Forgotten First Amendment Legacy of Charles Hamilton Houston," 40 *McGeorge L. Rev.* 25, 26 (2009).

80. James Barron, "Remembering Those Lost 18 Years Ago," *New York Times*, September 11, 2019.

81. Charles H. Houston, "The Highway," *Baltimore Afro-American*, April 12, 1947, p. 4.

82. Ibid.

83. Charles H. Houston, "Our Civil Rights," *Baltimore Afro-American*, February 5, 1949, p. 4.

84. *See generally*, James Cross Giblin, *The Rise and Fall of Senator Joe McCarthy* (New York: Clarion Books 2009).

85. Federal Bureau of Investigation report file number 100-662, Memphis, Tennessee, October 22, 1941, p. 2. NAACP summary BU file 61-3176.

86. Charles H. Houston, "The Highway," *Baltimore Afro-American*, January 3, 1948, p.4.

87. Charles H. Houston, "The Highway," *Baltimore Afro-American*, February 21, 1948, p. 4.

88. Charles H. Houston, "The Highway," *Baltimore Afro-American*, March 20, 1948, p. 4.

89. Charles H. Houston, "The Highway," *Baltimore Afro-American*, February 28, 1948, p. 4.

90. Ibid.

91. Charles H. Houston, "Along the Highway" *Baltimore Afro-American*, December 11, 1948, p. 4.

92. Charles Hamilton Houston, untitled tape recording [c. December 1949], Charles Hamilton Houston Family Collection.

93. Remarks of President Barack Obama – As Prepared for Delivery, NAACP Centennial New York, New York, July 16, 2009.

94. Charles H. Houston, "Our Civil Rights," January 29, 1949, p. 4. (An editorial predicting that the nation may have a black president one day, perhaps as soon as the next generation or two. In the same column he thought that there could be a woman president, exclaiming "Why not!") It is also noteworthy that newly elected Vice-President Kamala Harris, the first woman elected to the office, acknowledges Charles Hamilton Houston as one of the greatest inspirational influences. https://www.washingtonpost.com/politics/2020/06/19/there-was-this-tool-that-they-had-figured-out-was-powerful-kamala-harris-working-system-justice/. Ironically, years before she was elected she when serving in the U.S. Senate she spoke about Houston in a Commencement address at Howard University. https://www.c-span.org/video/?428436-2/senator-kamala-harris-delivers-howard-university-commencement-address

95. "Panel Marks Launch of Houston Commemorative Stamp," *Harvard Law Today*, February 25, 2009.

96. Among the Medal of Freedom winners are Thurgood Marshall; the first black federal judge, William Hastie; the first black female federal judge, Constance Baker Motley; and the first black Secretary of Transportation William T. Coleman; all Charles Houston mentees.

97. Maryland Delegate Sandy Rosenberg interview, author's interview, August 6, 2018, Baltimore, Maryland. *See also* John D. Bessler, "The Abolitionist Movement Comes of Age: From Capital Punishment as a Lawful Sanction to a Peremptory, International Law Norm Barring Executions," 79 *Montana L. Rev.* 7 (2018).

98. Michael Dresser, "O'Malley Signs Death Penalty Repeal," *Baltimore Sun*, May 2, 2013.

99. Press Release, UMD Right Now, Board of Regents Approves President Loh's Recommendation to Change Name of Byrd Stadium to Maryland Stadium, December 11, 2015.

100. Mark Hansel and Barry Horstman, Panel: "Inequality in the Urban Schools", *Cincinnati Post*, March 19, 2005, p. A. (Journaling Charles H. Houston, Jr.'s remarks at the dedication of the National Underground Railroad Freedom Center).

101. C-Span, Remarks of Charles H. Houston, Jr. at Duquesne University, March 26, 2004, on the occasion of the 50th anniversary of the celebration of *Brown v. Board of Education*.

102. Walter Isaacson, "The Genius of Jobs," *New York Times*, October 29, 2011.

103. Ibid.

104. Walter Issacson, "What Makes a Genius? The World's Greatest Minds Have One Thing in Common," *Time*, November 17, 2017.

105. Charles Hamilton Houston, untitled tape recording [c. December 1949], Charles Hamilton Houston Family Collection.

Acknowledgments

I would like to pay special tribute to the many fine archivists and librarians who have helped me identify the original source material that makes such a project possible. Among them are Robert Poole, formerly of the University of Baltimore School of Law Library, Joellen El Bashir of the Moorland Spingarn Research Center of Howard University, Bill Sleeman, curator of the Nicholas-Gosnell Papers at the Thurgood Marshall Library of the University of Maryland School of Law, Raymond F. Trent of the University of Pennsylvania Law Library and the many fine professionals at the Library of Congress. The staff of the McKeldin-Jackson Oral History Collection at the Maryland Historical Society and the personnel of the Maryland State Archives were of great assistance. I would like to note the National Civil Rights Museum in Memphis, Tennessee, for outstanding preservation and presentation of several of the NAACP documentary movies recorded by Charles Houston in the 1930s of the poor conditions in segregated Southern grade schools.

The Reginald F. Lewis Museum of Maryland African-American History & Culture should be acknowledged for its many artifacts that served me well, reinforcing the work on some of the chapters and the irreplaceable work of the late Judge James F. Schneider on Maryland lawyers and Baltimore City courthouses. Without the black press, telling Houston's story would be impossible. Most notably, the *Baltimore Afro-American* allowed Charles Houston a platform to write freely and for the many years it reported on his work with great precision. The root of this book was largely provided by the archives of that newspaper and the help of its publisher emeritus, Jake Oliver. *The Pittsburgh Courier* and *The Chicago Defender* should also be given well deserved praise for the chronicle of events that is covered in these pages.

All biography is a product of the work that has gone before. The indispensable contributions of Genna Rae McNeil's *Groundwork* and Richard Kluger's *Simple Justice* are unmatched resources in revisiting the story of

Charles Hamilton Houston. Geraldine R. Segal's, *In Any Fight Some Fall* added more personal family insight to my contribution.

The interviews of Thurgood Marshall captured by the work of the late and legendary Carl T. Rowan and national news journalist Juan Williams have been indispensible in my attempt to fully understand Houston's effect on lawyers he mentored. I have enjoyed the support and counsel of my outstanding colleagues at the University of Baltimore School of Law; many are cited in this work. I would like to particularly mention F. Michael Higginbotham, Michael Hayes, Jack Lynch, Steve Grossman, Arnold Rochvarg, Mike Meyerson, Cassandra Jones-Havard, Gilda Daniels, Audrey McFarlane, Garrett Epps, Eric Easton, Tim Sellers, John Bessler, Nienke Grossman, Dionne Koller, Amy Sloane, and Christopher J. Peters. Each have provided insights that helped me set priorities for what I decided to include. I would also like to thank my administrative assistant Deborah Thompson for all her technical support.

I have appreciated the prayers of loved ones and friends that have encouraged me on the long journey toward completion. I am particularly grateful to the love of my life, my wife Dreama Anderson, and my children Kristen, Danielle and Ivan who have loved and endured me during this process. My mother, Dr. Aquilla Alaba Rice, provided much of the inspiration for the book, as one of the first women of color to attend and graduate from the University of Maryland at College Park.

Insights from the *New England Law Review*'s 1993 symposium and the *Harvard Law Review* 1998 symposium on Charles Hamilton Houston each provided a valuable record from those who worked directly with him. William A. Elwood's collection of videotape interviews produced through the University of Virginia of many civil rights pioneers who were touched by Houston added key details that showed depth and complexity of this singularly unique lawyer. Special thanks are due former University of Baltimore Law Dean Gilbert A. Holmes, under whose leadership this project began, and Dean Ronald under whom it was completed.

Michael Bowen Mitchell, son of Juanita Jackson Mitchell and Clarence M. Mitchell, Jr., generously provided me material from the Mitchell Family Papers. These documents filled in enormous historical gaps in the year 1934, when Houston started working with Michael Mitchell's mother and grandmother, and 1950, the year of Houston's death. Philip Stewart is also due special mention for providing me access to his father Dr. Donald Stewart, Houston's last client.

The late Dean J. Clay Smith's book, *Emancipation*, chronicling lawyers in the last two centuries, built a bridge to the origins of early black lawyers and provided a valuable measuring stick to evaluate Houston's contributions. I am also grateful to Dean Smith for the personal encouragement offered me in 1996 to pursue a study of this legendary black lawyer. My former law professor and lifelong Thurgood Marshall biographer Larry S. Gibson deserves special credit for keeping Marshall and Houston's memory vibrant to so many generations.

Finally, I would also like to express my appreciation the Houston family, who have given me their time, materials, and encouragement as I attempted to do some justice to a great, yet unsung American hero. I cannot say enough about the late Charles Hamilton Houston, Jr., the teacher and historian whose keen insights over the years of our association have unlocked new perspectives on his father's work. Any merit that is in the biography, is because of his help discussing material that had been uncovered. Any flaws are mine alone. Also deserving special mention is Charles, Jr.'s devoted wife Rose Jagus. During this almost 16-year odyssey since the 50th anniversary of *Brown v. Board*, she provided great care for her husband while he lived, worked and had great patience with me as we tried to finish this story of his legendary father together. If nothing else, I hope more people get to know about Charles Hamilton Houston's transformational impact on the world.

José Felipé Anderson
Baltimore, Maryland
August 2021

Index